Working with Developmental Anxieties in Couple and Family Psychotherapy

The family begins with the parental couple; it is they who create the family. This book explores the way in which the child or any member of the family can carry unresolved projections arising from the parents' families of origin: their *family within*, and the difficulties this internal family presents for the therapist.

The model developed in this book explores psychoanalytically-based ideas about infant development and applies them to the internal world of couples and families. It presents both a clear explanation of these theories as well as case histories that show how these ideas work in practice. The developmental model presented offers an original perspective on the wide range of problems that many couple and family therapists struggle with. These problems can be understood in the context of *the family within*, the way in which the family of origin dynamics have been internalised. This shared understanding between the couple and family and the therapist provides a path to greater maturity and therefore a greater capacity to cope with life's vicissitudes.

Working with Developmental Anxieties in Couple and Family Psychotherapy presents both a clear theoretical framework for understanding the development of the couple and family, and a practical application for these ideas. Case studies bring the model to life through illustrating both the problems of the family or couple and the difficulties of the work. It will appeal to psychoanalysts, psychotherapists, couples and family therapists.

Penny Jools has a PhD and a Clinical Masters in Developmental Psychology. She and her two colleagues and co-editors run a successful private clinic in Annandale, Sydney, that specialises in working with troubled couples and families. She has worked as an individual, couple and family psychotherapist for more than thirty years. Her recent international publications have been on couple psychotherapy.

Jenny Berg, MBBS, FRANZCP, is a child adolescent and family psychiatrist and psychoanalyst. Couple and family psychoanalysis is her area of expertise. She has regularly supervised interested private practitioners, taught child psychiatric trainees, and has been steadfast in maintaining an organisation (the Couple Child and Family Psychotherapy Association of Australasia) that aims to keep these ideas alive within the wider community in Australasia. She has also published internationally in this area.

Noela Byrne is a qualified social worker and an individual, couple and family psychotherapist. Until her recent retirement, she had spent over thirty-five years in both the public and private sectors. She has been involved in supervision and teaching to both psychiatrists and psychotherapists in training. Her past publications were in individual, couple and family psychotherapy.

'Couple relationships are the source of much joy and misery. They have huge significance for the well-being of family members and for the community at large, so they are worth understanding and supporting. This book helps us do just that. It describes the interior landscape of couple relationships, providing a lucid digest of the main psychoanalytic ideas and illuminating the dark valleys that hinder couples in their conscious quest to reach the sunny uplands they seek. It focuses on developmental anxieties associated with relationship problems and illustrates the process of working with these in vivid detail. The combination of clearly sign-posted theory and well-honed clinical experience provides valuable threads that will assist therapists in navigating the often labyrinthine tunnels that make up the internal world of couple relationships.'

Christopher Clulow PhD,
Senior Fellow, Tavistock Relationships,
London

Working with Developmental Anxieties in Couple and Family Psychotherapy

The Family Within

Edited by Penny Jools,
Jenny Berg and
Noela Byrne

Routledge
Taylor & Francis Group
LONDON AND NEW YORK

First published 2018
by Routledge
2 Park Square, Milton Park, Abingdon, Oxon OX14 4RN

and by Routledge
711 Third Avenue, New York, NY 10017

Routledge is an imprint of the Taylor & Francis Group, an informa business

British Library Cataloguing in Publication Data
A catalogue record for this book is available from the British Library

Library of Congress Cataloging in Publication Data
A catalog record for this book has been requested

ISBN: 978-1-138-07988-5 (hbk)
ISBN: 978-1-138-07989-2 (pbk)
ISBN: 978-1-315-11420-0 (ebk)

Typeset in Times New Roman
by Swales & Willis Ltd, Exeter, Devon, UK

Contents

Preface

The inspiration for this book arose from a series of lectures offered by the Couple Child and Family Psychotherapy Association of Australasia (CCAFPAA) to clinicians who were interested in learning more about object relations theory and its application to psychotherapy with families or couples. From this starting point, the idea evolved into producing a book that would cover both a theoretical framework for the psychotherapeutic work with troubled families and couples but also the application of the theory, covering the process and interventions by the therapist. Many of the chapters in the book have been written collaboratively, reflecting the ways in which our group has developed their thinking and clinical practice.

Originally, CCAFPAA was set up in 1998 as a state-based organisation known as the New South Wales Institute of Family Psychotherapy. Central to the establishment of the institute was Dr Charles Enfield, a child psychiatrist who had trained at the Tavistock clinic and who brought the ideas of Fairbairn and object relation family therapy with him in 1976 when he was appointed as Head of the Psychiatry Department at the Royal Alexandra Hospital for Children in Sydney.

As the association grew, a greater focus developed on the dynamics of the couple, who were regarded as the architects of the family. Often, when a child was presented as the problem, family work changed to couple work as the parents were able to acknowledge their part in the family's difficulties.

It is hoped that the chapters in this book will contribute to a greater understanding of the '*family within*', that is, to the internal objects that play such an important role in every intimate relationship.

Acknowledgements

This book has a long history. We would like to thank all the members of the Couple Child and Family Psychotherapy Association of Australasia (CCAFPAA) who have contributed to it, either directly in the form of their written contributions, or indirectly through the valuable insights they have provided through supervision groups.

We would like to thank Maurice Whelan for his helpful comments at a critical time in the book's development. We are grateful to Jill and David Scharff for the encouragement they gave us from our first meeting in New Orleans in 2004. We would also like to thank Jeanne Magagna for her support and enthusiasm for the project.

We would also like to acknowledge our husbands, Gary Bryson, David Cole and Brad Freeman for their support and critical input during the book's long gestation.

We would like to thank the couples and families who have given us permission to use their experiences, which not only form an important part of the book, but have contributed invaluably to our therapeutic understanding. Lastly we would like to thank each other for the way we have supported and extended each other in our work and in this volume.

Penny Jools
Jenny Berg
Noela Byrne

Permissions acknowledgement

Excerpt from 'What I Believe' from *Two Cheers for Democracy* by E.M. Forster. Copyright 1939 by E.M. Forster. Copyright © Renewed 1987 by E.M. Forster. Reprinted by permission of Houghton Mifflin Harcourt Publishing Company. All rights reserved. Also reprinted by permission of The Society of Authors, London.

Contributors

Editors

Dr Penny Jools, clinical psychologist and psychoanalytic psychotherapist and psychoanalyst
Penny has a PhD and a Clinical Masters in Developmental Psychology. Twenty years ago she and three colleagues set up a successful private clinic in Annandale that specialised in working with troubled couples and families. Dr Jools is past president of CCAFPAA, (Couple Child and Family Psychotherapy Association of Australasia). Her recent international publications have been on couple psychotherapy. Now retired from clinical practice she has used the opportunity to bring the work of the contributors into this volume, while miraculously not badly offending any of them. She offers supervision and consultation from Hobart where she now lives. She is a voracious reader of fiction.

Dr Jenny Berg, MBBS, FRANZCP, child adolescent and family psychiatrist
Jenny originally trained as a child psychiatrist and was fortunate enough to encounter her great friends and colleagues, Noela Byrne and Penny Jools, early in her career, to whom she is deeply grateful for the way things have turned out. Together they developed a shared interest in the application of psychodynamic principles to working with couples and families which has continued for over twenty-five years. Couple and family psychoanalysis is her area of expertise. Over these years she has continued to develop her understanding and skills, has contributed to the international discourse in this area and made friends along the way, has regularly supervised interested private practitioners, has taught child psychiatric trainees, and has been steadfast in maintaining an organisation, CCAFPAA that aims to keep these ideas alive within the wider community in Australasia. She hopes this book might contribute a little towards that later ambition.

Noela Byrne, social worker and psychotherapist
Noela is a qualified social worker and an individual, couple and family psychotherapist. Until her recent retirement, she had spent over thirty-five years in both the public and private sectors. She is a member of the New South Wales Institute

of Psychoanalytic Psychotherapy, past member of the British Society of Couple Psychotherapists and Counsellors and a founding member and past president of the Couple Child and Family Psychotherapy Association of Australasia. As well as her many years of clinical experience, she has also been involved in supervision and teaching with the New South Wales Institute of Psychiatry as well as with NSWIPP and CCAFPAA. Her past publications were in individual, couple and also family psychotherapy.

Contributors

Lissy Abrahams, Tavistock trained couple and family psychotherapist
Lissy is the founder of the Heath Group Practice, a therapeutic practice for children, adolescents, adults, couples and families in Edgecliff, Sydney. Here she works mostly with individuals and couples within a psychodynamic framework, as well as offering family dispute resolution services to separated or divorced couples. Prior to setting up the practice Lissy lived in London for nine years, where she trained as a psychoanalytic psychotherapist at Tavistock Relationships (formerly the Tavistock Centre for Couple Relationships). Following the training she remained at Tavistock Relationships and practised as a clinician, lectured on couple conflict and Attachment Theory, tutored, was a seminar leader, a member of the assessment committee and had a private practice. Lissy held positions on the Executive Committee and Membership Committee of the British Society of Couple Psychotherapists and Counsellors and was Vice President of the Couple Child and Family Psychotherapy Association of Australasia (CCAFPAA).

George Haralambous, clinical psychologist and couple and family psychotherapist
George is a clinical psychologist and couple and family psychotherapist who is a past president and has been an active member of CCAFPAA (Couple Child and Family Psychotherapy Association of Australasia) since its foundation. He has worked in a variety of settings, including an inpatient family therapy unit, and has been in private practice for over twenty years, where he has worked predominately with couples and families. As a professionally endorsed forensic psychologist, his work has included court appointments as a single expert witness for family law matters. George supervises widely, with individuals and institutions, and has maintained an active interest in the professional development of therapists, particularly from an Object Relations perspective.

Maria Kourt, clinical psychologist and psychoanalytic psychotherapist
Maria has a background in working with children, adolescents and their families in the community and the public health sector, where she also held a position as head of a psychology department.

She has worked in the Perinatal and Infant Mental health area, teaching Infant Observation and conducting clinical supervision groups for the NSW Institute of

Psychiatry as well as consulting for an organisation which works with Aboriginal parents and their infants. Maria is a current long standing executive member of NSWIPP (New South Wales Institute of Psychoanalytic Psychotherapy) as well as being a past treasurer and past vice president of CCAFPAA.

She has co-authored a number of papers in the areas of Attachment, Child Psychotherapy, Couple and Family Therapy and the Outcome Evaluation of short and long term Psychotherapy. She supervises and consults with individuals, couples and families in private practice in Sydney.

Laurie Lovell-Simons, psychoanalytic psychotherapist, Balint group leader and social worker

Laurie is a psychoanalytic psychotherapist in private practice working with individuals, couples and groups in her rooms in Sydney, Australia, as well as using Skype or phone. She is a long-standing training and supervising member of NSWIPP (NSW Institute of Psychoanalytic Psychotherapy), and an active member of CCAFPAA. She is also an accredited Balint group leader and trainer for the Balint Society of Australia and New Zealand and is a regular educator and supervisor in this field in Australia and in China. Laurie loves to walk in wild places, paint, sculpt and write poetry.

Julia Meyerowitz-Katz, Jungian analyst and art psychotherapist

Julia is a Jungian analyst and art psychotherapist in private practice in Sydney, Australia. Julia is an active member of ANZSJA (Australian and New Zealand Society of Jungian Analysts) and CCAFPAA. She has worked in a variety of settings and has contributed as an editor and advisor to the several peer-reviewed professional journals. She has published papers on working with children in art therapy, supervision of art therapy and working psychoanalytically with couples. Her most recent publication, co-edited with Dean Reddick, is *Art therapy in the early years: Therapeutic interventions with infants, toddlers and their families* (Routledge: London, 2017).

Part I

Theory and practice

Introduction

The family within: a developmental focus on family and couple psychotherapy

Penny Jools

This book is for psychotherapists who work with couples and families. The work of eight practitioners in this field will be presented. Each chapter will give examples from clinical practice. Some chapters are written by one person and some by two. This reflects the collaborative nature of our work. We see couples and families on our own, but we think about them together. We will also explain how we work with the people who come to us seeking help. The first five chapters describe the thinking and the theory that underpin our practice, building on ideas that are already current in the international discourse on couple and family psychoanalysis from an object relations perspective. The second part of the book provides detailed case studies that illustrate these ideas.

When working with couples and families the notion of 'the family within' is of central importance. 'The family within' refers to the way our significant relationships are profoundly determined by our family of origin. We all, for better or for worse, internalise a sense of the family we have come from. And it continues to live within each of us. When we establish a relationship with another and form a couple, and when a new family is formed, the nature of the new entity is shaped by what we bring from our past.

The notion of 'the family within' that is used by the practitioners who have contributed to this book is heavily influenced by psychoanalysis. Psychoanalysis was created out of an understanding of what takes place in a consulting room between two people. The theories and the technique that were initially developed in the field of psychoanalysis focused strongly on that dyad. While a person's family of origin was considered important, it took some time before a couple or a family were thought of as 'the patient' or 'patients'.

It is perhaps surprising that the psychoanalytic enterprise took so long to consider the couple and family as worthy of analysis in its own right, since, as Britton (1995, p. xi) pointed out more than twenty years ago:

> The family remains the locus in quo of individual development and the unit of social expectation: 'marriage', whether celebrated or uncelebrated, socially contracted or uncontracted, or simply conspicuous by its absence, remains at the centre of 'family life'. I think it does so because the idea of a couple coming together to produce a child is central in our psychic life, whether we aspire to it, object to it, realise we are produced by it, deny it, relish it, or hate it.

This volume reflects our own clinical experience, which has been discussed at length over many years in seminars and papers: we offer our experiences and our thoughts for discussion in the hope that it will make an important contribution to our knowledge of the psychic life of couples and families, building on an international tradition of psychoanalytically-based couple and family therapy.

All eight practitioners are psychoanalytically-trained psychotherapists. A training in psychoanalytical psychotherapy with its three components, a personal analysis, theoretical lectures and seminars, and clinical experience, provides a solid foundation to progress to work with couples and families. Our contributors continue an interdisciplinary tradition which has always been an important way of working for most of us with a background of working in the government sector. The contributors include a child psychiatrist, two social workers, three clinical psychologists, a couple psychotherapist and a Jungian analyst. All of us have experienced an infant observation as part of our training. Most of us have worked with young children. Both these experiences give us access to the primitive feelings, sometimes difficult to express in words, that are an important part of the child's experience. These feelings can be distressingly re-evoked in the intimate relationship with a partner and lead to a request for help.

Working with couples and families makes a considerable initial challenge to anyone, even the person trained to work with the individual: the couple or the family, not the individual, is the patient. We often sit in the consulting room with warring people. Their hurt and rage threatens our capacity to think. Sometimes, the atmosphere they create is so intense we wonder how they got together, why they stay together. When we can think we have to understand what this conflict means to each of the participants. We draw on our knowledge of the couple's history and the theoretical maps available to navigate the complex interactions before us. We are able to think about the family each has developed within and the way it has shaped their emotional development. We notice that they are seeing each other in black and white terms, and cast each other in roles, plays and scripts which have histories that determine how they experience each other.

In this book we pay considerable attention to the emotional impact on the therapist of destructive behaviour in the consulting room. We may have 'forgotten' our childhood experiences, but witnessing conflict in our patients can resonate painfully with our own early traumatic experiences. Therapists have to be aware of their own 'family within'. Much of the work of therapy is understood through the transference and counter-transference experiences of the therapist and how the projective identification distorts relationships. In work with couples and families, theses transferences, counter-transferences and projective identifications are more complex than in a dyadic relationship. Hence we underline the importance of the use of the self in this work and therefore the importance of supervision and a larger community of like-minded therapists to support the therapist in carrying these toxic emotions without enacting them in an unhelpful way. We are then in a better position to alleviate the suffering of those who seek our help and assist them to lead more fulfilling lives.

As psychotherapists we understand that it is our most intimate relationships that evoke and frequently provoke our sense of vulnerability, dependence and anxiety. Many of the parents in this volume seem to function well in the real world, hold down jobs, have friends, but find themselves dismayed at the emotional minefield unleashed in their relationships with their partners and families.

While Freud (1916/1917) acknowledged the impact on the unconscious of childhood experience and how it affected the adult psyche, it was later psychoanalysts, like Klein (1946) and Fairbairn (1952) who shifted the focus to very early experience. It is these very early primitive feelings that often create painful conflict in couples, but also affect us as therapists. The case studies in this book attempt to describe and understand these primitive feelings in our patients and in ourselves, and make clearer the family within that creates the dilemmas we are witnessing in the consulting room.

The theoretical material in the first five chapters will, we hope, provide a map that can assist in charting a passage through these often stormy waters. Our theoretical map or model is a developmental one. What does this mean? Our argument in these chapters is that the emotional growth of a couple or family can usefully be explored using a model of the emotional growth of an infant. For example, the infant's first experience in the world is sensory: feelings provoked by touch and being held and our other senses too, hearing, sight and taste. These sensory experiences are important in a couple's relationship, particularly their sexual relationship: couples' difficulties in touching and holding each other, we suggest, may arise from compromised early experiences. Does an infant raised in an orphanage have an adequate experience of touching and being held? What might this do to the same person's capacity to be available in an intimate sexual relationship in adulthood?

We know the world of the child is also full of conflicted emotions, tears one minute, laughter the next: many parents have had the experience of an enraged 2-year-old, faced with a frustration of their desires, who, hands on hips, yells 'I hate you'. This can also be the response of an adult partner to the ordinary frustrations of an intimate relationship. Families and couples, (unlike the 2-year-old) can be dismayed when the restraint they are able to show in their working lives, disintegrates at home, where at times hate can prevail over love, and restraint and reflection can go out the window.

While the young child may move quickly and painlessly from hate to love in the space of a few minutes, the ambivalent nature of any intimate relationship is harder for the adult to understand and accept. Holding the tensions between love and hate, where love can prevail, is one of the tasks of marriage, which sounds easy but isn't.

Family life is intense. The older child can exhibit jealousy and rage at the sense of exclusion from the parental relationship and become distressed and angry at the arrival of a new sibling. A 3-year-old may jump into bed on Sunday morning and insinuate himself between the parents. These manifestations of Oedipal issues can be difficult for a family to manage, especially if they resonate with the parents' own unresolved Oedipal anxieties.

Family life is also full of acceptance and love, and a bit like democracy, is a flawed system for raising children, but is one we value, notwithstanding, or perhaps because of, the variety of relationships the family now encompasses. As E.M. Forster said in 1938, as war was approaching: 'So two cheers for Democracy: one because it admits variety and two because it permits criticism. Two cheers are quite enough: there is no occasion to give three.'

Our argument in this book is that the very intensity of family life, the anxiety that these intense feelings provoke and the defences than can be mobilised against safely experiencing and understanding these feelings, is at the very core of our therapeutic work. Our task has been to provide a map to chart a way through the human dilemmas we encounter in our work, and thus help our couple to understand their family within, and how that is affecting the real life family they are trying to create.

In the thirty years our group has been working in the field, we find that it is often concerns about the child that bring the couple or family into seeking some form of therapy. Most parents want the best for their children and will seek help for them if they feel they are distressed. A focus on the couple often frees the child to get on with the normal developmental task of childhood. Crucial to the work is the idea that the couple/family is able to develop a reflective space to think about itself. We argue that this occurs through the emotional containment the therapist provides within the predictable safe space of the consulting room. The latter part of the book provides case studies that illustrate the developmental model, and the work of the therapist in helping couples and families to move on.

As someone who is intending to do this work, you may be wondering what kind of frame couple and family psychotherapy requires. Is it the same or does it differ from other therapy modes? Generally the frame refers to the contract that has been established with the patient (individual, couple or family) about how often they will meet, for how long and for how much. Mostly couple or family psychotherapy is shorter in duration than psychoanalytic psychotherapy; two to three years is a common time for therapy to last. We usually see the couple or the family weekly, for one hour, with therapeutic breaks often during school holidays. As an example of the way we work, one question that is often raised is: what happens when only one member of the couple turns up for therapy? You will probably want a strict rule about this, but in reality, like in most situations in therapy, the reason for the absence has first to be understood. Why is the other person not there, what is the absence expressing? What impact on the relationship will it have if only one of the couple is seen? The important thing here is to be able to think about the meaning of the situation, remembering that the couple or family is the patient.

How the book is organised

The book falls into three parts.

The first five chapters present our theoretical model for working with couples and families together with the application of these ideas to the work. This section crystallises our object relations model of psychic development in couples and families, as well as how we work using this model.

The second part of the book presents case studies by seven of the contributors, amplifying the concepts outlined in the first five chapters. These chapters highlight, as does the theoretical model, the role of early neglect, deprivation and abuse, and the impact of this on the couple relationship, particularly the sexual relationship.

In the final section we include a case study and discussion of attachment and its relationship to object relations theories. Finally we look at the use of affective learning groups as a way of helping attendees at a conference experience and process the material presented. The volume concludes with some clinical and theoretical questions that remain unanswered, questions that will hopefully lead to further discussions and thinking in this field.

Confidentiality

Couples and families whose cases have been cited in the following chapters have given permission for the use of their material. The identities of the participants have been disguised and in some instances the case material is a composite of several cases.

References

Britton, R. (1995). Foreword. In S. Ruszczynski and J. Fisher (Eds.) *Intrusiveness and Intimacy in the Couple* (p. xi). London: Karnac.

Fairbairn, R. (1952). *Psychoanalytic Studies of the Personality*. London: Routledge.

Forster, E.M. (1951) *What I Believe*. London: Harvest Book. First published in *The Nation*, 16 July 16, 1938.

Freud, S. (1916/1917). Introductory Lectures on Psycho-Analysis. Lecture XXXVIII: Analytic Therapy. S.E., Vol.16 (pp. 448–463). London: Hogarth Press.

Klein, M. (1946). Notes on some schizoid mechanisms. *International Journal of Psycho-Analysis*, *27*, 99–110 [Reprinted in M. Klein, *Envy and Gratitude and Other Works 1946–1963*. London: Hogarth Press, 1980].

Chapter 1

The couple and family in mind

Jenny Berg

Just as children change with age and experience, so do couples and families. Every couple and family face challenges in their development; the birth of a child, the loss of parents, retrenchment, and the 'empty nest' when children leave home are some usual examples. But not all couples and families have the capacity to deal with these changes.

In this chapter we examine how early experiences shape the minds of the individuals that later form the couple, and how this early experience then affects the couple's combined capacity to negotiate change. Common to all psychoanalytic theories is the idea that we are formed by our experiences as infants and children. The focus in object relations theory is on the impact on the personality of the earliest relationship between the mother and infant. Our infant feels anxiety because his[1] mother who provides also deprives, by being unavailable at times. And in an attempt to deal with his feelings about this apparent contradiction he does so by splitting the experiences into separate mothers, into good and bad parts.

We see this splitting and projection of feelings at the heart of many of the problems that couples and families bring to the consulting room. But how does this happen? How does this process that structures the mind of an infant later manifest in the minds of the people who together make up the couple, who go on to have an infant? How is it that some adults are able to develop minds that can connect with another in a loving way, while the minds of others are so divided within themselves that relationships with others are fraught and the normal challenges of development become problematic?

This idea of an internalised process, that we call internal object relationships, is a core psychoanalytic concept, and is fundamental for providing a model to help understand the workings of the mind. These 'relationships' are not easily accessible as they are largely stored in the unconscious part of the mind.

So what exactly do we mean by this term 'Object Relationship'? An 'object' is another, and in the first place most often a mother. The primary idea is that our relationships with others shape us psychically, and that relationships are most impactful during infancy. In our view the mind is essentially formed in these earliest dyadic relationships. The infant and the (m)other are involved in a mutually formative process. Changes occur due to the developmental maturation of the infant's mind as it organises experiences and participates in interactions. The parents also adjust to their infant's presence. Clearly the mother's capacity to support her infant's development is imperative for his healthy psychological growth. The understanding and support given by the father is containing for the mother–infant couple and vital for the overall family's healthy functioning. We start life as a couple, and we start families as a couple.

This first chapter outlines a case study, where a young woman presents with physical symptoms in the context of complex family dynamics. The chapter examines the dilemmas of this young woman and her family through the lens of a model of the growth of the mind derived principally from Klein (1946) and Fairbairn (1952). A gradual exploration and clarification of these models, maps of the internal organisation of the minds of the members of the couple or family, is an important part of the work of psychoanalytic psychotherapy. These models define the particular anxieties the couple or families in our consulting room face. They are also representative of essential anxieties that we all face in coming to terms with and understanding our separate existence in the world, including the world of relationships we are born into.

Additionally, concepts added by Winnicott (1953) and Bion (1962a) will be touched on in this chapter, and again later, to provide the contextual framework for facilitating this process of exploring, understanding and integrating these often split internal object relationships.

Moving between theoretical ideas and clinical material is a hallmark of this book; it will happen many times as you read.

Emma and her family

Emma was 17 when she presented, the youngest of four from an intact middle-class family. At menarche she had begun to suffer attacks of dizziness, nausea and ringing in her ears, which meant she missed a lot of school. Eventually she was diagnosed with Ménière's disease, an intermittent, debilitating and largely untreatable neurological condition.

Emma's neurologist had advised a low salt diet, and for three years Emma's mother Judy dutifully cooked special low salt food for her daughter. Emma rarely ate these specially prepared meals and continued to suffer debilitating attacks of dizziness.

The family was referred for therapy by Emma's psychiatrist because of her depression, which he thought had a lot to do with relationships within the family.

Over the years of Emma's illness various members of the family had upset Judy by eating Emma's 'special' food, which was always carefully labelled in the fridge.

John, Emma's father, was sceptical about the diagnosis of and treatment for Ménière's disease, and angry with Judy for what he saw as evidence of her indulgence of his daughter. He was the main offender when it came to eating Emma's special food. Emma's three older siblings were also rivalrous with her, although they could acknowledge how unwell she was. Judy felt stressed by the extra work-load of cooking for, looking after and worrying about Emma, as her daughter was so often unwell. She was upset that her family did not support her with this, but instead criticised her for favouring Emma. She was offended by this suggestion, and defended herself by saying that she cared equally for everyone in her family, a statement that we came to understand was scrupulously correct.

Parents' background history

Both Emma's parents had markedly rejecting experiences in their childhoods. Judy, the middle of three girls, had a difficult upbringing. Her father was physi-cally abusive and her mother had recurrent psychotic breakdowns requiring hospi-talisation. Judy never knew what it was like to be mothered, as her mother seemed emotionally absent even when not actually in hospital. Additionally, Judy was required to help out extensively at home and in the family retail business. She complied with these excessive demands but her father would still lose his temper over minor things and beat Judy or lock her away in a small pantry. It is unclear why she alone bore this burden, and nowadays she is angry that her sisters, who were not so compliant, had it easier.

Judy became a very perfectionistic person. She is scrupulous about things being done properly, and becomes agitated if this does not happen. She feels compelled to attend to the people in her world, exhausting herself in the process. Like her mother before her, she does not care well for herself, and feels quite uncared for. There is a right and a wrong way to do things, and very few people do things the right way as far as Judy is concerned. In this way she is like her father; things are never good enough. It is clear she does not intend to be judgemental, but people simply do not live up to her standards.

John, the younger of two boys, was much less academically capable than his older brother and so a disappointment to his parents, particularly his mother. As he could not compete academically with his brother, he instead developed a talent for being a joker. He thinks this further alienated him from his mother, as he was sent to boarding school at the same time as his brother, missing out on two years at home. He is a spontaneous and colourful character, who wants to live life to the full. At times he seems irresponsible, like someone who has never really managed to 'grow up'. He acknowledges that he is slapdash about things and that this often leads to conflict with his much more fastidious wife.

Both parents have reacted to their childhood experiences of emotional neglect, but in opposite ways. Judy tries to get her needs met by looking after others and unconsciously expecting something back. John tries to get his needs met by being entertaining and expecting appreciation in quite an entitled, childish way. Their marriage has not been a happy or genuinely collaborative one. He feels he can never do things right for her, an assessment she agrees with. She on the other hand feels overburdened and unappreciated. They both share a sense of being alone and unloved.

It is clear that Judy can clamp down on John's fun, a projected aspect of her own longed for adolescent experience, much like her own father did to her. John repeatedly provokes Judy to be critical of him thus replaying his mother's rejection of him. Despite these difficulties they ran a successful family business, which thrived on his people skills and her diligence. By the time of Emma's birth (the fourth child) Judy was overwhelmed and in a constant state of stress, trying to get things done. She complained that John was no help, and in her opinion often left her with all the work both for the children and for the business.

The nature of early object relationships

We have already said an 'object' is an 'other', and 'object relationships' are relationships that we make with the significant others in our life, in the first place usually our mothers.[2] It is important to understand that what is internalised is the affective experience of a particular kind of *relationship* with another, i.e. the internalised experience of the self in relationship to the other, along with the affect or emotion evoked by the experience.

These relationship patterns are dynamic; they are constantly being activated and reworked, and there is a two-way interaction between what occurs intrapsychically and interpersonally.

With development, revisions of these primitive object relationships occur, and more sophisticated understandings are laid down over earlier ones. With regression, more primitive experiences can again resurface. This can occur in situations of great stress or developmental crisis.

Mrs Klein and her opposing breasts

On the basis of Mrs Klein's observations of very young children she conjectured that there are a series of defence mechanisms used by infants to protect themselves from the distress that they feel in the face of the overwhelming anxiety that arises from intense dependence. These early experiences leave psychic records that are internalised in the unconscious mind. Because they are experiences perceived by the immature infant brain these records do not accurately reflect reality. Also, they are partly or wholly sensory perceptions and this means they are distorted by infantile phantasies, which shape them often intensely.

Klein's defence mechanisms also serve as a model for unconscious communication between infant and mother, a communication between minds. Nonetheless, while that communicative function is a helpful idea, it is the overwhelming anxiety of absolute dependence that we begin with, the relationship between the internalised experience of the (m)other and the vicissitudes that hunger and maternal absence have on these internal representations. And importantly it is the way that the conflict between these internal objects come to have a life of their own; and this, in Kleinian terminology, is between a good breast and a bad one: an available loving (m)other or an unavailable hating (m)other.[3]

This conflict between the forces of 'love' and 'hate' is faced by the newborn infant in order to cope with the reality that even 'good enough' mothers are unavailable sometimes. Even though our infant does not 'think' in these terms, he hates the frustrating mother/breast and this cannot be squared with his love towards the comforting mother/breast. Side by side these contradictory feelings are incompatible and arouse dangerous, chaotic and potentially annihilatory states of mind. In Klein's view the infant fears both his own demise from abandonment, and as a result of his projected rage, the demise of his mother, the source of all nourishment (Britton, 1989).

The solution, Klein suggested, for this conflicting situation is that the infant creates a defensive structure that *splits* these experiences into different parts, and keeps knowledge of the good part separate from the bad part. These split experiences (good and bad) are then *introjected*, which means taken inside the infant's mind: these are the internal objects.

In an attempt to maintain a link with a good mother, so as to be able to sustain himself, the 'bad' aspects are *denied* and *repressed* into the unconscious self. In this way the infant creates a *phantasy of an idealised*, as opposed to a 'good enough', mother. She is too good to be true because all the bad bits have been pared away. But the bad experience is retained, unconsciously, inside the infant's psyche. So *splitting*, the first defence available to the infant, is accompanied by *introjection* and *repression* of this bad experience of the mother. That is to say the bad object relationship is relegated into unconsciousness.

It is clear that this is all highly complex activity for a baby to be consciously engaging in, and that is the point. These defences occur at a deeply emotional, physiological level and are unconsciously generated and registered.

This level of psychic functioning represents the Paranoid-Schizoid Position (Klein, 1946), and because the mother/father is not related to as a whole figure, in which good and bad can be integrated, Klein termed this part object relating.

Things get more complicated now because we have to consider the two-person situation in psychic development. So when the previously unavailable mother returns to the infant, he can no longer bear the psychic effort of repressing the hated object relationship and now *projects* it into mother.

The infant then 'identifies' his mother with this bad projected object relationship and expects retaliation from the now *phantasied* persecutory mother. This process of ridding oneself of the intolerable internal experience into another is termed *projective identification*.

A mother who cannot contain the projected persecutory anxiety, such as Emma's mother, because she is too anxious herself, returns to her infant a doubly anxious experience, thus reinforcing the bad object relationship. There is a sense that the world is dangerous, and no one is available to help. This has implications for the later expression of dependent needs, and increases the difficulty in allowing one's self to be vulnerable.

In addition, Klein's concepts help us to understand that the experience of 'bad' internal objects can also be projected into relationships in the world, so the help offered by husbands, or other helping figures (such as medical professionals and therapists) is also unable to be seen as helpful and therefore not able to be used. 'If the mothers are not able to contain their infants' worries, the babies then receive a view of themselves that confirms their poor sense of themselves as unmanageable' (Savege-Scharff and Scharff, 2005, p. 38).

Klein and processes of incorporation: depressive level functioning

In the normal course of 'good enough' development for the infant, the containing mother survives the projected persecutory 'attack' from her infant, so the infant is proved wrong about his fears that his mother will damage him, or that he has damaged his mother. She has been able to ride out the emotional storm when the infant believed everything had turned bad and the source of life had disappeared. Only then is a benign view of himself in relation to the mother possible, and this allows the *Introjective Identification* of a good enough object relationship.

This process of *introjection*, of being able to take things in mentally, is facilitated by the neurological maturation of the baby which allows an increasing ability to tolerate frustration. It takes some time for the infant to put his two contradictory experiences together and realise they come from the same person; for the infant to realise that the mother he hates for abandoning him is the same mother he loves for loving and caring for him. What can then become established is not an idealised object relationship, but one that is responsive enough, often enough. And when this happens he begins to become 'concerned' for the angry hostile feelings he has towards his loving parent, and the stage of Depressive position functioning (Klein, 1935) is ushered in. This is what occurs in a securely attached mother–infant dyad.

This is also what happens in the course of a good therapy; the therapist is introjected as a good enough object, thus providing the opportunity for a reworking of original internal object relationships. The patient becomes able to expect that their dependent needs might be reciprocally met in an adult relationship, so that they can risk being vulnerable with those who care for them, and whom they care about, without fear of being damaged or damaging.

Bion and containment

Our ideas about how the infant's mind develops owe much to the idea of containment (Bion, 1962a). Bion thought that the overwhelming experiences which an infant needs to project into the mother were anxieties about annihilation, about survival when he is so utterly dependent, which he labelled 'beta elements'. How these anxieties are dealt with depends on the 'containing function' of the mother. Bion believed that the normal (ordinary 'good enough') mother would be responsive to these frightening feelings (*projective identifications*) from her baby. The mother would be able to relieve her infant of his overwhelming experience by her capacity to withstand and process these anxieties, through her use of what he termed 'alpha function', or her capacity to contain. She would then give back to her baby a more benign (metabolised) experience, and thus function as a container for what her baby could not contain himself. This process is linked to depressive position functioning, but Bion highlights the role of the mother/caregiver in helping her infant to integrate good and bad experiences into a whole maternal object that can be internalised.

As a result the infant gradually learns to take in things, to learn from experience. This internalisation of alpha functioning, or thinking for itself, then continues into adult life and provides the basis for resilience and the capacity to deal with difficult things.

Bion's ideas about containment also provide a model for therapy, where the therapist tries to understand and re-process the previously unconscious affects from the patient's earlier experience, integrate the split thinking, and help the patient (couple or family) move forward. The importance of containment is further discussed in a later chapter.

Perhaps with these concepts in mind we could now speculate further about Emma's infancy. When Emma cried and it was hard to settle her, Judy felt bad. Apart from her baby's needs, Judy's unmet dependency needs were evoked; these began with own early neglect, at the hands of her parents, and were replicated in her marriage. Judy would no doubt have tried to soothe her baby; however, as she was *projectively identified* with the infantile distress, she would have returned to Emma unmetabolised, uncontained 'beta elements' of her own.

This overwhelming situation created chaotic feelings for both infant and mother, and baby Emma may have continued to be distressed, or alternately may have dissociated and quietened down.

This situation for the mother–infant dyad of Emma and Judy is not helped by what John brings from his family background. The emotional neglect in his family of origin has left him rivalrous with his own children for Judy's love. It is as if there is not enough to go around. He is therefore unable to provide Judy with the love that she needs (if she could accept it) or the necessary support for her parenting, which she just might be able to use. This inability of the couple to function as a satisfactory unit (parental couple) who can be there mutually for each other reinforces splits between good and bad in the couple's combined psyche – John's shameful view of himself as incompetent, as a child – and Judy's long-suffering view of herself as the only grown-up, unfairly having to do everything. This unsatisfying couple relationship is also internalised by Emma through the mechanism of introjective identification, so her relationship with herself is problematic: she is off balance; sick.

Winnicott and Holding

Winnicott saw that the 'good enough' mother when caring for her newborn infant would become preoccupied, a state of mind that he termed 'Primary Maternal

Preoccupation' (Winnicott, 1960). This allowed her boundaries to envelop the newborn, to lend an auxiliary protective ego, until the infant had developed sufficiently to start to manage some things on his own. Winnicott next suggested the facilitating mother would provide a 'holding environment', one where she was present and available for helping, but was also aware of the importance of not imposing herself when it was not necessary.

With this Winnicott implies that the attuned mother intuits when her developing infant can be tested a little, to learn from experience. So, the infant learns that outside reality is not always there to fulfil his desires. The mother needs to be in a state of mind which allows her to make these judgements, and to do this she has to be able to bear that her infant must tolerate some distress. And the mother's capacity to tolerate distress is aided by the presence of a comforting third – traditionally the father, but it could be another, who holds and supports her during this time.

Judy's own history of neglect and abuse, coupled with her own unconscious hostility, made it very difficult for her to allow Emma to suffer any distress, so limiting Emma's capacity to learn from experience. Emma remained full of fearful anxieties, her own and her mother's, which never dissipated, as she was never helped to face them, and thus achieve some containment of them.

Fairbairn, splitting and endopsychic structure

While the idea of the infant's need to split the object into good and bad was the foundation of Klein's theory, Fairbairn offered a more subtle mapping of the intrapsychic processes involved. His theoretical model is particularly relevant to the forms of splitting we see working with couples and families. Unlike Freud and Klein, Fairbairn was concerned with the *actual* experience of the mother. Babies are helpless and need care and protection to survive; the imperative of survival requires that the baby engages its mother. So Fairbairn believed that 'the infant is born object seeking' (Fairbairn, 1952, p. 138) and that this 'drive to relate' was the organising principle for the development of the self or ego. To deal with his mother's failures to be available for safe relating an infant uses splitting processes which structure his mind in a way that is represented in Figure 1.1.

The central area of this diagram contains what Fairbairn (1952) termed the 'ideal object relationship' between the central ego (or self) and the 'ideal' object, a relationship associated with feelings of satisfaction and security. Fairbairn used the term 'ideal object' which can be confused with idealising, and suggests something akin to perfect. This type of object relationship is better thought of as a 'good enough' one, with a good enough object, borrowing the term from Winnicott (1953). In healthy individuals this constitutes the largest part of the mind and is available for conscious relating.

On the top and bottom of the diagram are the other two main types of object relationships, both of which are frustrating and unsatisfying: the exciting and the rejecting object relationships.[4] They are associated with unbearably painful emotions and are defended against by being pushed, or '*repressed*' into unconsciousness by the

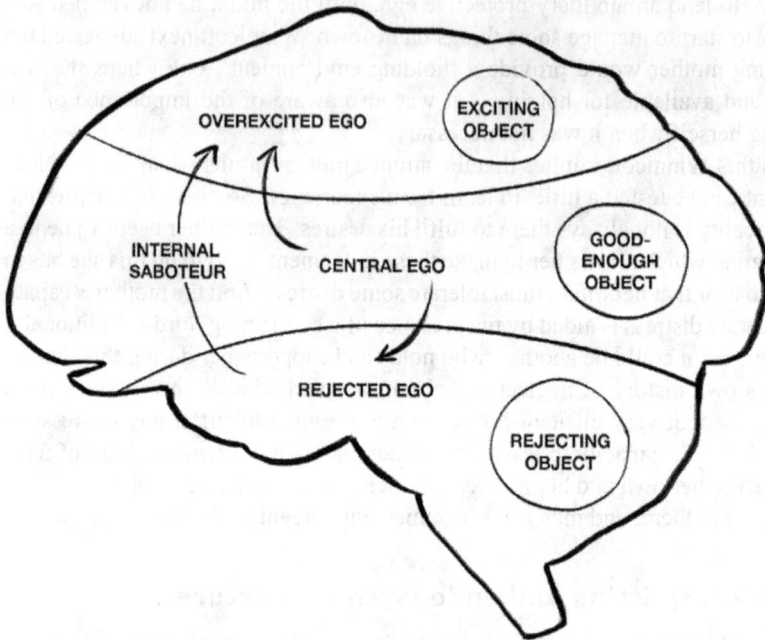

Figure 1.1 Fairbairn's three main types of intrapsychic object relationships (Diagram: S.J. Bryson)

(Source: Modified from *The Sexual Relationship: An Object Relations View of Sex and the Family*, courtesy of Routledge and Kegan Paul. Copyright © David E. Scharff, 1982. Reprinted by kind permission)

central ego. This involves the splitting of the self in the face of the perceived failure of the object (mother) to be 'good enough'. Parts of the ego are bound up in these repressed processes and are unavailable for normal flexible relating. Consequently the ego or self is weakened by the degree to which these splits exist.

This is an important distinction from Klein, who thought that splits existed in the internal objects largely because of the infant's primitive phantasies and was not so focused on the real relationship between the mother and infant.

Fairbairn used the term 'exciting' not primarily to reference sexual feelings; the state here is of being overly anxious, or hyper-aroused in a way that is unpleasant or frustrating, not satisfying. It has significant physiological and physical aspects to it, as most intense feelings do, and is associated with yearning and painful longing, with desperate, anxious arousal. The excited ego represents that part of the self that craves nurture.

The rejecting object relationship, between the rejected ego and the rejecting object, is also associated with feelings of frustration, but here there is anger and despair. The rejected ego represents the part of the self that eschews care. This could result from a mother who is unable to be attentive to her baby, unavailable for external or internal reasons. The infant is then not able to expect care, or rejects it when offered. This may have been Judy's experience as a baby at the hands of Emma's grandmother, who was severely unwell with a post-partum psychosis.

Fairbairn hypothesised that such an infant, one with a 'rejecting' mother, may give up expecting to have their needs met, and that a secondary tendency to repress the search for the object may arise (from the rejected ego) in the service of avoiding the repeated pain of rejection and disappointment. Fairbairn called this tendency the *Internal Saboteur*, and thought that it resulted in cases of schizoid withdrawal – a retreat from relating. However, below this withdrawal there may well be locked away pockets of unmetabolised experience.

These painful feelings from infancy may be felt as physiological experiences of distress, e.g. difficulty with feeding, skin irritation, sensations that are fragmentary, and outside conscious expression. Fairbairn hypothesised that these physical sensations may represent dissociated memories, uncontained splits in the experience of the self.

It is possible to think about Emma's dizziness and her failure to respond to medical interventions in this regard. These physical symptoms could be seen as an unconscious expression of the rejecting object relationship, and a sign that this may be so is that they cause frustration and anger in others, particularly between the parents.

An example of a rejecting object relationship, reinforced by secondary repression of the Internal Saboteur at work, can be seen below where Judy rejects both the help of the therapist and the affection of her husband.

Judy: (Angrily) *I don't know why John doesn't help; why he can't see how much I do and think about doing more? He's actually unhelpful. Why eat Emma's special food? As if I don't have enough to do!*

Therapist: *Well I don't know why John does that, but perhaps Judy you expect too much of yourself, and you are wearing yourself out? Maybe John can't keep up with how much you do?*

John: *It is so true: you do your job, run the business, look after the family and all the relatives, and fuss over Emma even though she doesn't really want you to. The special food, you've done it for years now, it doesn't help anyway, and I eat it because sometimes when I finish work I'm hungry. You seem cross all the time that I don't do as much as you, but nobody could, you don't stop. . .*

Judy: *I don't think that is fair, she's really unwell John, and she's been that way for a long while now. I really wish you would help more with her. . . . I feel you resent the fact that she is sick . . . and you don't do much to help me.*

John: *I do resent it, you are so constantly doing stuff for her, for everyone actually. And anyway I do help Emma in my own ways. I took her for driving lessons. You are always so worried about everything – about doing everything right; with you there's never any time for fun. . . .*

Therapist: *Is John right? Is it hard for you not to be always looking after others, to get something for yourself. . . . Maybe it is even hard for you to come here, it feels like another demand, not something that is helpful.*

Judy: (Angrily) *Well it doesn't feel very helpful actually, I don't know how any of this helps with Emma's problems. You seem to be implying that I'm doing too much, but I can't not do what I do because no one else will do it. Coming here just takes time, and even though sometimes I think it helps, it doesn't make John any less lazy . . . and that is what I need – him to be more responsible, less needing attention himself.*

Therapist: *I think that you both might need care and attention; John is just better at asking for it. You feel I have been critical of you for caring for Emma – like John was, like your father was . . . and you are angry with me about that. I appreciate you are trying to do the right thing but I can also see that John would like to be with you in a way that might be good for you. It might not cure Emma, but it might help the two of you to manage together better, it might bring you closer.*

John: *I would like that . . .* (He reaches for her hand)

Judy: (Still angry . . . is reluctant to have him hold her hand) *I can't see it. . . . I don't really think he's interested in me and what I think about him. . . . I think he just wants to be going out and showing off so that other people will think that he is charming and funny. . .*

John: *Well, I do care what you think . . . but mostly I think that you think I'm not up to much.*

Judy is unable to escape her rejecting object relationship dynamic – she expects criticism and rejection, and cannot allow for more loving interactions such as a therapist who might want to help and a husband who might care for her.

The case material that follows sheds some light on the circumstances in Emma's family at the time of her birth, and on how these frustrating object relationship cycles are passed through the generations.

Therapist: *So what was it like for you both when Emma was born?*

Judy: *Terrible. I was so overwhelmed, so tired. I had so much to do. Four children, and the business to run, and John wasn't around much, and when he was around he wasn't much help. Emma wasn't too unsettled. But I felt terrible, I wasn't sleeping at all. So I would go and check on her to see if she was sleeping, which she was, but by checking I'd wake her up, and then she'd be hard to settle.*

John: *I thought that Judy had postnatal depression, she was down all the time, no energy, not like she usually is. But she wouldn't consider the idea . . . it was like I'd said the wrong thing to mention it.*

Therapist: *Is that right Judy? Did what John thought upset you?*

Judy: *I didn't want to think that I was like my mum, I just wanted to carry on. It would have been better if John had been more helpful.*

John: *Actually I tried to be helpful. I was out front in the shop, which I admit I liked. Judy was doing the behind the scenes stuff, like she always did. She said she needed to be there to hear if Emma cried. It wasn't different to usual. Maybe it should have been, maybe that was my mistake. I loved the kids when they were little, and I did a lot for them; still do, even though now I think they are very indulged. I tried to help with Emma, but Judy was not happy to hand her over to me, I didn't do it the right way.*

Judy: (Upset, tearful) *I felt she was rejecting me, just like I feel she is now. . .*

Therapist: *So you felt like your baby was rejecting you, like you had felt rejected by your mother . . . that must have been terrible.*

Judy: (Crying) *It was. . . . I kept trying to make it okay, but nothing I did seemed to make it any better, she didn't seem to need me.*

John: *Judy was in a real state, worrying about Emma all the time. It didn't help when I told her she was doing fine, and the other three children had all done well. It's the only time my mother has actually been helpful. Judy seemed to let her help a bit when no one else could.*

We again see in the clinical vignette a complex feedback cycle of the rejecting and exciting object relationships at play between both John and Judy, and Judy and Emma, with little room left for good enough object relationship functioning to occur.

Perhaps Judy felt ambivalent about having this fourth baby, and could not express her negative feelings about this. Emma was the second daughter, as was Judy, and this coincidence may well have evoked in Judy uncontained infantile states of mind from when her own mother was psychotic. Judy just felt terrible. To counter these unconscious feelings Judy needed to 'check' on Emma to ensure she was alright, that she had not been harmed by her hostile feelings. So Judy would anxiously intrude on Emma and even wake Emma when she was sleeping.

In fact Emma settled quickly and was not a needy baby. However, Emma's reaction left Judy feeling rejected; she said she felt her baby 'didn't need' her, making her unavailable like her own mother had been and thus reinforcing the rejecting object relationship. Ostensibly caring, this is a frustrating object relationship for both mother and infant. Judy needed baby Emma to confirm that she was not a rejecting mother, like her own mother was, but this was clearly not something baby Emma could do, contain Judy's destructive anxieties. As a baby Emma, who was exposed to too much anxious attentiveness, may well have felt overwhelmed and even dizzy with this experience, and while she looked like a quiet, good baby she had retreated to a schizoid, dissociated state.

Emma introjected and repressed an excess of anxiety in relationships, and experienced predominantly frustrating object relationships in her unconscious mind.

As a result of this internal psychic world she was unable to feel secure within herself, there was not enough ego available for good enough object relating, and she now continues to express, unconsciously, her internalised sense of things 'not being right', of being overwhelmed and uncontained through a psychosomatic symptom – dizziness, things spinning out of control. Emma's further defence of retreating and becoming dissociated from this excess of anxiety also seems now to be challenged by adolescent development. It is notable that the onset of Emma's dizziness coincided with her menarche, and it is worth considering the need for her separation/individuation as a causative factor here.

The vignette above also demonstrates that John is seen by Judy as an unhelpful partner; it is likely that Judy's rejecting object relationship dynamic has painted them into a corner here, one which fits with John's own rejecting intrapsychic world. His attempts to help were not acceptable, he felt relegated to being incompetent, and no doubt felt angry about this. He is used to feeling a disappointment and expecting not to be cared about. John expresses this in 'it's the only time my mother has actually been helpful', a comment which backs up his previous statement that he believes that Judy doesn't think he's 'up to much'. He seems to hold more of the longing for the couple to have a space for themselves, though his resentment at being left out sabotages his chances of winning Judy's care.

Emma's illness and Judy's anxieties are legitimised through the medicalisation of her symptoms. But outside the family, doctors who are consulted to help Emma also fail to 'get it right' like Judy. Medical treatments repeat the anxiety provoking frustrating object relationship sets that Emma is so familiar with. And this can be anticipated to carry through to a potentially difficult transference relationship with any help that is offered from a therapist.

Emma's untreatable symptoms keep her enmeshed with her worried mother, unable to function and to be independent, but at the same time resentful of this enforced dependency. Moreover Emma's dependent needs are not appropriately met, as she is now cared for as a sick person, not someone whose need for care is normal.

Emma's case demonstrates how this concept of the secondary repression from the rejecting ego or 'internal saboteur' applies to a psychosomatic presentation, where displacement of the need for care onto a physically elusive condition both elicits care and rejects it at the same time.

Summary

Emma and her family's story demonstrates how the emotional relationships that we are exposed to in infancy and childhood are internalised and can be understood to shape the developing unconscious mind. The theories of Fairbairn and Klein are particularly useful in understanding these internal worlds of couples and families and the capacity of these internal worlds, the 'mind' of the couple or family to deal with the challenges of life. Klein suggested that the infant's mind is shaped by unconscious processes, which she conceptualised as phantasies, informed by strong inner anxieties. She further suggested that these anxieties have an innate developmental progression. She thought that, irrespective of the reality of the relational experience, the infant struggles with loving and hateful feelings towards the mother and uses the defences of splitting, introjection and projection, and introjective and projective identification on the path to normal development. If this development proceeds well enough the infant achieves Depressive Position functioning. If development is compromised, the infant can remain in a world split between good and bad, that is at paranoid-schizoid functioning.

This helps to explain the persecutory fear that Judy suffers that she will not be able to help Emma her daughter, despite her conscious efforts to do so, as Judy, or the maltreated child part of her, is unconsciously identified with both the needy child aspect of her daughter, and also the part that is rejecting of 'bad' mothering. Judy unconsciously needs Emma to remain sick to carry all her difficult needy and angry feelings, which Judy has no conscious connection with, while Judy consciously does everything she can to care for her daughter. In fact she does too much, and Judy feels exhausted by her efforts and experiences resentment about being unappreciated by Emma, and her family. These unconscious processes render her quite helpless to make any difference. The family remains stuck in a paranoid-schizoid way of dealing with the world.

Experience is relational Fairbairn argued; the infant is born other (object) seeking and the template for the mind arises from the sets of relationship experiences that we accrue with our primary others. Fairbairn was concerned with the real relationship between the mother and the infant, and the differences between good enough and inadequate parenting become represented in terms of structures the infant mind develops. His model includes a division of the frustrating object into an exciting and rejecting one, with the idea that the exciting object is exciting of anxiety in an unsatisfying way. By extension, Fairbairn's model also valorises the real relationship between the family or couple and the therapist.

Using Fairbairn's framework, the internalised 'bad' relationship between Emma and her mother could be further understood as having both an overly exciting and an overly rejecting component, which vacillates in an unstable, insecure way between these poles, generating a great deal of distress and anxiety. There is little time spent in a good enough state of relating where there is a stable sense of a competent self, and an accompanying sense of satisfaction and comfort that can be found in relationships. These concepts apply also to the marital relationship, and the nature of the transference relationship with the therapist. Emma's somatic symptom of dizziness could be a derivative of her early infantile experience. For Judy, Emma's illness is again something she can't do right, eliciting a rejecting object relationship, further reinforcing her earlier experiences of lack of care, and her internal saboteur, which harshly crushes any hope of care being available. She unconsciously remains unable to accept any care. John's childhood dynamic of being rejected adds to this stuck situation, as he resents being left out by Judy, and he cannot join together with her in support of their coupledom; rather he tries to elicit more exciting object relationships with others, including the therapist.

If Klein and Fairbairn provided ideas about the internal structure of the mind, Bion and Winnicott provided some invaluable links between these internal structures and the role of the outside world.

Bion's ideas about containment, which he thought led to the growth of thinking, require the presence of another. For Bion it is the capacity of the mother to transform difficult emotional experiences (beta elements) and return them to the child in a detoxified way that allows the child to take in experience and make sense of it, to learn from experience. This has ready applicability to the therapist's endeavour. Winnicott's ideas are also relevant to the therapeutic process. Just as the mother holds her baby, and establishes a sensitive routine which provides physically for the mother–infant relationship, so the therapist through the use of the therapeutic frame, provides a safe and reliable context for the work of therapy. The sensitivity of the mother to judge when to help and when doing so would intrude on the infant's capacity for development is a very significant idea. Sadly Emma's parents were initially unable to contain her anxieties and their own. Nor were they able to provide a 'holding' environment for her development since they were not able to function as a united parental couple.

Conclusions

In this chapter we have highlighted how ideas about internal object relations from Fairbairn, Klein, Winnicott and Bion come together to shape a theoretical model of the infant's mind. More importantly we use these ideas, in the case study about Emma and her family, to think about the mind of the couple and family and its capacity to accept the challenges of life, which is what this book is about.

To negotiate these anxieties however cannot be done alone – the mind is formed by relationships, which are also the source of the anxieties. Both Bion and Winnicott in different ways emphasise what Fairbairn began, the idea that it takes another to make a mind. The passing of experience from the infant to the mother and a returning back of something to the baby, hopefully detoxified and less anxiety provoking, is essential for healthy development. The therapeutic implications of this we will continue to draw on.

As we are couple and family therapists we will add that the baby comes from a couple to make three, and note that the mind has its origins in a series of dyadic and triadic structures.

Notes

1 We are using the masculine pronoun, rather than the female or neutral, for the sake of simplicity of explanation. No deference to patriarchy is intended.
2 Many others could be the chief carer for an infant. The use of the word 'mother' here is not meant to exclude others.
3 Melanie Klein was working at the same time that Ronald Fairbairn was developing his model of the mind; they corresponded and influenced each other's thinking. (In her 'Notes on some schizoid mechanisms' (Klein, 1946) she is concerned about the infant's

relationship with another, the real external object, and does not only see development as driven by instinctual pressures seeking satisfaction, the classical Freudian position. However she stayed loyal to Freud's topographical model of the mind and retains instinctual drives in her theoretical position.)

4 Fairbairn's original terms for these were the 'libidinal' and 'anti-libidinal' object relationships. These are Freudian terms, but Fairbairn was not of the opinion that the forces at work were instinctual drives; rather they were the result of the interaction between the infant and his parent. For the sake of clarity we prefer to use terms which describe the quality of the object relationship being invoked.

Bibliography

Bion, W.R. (1959). Attacks on linking. *International Journal of Psycho-Analysis, 40,* 308–315.

Bion, W.R. (1962a). The psychoanalytical study of thinking. *International Journal of Psycho-Analysis, 43,* 306–310.

Bion, W.R. (1962b). *Learning from Experience*. London: Heinemann.

Britton, R. (1989). The missing link: parental sexuality in the Oedipus complex. In J. Steiner (Ed.) *The Oedipus Complex Today* (pp. 83–101). London: Karnac.

Fairbairn, W.R.D. (1952). *Psychological Studies of the Personality*. London: Routledge & Kegan Paul.

Fairbairn, W.R.D. (1958). On the nature and aims of psychoanalytic treatment. *International Journal of Psycho-Analysis, 39,* 374–385.

Klein, M. (1935). A contribution to the psychogenesis of manic-depressive states. In M. Klein, *Love, Guilt and Reparation and Other Works 1921–1945*. New York: Free Press.

Klein, M. (1946). Notes on some schizoid mechanisms. *International Journal of Psycho-Analysis, 27,* 99–110 [Reprinted in M. Klein, *Envy and Gratitude and Other Works 1946–1963*. London: Hogarth Press, 1980].

Savege-Scharff, J. and Scharff, D.E. (2005). *A Primer of Object Relations Therapy*. Lanham, MD: Jason Aronson.

Scharff, D.E. (1982). *The Sexual Relationship: An Object Relations View of Sex and the Family* (p. 217). Boston: Routledge & Kegan Paul.

Winnicott, D.W. (1953). Transitional objects and transitional phenomena. *International Journal of Psycho-Analysis, 34,* 89–97.

Winnicott, D.W. (1960). The theory of the parent-infant relationship. In *The Maturational Processes and the Facilitating Environment* (pp. 37–55). New York: International Universities Press, 1965.

Chapter 2

The developmental framework

How couples and families grow

Jenny Berg and Noela Byrne

Introduction

In this chapter we will consider anxiety and its relationship to the emotional growth of a couple or family. 'Anxiety' is a word in common usage and at one level it is an emotion that everyone has experienced. However, we contend that anxiety is central to understanding the internal psychological world of the couple and family. Also, and importantly, anxiety can manifest unconsciously in a way that a couple or family is unaware of. A simple example is the child who develops a stomach ache every Monday morning of the school term and protests his reluctance to attend school.

As a couple forms and develops and progresses towards being a family, different anxieties are stirred up. If these anxieties are able to be managed in a 'good enough' way, development proceeds such that the couple and family cope with the stresses inherent in the cycle of life. The previous chapter described some of the ways in which internal object relationships structure our minds in ways that are flexible, or inflexible, open or closed to change. When developmental challenges or crises arise they can reveal fault lines in the minds of the parents and the family. As a result, the parents are not able to manage the anxieties that are stirred, and need help to move on. To understand these points where couples and families get stuck, and ultimately what might be required therapeutically to free them up, we will outline a *schema of developmental anxieties*, one which we all negotiate in the process of psychological growth. These ideas, seminal to the thinking in this book, will be illustrated by some work with a family in difficulty, where the initial referral was for a child.

What is anxiety?

Anxiety is a feeling that is at the basis of all other more well-elaborated emotions. Bion defined anxiety as a 'premonition of emotion' (Emanuel, 2000). This phrase captures both the sense of something unknown, a premonition, and also the unease that the feeling of anxiety evokes. It feels as if something is wrong. It is also a helpful conceptualisation as it locates the experience of anxiety at a perceptual or sensory level, in the body. We all know the experience of acute anxiety. It is mediated through the sympathetic nervous system, and triggered as part of the body's fight or flight response to danger. Flight from a raging bushfire is an Australian example of a situation that would arouse fear in all of us. Anxiety is also provoked by any change, even one that seems positive, like a move to a new house or a holiday to an exotic destination.

Pathological anxiety

When the amount of anxiety aroused overwhelms one's coping mechanisms it becomes pathological. This can occur with external danger or can be in response to internal triggers, where the threat is not clear. It often results in distressing symptoms. For instance, people with panic attacks usually feel so dreadful they imagine that they are dying. This gives a clue to the primitive mental states under-lying the anxiety – there is an inchoate fear of destruction or annihilation, of ceasing to be. In social phobia there is a fear of being unacceptable, a fear of not being a part of the group, of being ostracised, rejected and abandoned.

Anxiety – a central psychoanalytic concept

The object relations view we hold maintains that the primary source of anxiety is aroused by the infant's helplessness, the fact of dependence on an 'object', or (m)other for survival.

We believe that there is an innate sense of the need for dependence, to be in a sustaining relationship and that infants are programmed to strive actively to meet this need, in order to survive. Anxiety about survival is aroused normally when the 'good enough' mother is unavailable, and excessively with the experience of either an overly distant, rejecting mother who incites abandonment anxieties, or an overly anxious, 'exciting' mother who elicits engulfment anxieties. The way in which these relationships are internalised is what structures the infant's mind, and therefore their capacity to deal with these anxieties.

Developmental anxiety

This brings us back to the concept of developmental anxiety, the idea that anxiety is especially important as a 'driver' of the process of psychic growth. The idea here is that there are stages in psychic functioning which are linked to pivotal develop-mental challenges that occur in infancy and very early childhood. We believe the anxieties attendant to these developmental challenges represent stages (or positions) of infantile development, and that they form a hierarchy of experiences from primitive and inchoate to more mature and definite (Klein, 1946). These stages need to be negotiated for psychic maturation, so that infantile dependency can be replaced by a capacity for 'mature interdependence' (Winnicott, 1960).

Infancy is a time when there is a need for a containing presence to prevent the infant from being overwhelmed by strong feelings. The experience of having these anxieties contained (Bion, 1962) structures the infant's psyche into one that coheres, and it is the task of the mother to provide this for the infant, and the parents in the couple to give this to each other. Successful passage through these stages also requires a facilitating environment (Winnicott, ibid.). Likewise it is the task of the therapist within a safe and predictable therapeutic structure to provide the containment that the couple or family are lacking.

Developmental anxieties and their defences

Knowing about normal development is essential to help us to know what healthy psychological functioning 'looks' like, and also what is pathological, what happens when development has not progressed, and has become stuck. Table 2.1 is a summary of our developmental model and a key to diagnostic and therapeutic work with our patients, including the work with the couple described in this chapter. If the current level of functioning within the couple or family is ascertained then we, as therapists, can anticipate the defences the family may use, and this can helps us to contain the emotions involved. Knowledge of these developmental positions or stages also informs the sort of therapeutic interventions that are most likely to be effective.

The table shows the sequence of developmental stages with the attendant anxieties and defences seen in each position. We have already discussed (in Chapter 1) the stage described as the Paranoid-Schizoid position by Klein (1946), characterised by the defences of splitting and projection. This is what occurs to the infant's fragile sense of self in the face of the frustration of the unavailable (m)other. The Autistic-Contiguous position is hypothesised to exist prior to the paranoid-schizoid phase (Ogden, 1989). Here anxiety is located in the body, resulting in fears of bodily disintegration, of leaking or spilling out, of falling apart. The defensive strategy here is an attempt at merger, to cling to the other, in an 'adhesive' way; to use the other to plug holes in the sense of self. Some authors (Tustin, 1994; Mitrani, 2011) dispute that this is a normal developmental stage and argue that these anxieties only become manifest if trauma is suffered early in infancy causing a major disruption to the mother–infant relationship.

Included in our model is the idea of narcissistic object relating, which we consider falls between the autistic-contiguous and paranoid-schizoid stages – the shaded area on the table below – which subsumes what has been a difficult defensive structure in the couples and families we have worked with. We conceptualise this as being the area of 'borderline' relationship pathology, where the state of psychic functioning of the individuals in the couple is bordering on the edge of psychotic processes, as the phenomena that are occurring are so primitive.

Normally, movement from the merged state of very early relationships (mother–infant, or of 'being in love') to one of greater separateness proceeds without evident trauma. However, if this is not the case, if there is a lack of containment, the

Table 2.1 Schema of developmental anxieties

Developmental stage	Experience of anxiety	Transference/ counter-transference	Defences	Therapeutic strategy
Autistic-contiguous	**Disintegrative anxieties, dissolving Falling, spilling, sexual/ somatic symptoms**	**Overwhelming affect Somatic responses, difficulty thinking**	**Merging, denial of separateness**	**Holding and containment**
Narcissistic	**Fear of separation/ annihilation (claustro-agoraphobia), sexual inhibition**	**Merging/ domination and control**	**Projection, denial, rage**	**Identify shared narcissistic wounds, i.e. shared failure of containment in f.o.o.,* explore sexual difficulties**
Paranoid-schizoid	**Persecutory feelings**	**Idealisation or denigration**	**Projection and splitting, denial of contribution to couple's problems**	**Naming of splits – making sense, trauma interpretation**
Oedipal	**Feelings of exclusion, rivalry, jealousy, intolerance of third**	**Feelings of exclusion from couple, pressure to form alliance with one or other**	**Some regression to splitting, ambivalence, difficulty in separating from f.o.o.**	**Interpretation of feelings of jealousy, focus on shared anxiety**
Depressive	**Despair, sadness at damage Attempts at reparation**	**Despair in therapist Stuckness, sadness**	**Manic control, contempt, valuing and dependency on therapist**	**Interpretation of ambivalence, acknowledgement of loss of therapist**

(Source: Berg, Byrne and Jools)

*(f.o.o. – family of origin)

separateness feels like rupture; intense anxiety can ensue when the other fails to be available in a phantasised perfect way. Strenuous efforts to control the other, often unconscious at first, can cause great conflict when they do not produce the desired result, as the story of the couple in this chapter will demonstrate. Some of the devastating feelings released take the form of claustrophobic and agoraphobic anxieties, of entrapment or abandonment. The feelings generated are catastrophic and may have some relationship to early Oedipal anxieties (Britton, 1989; Feldman, 1989; Fisher, 1999).

The Oedipal stage is the next stage to be negotiated, in which rivalry and jealousy are paramount in the face of the threat imposed by the intrusion of a third. Here there is an emerging, if painful, recognition of the separateness of the other.

Last there is more integrated depressive level functioning, where there are stable object relationships and the other is viewed in a realistic fashion. This entails a respectful awareness of the other as a truly separate person, different from what we might phantasise about, and a concomitant concern for their well-being, not just a need to use them ruthlessly to ensure one's own survival.

These stages are characterised by specific defensive strategies, which is one of the ways we recognise that the person is functioning in that position. Understanding these defensive strategies, and what they mean developmentally, as we stated previously, also leads to the use of different therapeutic tools. These stages or positions are elaborated in the next part of this chapter in the context of the complex case material that is described.

In discussing this hierarchy of developmental anxieties and movement up or down the table, we often use the term 'position' for the resting places, after Melanie Klein, as opposed to 'stage'. A stage suggests a static, linear developmental sequence, whereas a position implies something more dynamic or dialectical. It is important to understand that in an adult these positions co-exist and operate simultaneously, both normally and in pathological situations, an issue that can be quite confusing in therapy. One implication is that the patient may be moving between positions within the course of a single session.

It is also important to know that this is a dynamic sequence; once more mature levels have been reached couples can and do still regress, and this needs to be tolerated and worked through, even when this regression is seized upon by patients as evidence that the situation really is hopeless. The therapist's capacity to tolerate and understand these regressions helps the couple to have a more tolerant and flexible view of themselves and their relationship, with its ups and downs.

This continual movement is evidence of development and growth. Healthy families have greater flexibility in relating. They can get cross with each other and recover from that to go on really caring and thinking about each other. Couples and families who are stuck use rigid, maladaptive ways of relating, such as not talking for days on end. They are more likely to have difficulties with very early aspects of object relating, or may withdraw from the anxiety of relating into a psychic retreat (Steiner, 1993).

Last, and using a slightly different lens, this developmental sequence repre-sents a tool that can be used as a method for assessing and measuring change in therapy. And it may also be a tool for psychodynamic research.

Therapists working with couples and families need containment for the work. We present the case material that follows to illustrate the value of the schema we are presenting to contain the therapist's anxieties, as well as the couple's. An awareness of this way of understanding the family's developmental anxieties and defences can provide a space to reflect that the overwhelming affect in the con-sulting room may have eclipsed.

We also wish to acknowledge the value of supervision both for working at the depth required, and for containing the therapist's anxiety at what those depths reveal. The learning, as with any psychoanalytically-based practice, is mostly done through ongoing supervised clinical work and the safe reflective space pro-vided by personal analysis or therapy.

The material that follows covers four years of therapy, initially with a family and then with the couple. We will be using work with this family to illustrate and enlarge on the developmental anxieties that we have briefly described above. The work was continually supervised and the dynamics that emerged stimulated the ideas we describe in this chapter.

Xanthe and her family

Xanthe, (aged 11) was suffering with bulimia nervosa. She had been a poor feeder even as a baby, and her fussy eating had dominated much of the shared family time. Recently she had refused food altogether for prolonged periods, but would then reactively binge and vomit. This binging behaviour provoked her parents to seek help, as to them this seemed to indicate that Xanthe was out of control.

Wendy (aged 46) was distressed and tearful throughout the initial sessions, in a way that felt overwhelming. She was beside herself as to why a clever girl like Xanthe had chosen to starve herself like this. She suspected that Xanthe did it on purpose, to provoke the anger that Wendy felt. Wendy also felt angry with her husband, Hilton, who was often away from home on business, leaving her on her own to deal with Xanthe.

Hilton (aged 54) smiled incongruously during the early interviews while his wife wept, giving the impression of being emotionally detached. He explained that to provide for the family he had several significant business ventures, which required a great deal of him, including overseas travel. He knew that Wendy found this difficult, but he maintained that travel was necessary to earn the income that supported their current lifestyle.

During the first session Wendy spontaneously revealed how much her father's death ten years previously had affected her. He had become ill while she was pregnant, and died when Xanthe was an infant. When pregnant, she had been filled with an impending sense of loss that prevented her from connecting to her developing baby. She also had not had time to grieve for her father, due to the demands of looking after Xanthe.

Family of origin

Wendy idealised her father, a view Hilton shared. He was seen as the caring available parent, even though he too, like Hilton, was often away from home when she was little, on business trips abroad.

Wendy described her mother as angry and hard to please. She suffered from severe postnatal depression after Wendy's younger sister was born, when Wendy was 6. Wendy became mother's little helper at this time, even changing the newborn's nappies. Eventually Wendy's mother improved, and her parents stayed together, a seemingly stable and functional couple.

Hilton's father was an alcoholic, and unpredictably violent to his mother. Hilton was clearly frightened of him and his childhood memories are few. He recalls his mother bearing visible bruises, yet acting as if nothing was wrong. He felt confused by this denial of reality, and by his mother's lack of response to the abuse. His father left home when Hilton was 11 years old, and Hilton followed before he completed high school. Wendy thought Hilton's mother was cold. Hilton made no comment on this, but angrily described his father as reprehensible.

When he met Wendy in his late twenties Hilton was a successful trader, living a lavish lifestyle, with no thought for a family or the future. Wendy admired Hilton for his quick mind and success, and very much sought him out. She provided him with his first taste of emotional sustenance, encouraged him to study and develop a more reliable career. Hilton felt very flattered by Wendy's attention, but admitted he felt overwhelmed by the intensity of her pursuit; it was more attention than he was used too, and felt a little claustrophobic.

The couple shared an unrealistic view of Wendy's father, as an idealised parent, an 'exciting' father object, and an experience of 'rejecting' mothering. So idealising Wendy's father for this couple functioned as a defence against a recognition of their split off and repressed 'rejecting object'. They share a split unconscious internal parental couple, based on their childhood experiences of their parents, and we will see the impact this has on their capacity to be partners and parents.

In their early relationship Wendy had transferred this idealisation of the father onto Hilton; through his role as the provider they shared an unconscious phantasy of his making good for what had not been available.

Autistic-contiguous anxieties

Let us revisit the developmental hierarchy outlined above to further illuminate this family's dilemmas. The earliest stage in our developmental hierarchy is the Autistic-Contiguous position. Thomas Ogden (1989) synthesising the work of others (Meltzer, 1975; Bick, 1968; Tustin, 1986) described what he considered to be a new normal phase of psychic organisation, the Autistic-Contiguous position occurring earlier than Klein's positions (Klein, 1946).

The phase involves the development of a sense of body self, the starting place for a stable internal sense of self. Starting from Freud's statement that the 'ego is first and foremost a body ego' (Freud, 1923), Ogden suggested that infants learn the limits of themselves through sensory perception, and that the sensation of touch helps to define the self and to distinguish self from other. Skin, usually via the sensation of touch, or the lack thereof, becomes a primary boundary for the experience of relationships with others. Other senses are also capable of being soothing, for instance the sound of a mother's voice. 'Good enough' holding and handling (Winnicott, 1960) in the psychosomatic partnership of the mother–infant dyad soothes overwhelming sensory experiences, creating a sense of boundedness and gives 'a sense of going on being' (Winnicott, ibid.); the self as a separate physical entity.

It follows that either intrusive or insufficient handling at this stage could cause a disruption in this rudimentary sense of self. Bick (1968) describes this disruption as an experience of the 'disintegration of the sensory surfaces' with feelings of leaking, dissolving, disappearing or falling into shapeless, unbounded space.

The defences characteristic of this position can include:

1   psychosomatic displacement of anxiety into the body, especially internal organs, which then become significant problems in their own right; Xanthe's anorexia and bulimia are representative of this;
2   second skin formation (Bick, 1986): the use of repetitious sensory experiences – rocking, exercising, cutting, touching, staring at patterns until mesmerised. In older children and adults repetitive counting or intoning of words, or simply continuous talking, can have a similar function. These have an obsessive quality. We would argue that sensations of emptiness or hunger from self starvation, the continual muscular tension of anorexic exercises, repetitive vomiting, and the presence of regurgitated food and acid in her oesophagus functioned in this way for Xanthe;
3   'adhesive identification' – Meltzer's (1975) term for the narcissistic fusion displayed by Wendy and Hilton. This form of defence can be seen as an unconscious need to stick the other onto you to avoid psychically falling to pieces, disintegrating. This is a more primitive mechanism than introjective or projective identification because it is as if there is no sense of an inner self for projecting or introjecting into, there is a need for absolute sameness. Difference is intolerable. This idea is a way of understanding the very controlling dynamic seen in narcissistic ways of relating.

Sexuality and autistic-contiguous anxieties

The adult sexual relationship is coloured by aspects of the mother–infant psychosomatic partnership (cf. Scharff, 2008), i.e. anxieties relating to the skin and its permeability. When good enough internal objects are established, a couple's sexual relationship can be nurturing and replenishing, maintaining psychic integration. When the internal objects are not so stable, sex can become overwhelming, with phantasies of psychic disintegration, accompanied by fears of engulfment or abandonment (Britton, 1989).

Additionally, early traumatic experiences may result in encapsulated object relationships (Hopper, 1991) that have become dissociated from consciousness. Such traumas include the impact of intrusive physical events, sexual abuse for example, or the deprivation of physical care, or emotional neglect, on the developing ego of the infant or child. These overwhelming experiences are unmetabolised, hinder psychic development, and may be re-evoked along with accompanying extreme anxiety in physically intimate relationships. This anxiety may be condensed and projected onto the main organs of sensation, the skin and genitals, so sex is problematic and either avoided, or compulsively sought in a dissociated and counter-phobic way.

Narcissistic anxieties and defences

Patients with such deeply dissociated and painful internal object relationships have a 'damaged' or depleted sense of self and are likely to have strong narcissistic defences with a longing for fusion, and an intolerance of separateness. In our developmental model, narcissistic relating generally occurs between the Autistic-Contiguous and Paranoid-Schizoid Positions. In normal life, a couple can negotiate the movement through the narcissistic position to a healthier way of relating. In the case of Wendy and Hilton, this proved to be both painful and difficult.

We now return to Xanthe's family and the impact of these primitive anxieties.

The narcissistic marriage and the Autistic-Contiguous Position

It seemed that in their early marriage Wendy and Hilton had unconsciously formed a narcissistic union, where there was pressure to always be of the same mind. Wendy, despite her own career, devoted herself to looking after Hilton, unconsciously projecting her neediness and longing into him and looking after this aspect of herself in him, in a very controlling way.

'I spent a lot of time looking after him', said Wendy. This included supporting the development of his career by becoming the corporate wife, and by crafting their relationship to be rewarding and exciting. In this way she avoided being needy and dependent herself. This repeated the way she coped as a child, particularly after the birth of her sister.

Hilton initially enjoyed being idealised and was outwardly happy to receive all this attention, as it was in direct contrast to the experiences he had with his distant and unpredictable parents. 'We had a fantastic life together, lots to talk about and do; theatre, movies, dinner parties, trips.' Hilton recalled how avidly Wendy had assumed this role, organising a hectic schedule of social and cultural pursuits and declining opportunities where they would not be together – something that, over time, he came to feel was claustrophobic, leaving him no room to be himself.

However, an early sign that something was wrong showed up in their sexual difficulties. Hilton was hypersensitive to touch and found skin contact aversive, despite being filled with desire. Wendy assisted in a desensitisation programme, but was subsequently anorgasmic herself, and now Hilton was unable to touch her in a satisfactory way. Wendy could not describe her experience clearly, his touch was not directly aversive, but Hilton did not seem able to pleasure her, although she could bring herself to orgasm. She was not able to suggest how Hilton try things differently for her, nor any fantasies she might have. She felt she should be able to have orgasms with Hilton, as she had been orgasmic in prior relationships, and would not consider that she contributed to the dynamic in this relationship. Unfortunately her distress and anger added to Hilton's own poor sense of his worth, and led Hilton to begin to avoid sexual contact with her.

This shared psychosomatic difficulty represented the deepest level of disturbance present in this couple. They both lacked a sense of containment at the level of the skin, a boundary that would hold them. This lack in part stems from their early experiences of not being held (Winnicott, 1960; Bick, 1968).

Their narcissistic marriage was a defensive arrangement; a shared phantasy of fusion provided a veneer of containment, but underlying disintegrative anxieties were exposed in their sexual dysfunctions. Their stuck together psychic state, a couple version of an adhesive identification (Meltzer, 1975), left no room for separation and difference. For a satisfying sexual relationship, two separate individuals come together; in their case two fused individuals could not be separate.

In this family, Xanthe presented with somatic difficulties, an inability to keep food down. It is often the case in our experience where children are presenting with somatic problems (difficulties with toileting, eating and sleeping) that these problems can represent a projection of the couple's own unconscious somatic difficulties.

Paranoid-schizoid anxieties

The next stage in our developmental model is termed paranoid-schizoid functioning, characterised by the defences of splitting and projection. Klein (1946) thought that the infant's mind was incapable of dealing with the conflicting feelings of love and hate aroused from alternately being nurtured and frustrated. In order to deal with this dilemma, the infant splits the maternal object into good and bad mothers. The infant then defends against the anxiety aroused by being angry with his unavailable mother, whom he depends upon, by projecting these feelings into his mother. But the process, according to Klein, becomes more complicated because the infant then identifies with these angry feelings and fears retaliation from his mother who, coloured by the anger projected into her, is now felt to be angry with the infant. This is the defence mechanism called Projective Identification by Klein.

The position is called paranoid because of the persecutory anxieties that occur, that is the fears of attack or damage to the self, and schizoid because of the defensive splitting and withdrawal (of the self) which occurs in an attempt to deal with these anxieties.

So this is *Part Object relating*, where there is splitting and either idealising or devaluing of the object. It is a situation which is normally transitory, and with good enough care, the infant internalises a satisfactory experience, allowing dependency to be tolerated and needs met in an adequate way. The infant learns not to expect retaliation from his mother. The nurturing and frustrating parts of the mother become integrated and the infant achieves what we call the depressive position, with a sometimes stormy passage through Oedipal issues. The integration of good and bad parts of the mother, that is to say the capacity to see the parent as a whole person, is necessary for the development of a strong self that can survive the inevitable frustrations of relationships, and life itself.

If the infant's physical and psychological environment is compromised, the need to project bad experiences persists and becomes a pathological defence. The fact that parts of the self (that part of the ego involved in the experience) are split off and projected out as well means the infant's developing sense of self is weakened.

Paranoid-schizoid functioning is the most common mode of object relating that we see when couples or families present for help, for example warring couples who continually argue and threaten to leave the relationship. They are unlikely to be able to carry out the threat as they have projected so much of themselves into the other that they are not psychically separate. This is why recommendations made by some couple therapists that the couple separate seem to fall on deaf ears. Fairbairn (1952, p. 111) hypothesised about this situation for the infant, who is unable to reject the mother for her failure, and continues to long for her:

> Unlike the satisfying object, the unsatisfying object has, so to speak, two facets. On the one hand, it tempts and allures. Indeed its essential 'badness' consists precisely in the fact that it combines allurement with frustration. Further it retains both these qualities after internalisation .... In his [the infant's] attempts to control the unsatisfying object, he has introduced into the inner economy of his mind an object which not only continues to frustrate his need, but also continues to whet it.

The impact of a third, the birth of Xanthe: disillusionment of the idealised couple

From Wendy and Hilton's early history it became clearer that the dual impact of Xanthe's birth and the death of Wendy's idealised father challenged the couple's fragile narcissistic link. Aware at some level that their relationship was in trouble, the couple went on to have a child, perhaps in an attempt to fix the marriage, a defensive way to glue them together. However the reality of Xanthe's infantile needs fractured their carefully constructed system for nurturing themselves. Wendy felt compelled to be a full-time mother, to give her daughter the care she felt she never had herself. But she did not enjoy mothering. Xanthe would not feed properly and Wendy became worried and upset. She tried to be patient and calm;

however, the reality was that she was tense, irritable and overwhelmed. She real-ised she was behaving like her own mother, which filled her with horror and guilt. She looked to Hilton for help, but he also found Xanthe's distress difficult to man-age, no doubt because of his own inadequate experience of being held as an infant.

Additionally, Wendy's rigid routine for Xanthe precluded Hilton doing any-thing spontaneous with his daughter. He could only do as Wendy wanted, and felt Wendy was critical even of these attempts. In one family therapy session he remarked: 'I don't bring things up anymore, there's no point. I have to do things her way or not at all.'

Hilton had not only lost his attentive partner, he also had to contend with Wendy's constant irritable unhappiness. He also felt distressed that they now slept in separate rooms, as his parents had done before they separated. He was con-cerned that they, like his parents, would end up divorced. Unable to contain his own and the family's distress, and fearful of behaving like his own violent father, Hilton retreated to his career.

Wendy was angry with him for not making things better, and he was bitter about no longer having an admiring partner, but one that left him feeling blamed. They were both disappointed in each other. The couple had lost what had felt good between them, their phantasy of an idealised couple, and their phantasy of Hilton as an idealised father. Neither understood why this had happened and tended to blame each other. They were both using defences that occur at a paranoid-schizoid level, splitting and projection.

It was clear that the couple's unresolved Oedipal issues, which left no room for a third in the relationship, also contributed to their difficulties. We see this issue in families who come for help where the burden of caring for children is something that divides the parents. The parents have been children who have not been adequately nurtured themselves, and become unconsciously rivalrous with their own children for care (cf. the case of Emma in Chapter 1). Thus we have a transgenerational transmission of this difficulty in parenting, where the responsi-bility for the needs of children is felt to be overwhelming.

After six months of family sessions, Xanthe's eating had improved as the cou-ple's unhappiness with each other came more to the fore, and she no longer was the focus of their attention. They agreed to move to couple therapy rather than continue their fighting in front of Xanthe, who was referred to an individual child psychotherapist.

At this stage in the couple therapy Wendy railed against Hilton for his not 'being there', and the more she railed the less he was able to be present. She was not able to ask for help, to be vulnerable, but instead became angry and demanding, treating Hilton in the way her mother had behaved towards her. Hilton repeatedly asked Wendy to modify her hostile and blaming behaviour, explaining that he could not 'be there' for her as her manner was overwhelming for him. This repeated his traumatic childhood experience of being at the receiv-ing end of his father's hostile behaviour. Consequently, he moved into a familiar schizoid withdrawal.

Wendy was unable to take back her angry projections and Hilton could not let his defensive barrier down; thus they recreated the unheld, uncontained experiences from their early childhoods. Their trading of mutual projective identifications was gridlocked, and their communication difficulty spiralled downwards.

Hilton's affair: Oedipal rage, mayhem and murder

During this difficult time for the couple and their therapist, Hilton had an affair while overseas, and then, wracked by guilt, confessed to his wife. Wendy deteriorated into a suicidal depression, but was unable to see the therapist's concern in her offer of a psychiatric referral. Instead she accused the therapist of siding with Hilton to make her the 'sick' one. The therapist was caught up in a projective split. The couple separated. Without disclosing it, Wendy sought a therapist for herself.

After a brief time the couple reunited, as Hilton could not abandon Wendy when she was so unwell. A period of manic sexual activity occurred, where the couple used intense bodily sensations to try to stick them back together, to reinstate the good. Wendy wanted everything to return to the way it was early in the relationship, and increased her accusations that the therapist was the cause of their problems.

The destructive effect of an affair on the couple, whose relationship was already fragile, was clear. Hilton had to some degree inevitably internalised his abusive father, and was overtly angry about Wendy's endless attacks on him. His retaliation, the affair, caused his wife to decompensate in a psychotic way.

It was hard to confront this destructive acting out, in part because of Hilton's concern for his suicidal wife, whom the therapist was also very worried about, but also because of complex counter-transference feelings. Their reuniting represented a psychological regression back to autistic-contiguous modes of relating, leaving the therapist to carry all the rejecting object relationship projections that had been previously located in Xanthe.

In the counter-transference, the therapist felt sick, overwhelmed by the hostile denigration being violently projected into her, and helpless through the feeling of being excluded. It was hard to hold on to the belief that she had anything good to offer as the reality of the destructive anxieties evoked by Hilton's affair and Wendy's enraged attacks disappeared behind their sexualised reconnection. These anxieties of being excluded and feeling worthless are common when working with Oedipal-level difficulties in a couple.

Depressive position anxieties

Bion (1962) notes that containment of destructive aspects of object relating that hails from the Paranoid-Schizoid position promotes the development of the Depressive position, whole object relating and Oedipal resolution. Britton (1989) also writes about the interdependence of these two psychological positions; one does not occur without the other. They are entwined. Oedipal anxieties can be only dealt with when depressive position functioning is possible. Likewise, the Oedipal position is never fully resolved (Fisher and Ruszczynski, 1995), but some resolution is a necessary prerequisite to depressive level functioning.

In depressive position functioning, good and bad experiences are integrated so that the rejecting and the exciting mother (or object) is recognised to be one and the same. If successfully worked through there is a reversal of projective identification and parts of the self that were projected into the (m)other are taken back. The self is stronger as it is no longer split, and both the mother and the self, freed from projection are seen more realistically. Curiosity about, and interest in the other, develops with this awareness of separateness.

However, there is also mourning for the loss of the idealised self, the idealised other, and the idealised couple as part of coming to terms with reality. Additionally, there is a realisation of one's capacity to do harm, with strong emotions of sadness, grief and self-reproach for past angry attacks on the other. This leads to concern for the other and a desire to make reparation. Resolution of this depressive anxiety is an ongoing process. We regress from this position when under stress and re-achieve it again later, and with each re-establishment it becomes stronger. It is important to help the couple or family to understand this, or they will see the inevitable, but hopefully now shorter lived, return to paranoid-schizoid functioning as a sign that they are no better.

Once there is awareness of a whole (m)other there is also awareness of the others who are in relationship with (m)other. Here the achievement is of Oedipal resolution, which allows movement from dyadic to triadic functioning. Once these positions are successfully negotiated a capacity for *Whole Object* relating is established. This is a complex capacity which allows an individual to be a separate self, with opinions and feelings, and yet to be in relationship with others, even if they have different feelings and opinions. These differences can be acknowledged and allowed, not seen as a threat to one's self.

Unresolved depressive position anxieties: narcissistic defences used

In the early stages of depressive position functioning when the (m)other (loved object) is seen as a whole person, with a life of her own, the child, and later the adult, faces the possibility of loss. This is because when the partner is no longer 'under control', and is recognised as separate, with their own mind, they are capable of choosing whether to stay or leave the relationship. Wendy's struggle with allowing Hilton a greater degree of separateness was catastrophically undermined by her husband's affair. The fear of loss could no longer be denied, hence the intense manic sexual activity that Wendy and Hilton engaged in at the end of their short separation, which provided a retreat to an illusory fantasy of fusion.

Working through to the depressive position: mourning the loss of the idealised (exciting) father

Wendy continued to make angry attacks on the therapist, whereas Hilton acknowledged his need to own his individual issues, and began his own therapy. This indicated his capacity to think his own independent thoughts, and to begin to feel free enough to voice them. This change in their dynamic exacerbated Wendy's feelings of Oedipal jealousy of the therapist, as someone able to recognise and understand Hilton's pain. She wanted to be the only one who could care for Hilton, because she needed to continue to project into him the intensity of her own need and longing that she could not tolerate. She saw their couple therapist as a rival and angrily rejected compassionate attempts to offer understanding to her, because this exposed her to her own vulnerability, of which she was contemptuous.

In one session the couple were arguing about money, in this instance the issue was who was more responsible for their habit of dining at the more expensive restaurants in town.

Therapist: *Well I think that you both like nice restaurants. And why wouldn't you? However this is connected to the idea raised before – overspending to mask loss. You have both shared a fantasy of a good providing father, who makes all things possible. Wendy wanted Hilton to be that good father, like she felt her father to be, and Hilton felt good about this role, one in contrast to his own father. And now you share bad feelings because this fantasy is fading.*

(Wendy starts crying slow tears, and Hilton is attentive and comforting to her.)

This opportunity to interpret their shared unconscious phantasy, regarding idealised fathers and idealised marriages, highlights their joint attempt to conscript Hilton into filling an unrealistic role. This shared idealisation prevented them from being able to accept the ordinary realities of a marriage, which cannot provide without also sometimes frustrating. This was followed temporarily by some shared acknowledgement of these losses, actual and phantasised, a diminution of anger and distance, and more acceptance of the reality of their marital situation.

Ending therapy

The couple's therapy ended abruptly at Wendy's instigation, after the couple therapist tried to address the feelings of exclusion and rivalry in the room. Wendy viewed the therapist enviously as a rival for her husband, and accused the therapist of having caused the relationship difficulties. She minimised the issues Xanthe had presented with, and was unable to acknowledge the work of the therapy. Although she could see the changes that Hilton had made (he was more available and had developed a capacity to contain her anxieties), she was unable to acknowledge that her life was any better because of these changes.

She was unable to express any appreciation of him, and would repeatedly say: 'Where has all the good gone?'

So Wendy was still full of persecutory anxiety, wanting to return to an idealised state using denial (of her contribution to the problems), splitting and projection of blame. She was functioning on the border of a narcissistic/paranoid-schizoid level of psychological development.

By contrast, there appeared to be a genuine development in Hilton, within himself and in the way he related to Wendy, and the therapist. The fused entity of the couple was split with Wendy enviously attacking the good, the compassionate understanding the therapist provided, and Hilton having more depressive position functioning, showing gratitude and wanting to make reparation.

We have commented on this couple's shared experience of lack of maternal containment. As a result, defensive splitting had led to the phantasy of an ideal, all-understanding object and a bad object, a source of malignant understanding. Britton (1998) hypothesises that the union of these good and bad parental objects is experienced as catastrophic, threatening chaos and fragmentation. Balfour (2005, p. 25) suggests that when both partners have been unable to arrive at a resolution of such Oedipal anxieties, there is no capacity to sustain a triangular space:

> This seems to reflect an internal situation that both parties shared – a belief that coupling with another person will not lead to a situation of give and take, based on a linked separateness. Instead it will lead only to a tyrannical relating where one partner dominates and the other is tyrannically colonised.

It seemed that neither Wendy nor Hilton were able to tolerate the experience of couple therapy, where the therapist represented the third in a triangular situation. Wendy perceived the therapist as a rival and Hilton had, to some extent, paired with the therapist to the exclusion of Wendy. Perhaps the therapist represented for him the good (m)other/parent that he never had. There may have been an eroticised aspect to this, not brought into the therapy room, but acted out in the affair, and which helped to fuel Wendy's sudden departure. Thus both partners in the marriage used narcissistic ways of defending themselves against the necessary disillusionment and subsequent acceptance of separateness and love needed in a real marriage. They both had early Oedipal issues, his abusive father, her depressed mother, and therefore could not withstand the intrusion of a third, their daughter Xanthe, into the relationship, nor the later intrusion of Hilton's affair and Wendy's projection of her anxieties about this into the couple therapist.

This was mirrored in the counter-transference experienced by the therapist. Wendy's rejection of the therapist and denigration of all their painstaking work as harmful was difficult to bear. In contrast, Hilton's gratitude and capacity for understanding led to a feeling of collusion between the therapist with the husband. This collusion, with its corresponding sense of exclusion, seemed to resonate with the couple's shared belief that only an idealised coupling, that excludes the third, can be tolerated.

Consequently, at the end of therapy, Oedipal anxieties remained unresolved for both, though Hilton had moved further towards a depressive level of functioning than Wendy.

Summary

In this chapter, we have presented a developmental hierarchy of anxieties, one that looks at how anxieties inherent in growth and maturation impact on the internal object relations the child has developed, as outlined in Chapter 1. These internal object relations will either help or hinder the infant's and later adult's capacity to deal with life. Our focus here is on one couple in particular whose early compromised experience led to narcissistic difficulties in their marriage. An early idealised narcissistic fusion led to sexual problems and was further exacerbated by the birth of their child. As is illustrated in the table earlier in the chapter, defences of splitting and projection, resulting in idealisation and denigration were used against each other as they emerged unhappily from their narcissistic fusion. The child in this family, no longer hostage to the parents' projections, improved greatly. Subsequently, the husband's affair, in part retaliatory for the angry protestations about a developing sense of separateness in the couple, had a catastrophic effect on the couple relationship. The wife was precipitated into a suicidal depression, fuelled by Oedipal anxieties and narcissistic defences. In the wake of the affair the couple's murderous phantasies were directed at the therapist through the act of terminating the therapy.

References

Balfour, A. (2005). The couple, their marriage and Oedipus: Or problems come in twos and threes. In F. Grier, (Ed.) *Oedipus and the Couple*. London: Karnac.

Bick, E. (1968). The experience of the skin in early object relations. *International Journal of Psycho-Analysis, 49,* 484–486.

Bick, E. (1986). Further findings on the function of skin in early object relations: Findings from infant observation integrated into child and adult analyses. *British Journal of Psychotherapy, 2(4),* 292–299.

Bion, W. (1962). *Learning from Experience*. London: Heinemann.

Britton, R. (1989). The missing link: Parental sexuality in the Oedipus complex. In J. Steiner (Ed.) *The Oedipus Complex Today*. London: Karnac Books.

Britton, R. (1998). Subjectivity, objectivity and triangular space. In *Belief and Imagination: Explorations in Psychoanalysis*. London: Routledge.

Emanuel, R. (2000). *Anxiety. Ideas in Psychoanalysis* (p. 6). Cambridge: Icon.

Fairbairn, R. (1952). *Psychoanalytic Studies of the Personality*. London: Routledge.

Feldman, M. (1989). The Oedipus complex: Manifestations in the inner world and the therapeutic situation. In J. Steiner (Ed.) *The Oedipus Complex Today*. London: Karnac.

Fisher, J. (1999). *The Uninvited Guest*. London: Karnac.

Fisher, J. and Ruszczynski, S. (1995). *Intrusiveness and Intimacy in the Couple*. London: Karnac.

Freud, S. (1923). *The Ego and the Id*. S.E. Vol. 19 (pp. 12–66). London: Hogarth.

Hopper, E. (1991). Encapsulation as a defence against the fear of annihilation. *International Journal of Psycho-Analysis*, *72*, pp. 607–624.

Klein, M. (1946). Notes on some schizoid mechanisms. *International Journal of Psycho-Analysis*, *27*, 99–110 [Reprinted in M. Klein, *Envy and Gratitude and Other Works 1946–1963*. London: Hogarth Press, 1980].

Meltzer, D. (1975). Adhesive identification. *Contemporary Psychoanalysis*, *11*, 289–310.

Mitrani, J.L. (2011). Trying to enter the long black branches: Some technical extensions of the work of Frances Tustin for the analysis of autistic states in adults. *International Journal of Psycho-Analysis*, *92*, 21–42.

Ogden, T. (1989). *The Primitive Edge of Experience*. New York: Aronson.

Scharff, D.E. (2008). *The Sexual Relationship*. Northvale, NJ, London: Jason Aronson.

Steiner, J. (1993). *Psychic Retreats: Pathological Organisations in Psychotic, Neurotic and Borderline Personalities*. London: Routledge.

Tustin, F. (1986). *Autistic Barriers in Neurotic Patients*. London: Karnac.

Tustin, F. (1994). The perpetuation of an error. *Journal of Child Psychotherapy*, *20*, 3–23.

Winnicott, D. (1965). The theory of parent–infant relationship. In *Maturational Processes and the Facilitating Environment* (pp. 37–55). London: Hogarth.

Chapter 3

The dynamics of coupledom

Noela Byrne and Maria Kourt

In 1916 Freud anticipated the study of the interconnectedness of couples and family relationships when he said: 'It is a very remarkable thing that the unconscious of one human being can react upon another without passing through consciousness . . . descriptively speaking, the fact is incontestable' (Freud, 1916/1917).

In this statement Freud anticipates the thinking about couple dynamics that would develop some three or four decades later. It can be read as acknowledging that couples communicate in an unconscious way. At a deeper level he is also suggesting that we seek a partner to meet unconscious, repressed needs.

In the first chapter of this book, theories about internal object relations and how they relate to the structuring of the infant mind were traced through the ideas of Klein, Fairbairn, Winnicott and Bion. In the second chapter we outline our model for a developmental hierarchy of anxieties in couple and family psychotherapy. In this chapter, we will be following the development of psychoanalytic ideas and their application particularly to couple therapy through more recent decades. In speaking of couples we are not referring to just those in a traditional heterosexual marriage, but any intimate sexual relationship.

As Australians, we are in a unique position geographically to be influenced by ideas from both Europe and the United States. This chapter thus reflects the input to our thinking that we have received both from Europe, notably clinicians working at the Tavistock in London, and from Jill and David Scharff, based in Washington DC. The theorists cited in the first two chapters of this book are the founding fathers and mothers of object relations psychoanalysis and originally their ideas were applied to work with individuals (children and adults). Initially, work with couples and families was not psychoanalytically based. It was a later generation of therapists, in both Europe and the Americas, trained in object relations, who applied this thinking to couples, starting with Enid Balint, at the then Family Discussion Bureau (later Tavistock Relationships). It was this application of ideas and observations that Henry Dicks collated and published. With his emphasis on repression, splitting and projective identification Henry Dicks (1967) revolutionised thinking about the dynamics of couples and provided the bedrock for later developments at the Tavistock Relationships (cf. Box *et al.*, 1981).

In this chapter we will highlight the contribution of Henry Dicks, after which we will move on to the later contributions of others from both sides of the Atlantic. These ideas will be illustrated through vignettes from therapy work with a couple over an eighteen-month period.

Many of the ideas that we have found useful in our work with couples resulted from a fruitful cooperation between Jungian and Kleinian analysts at the Tavistock. For instance, there has been an emphasis on the importance of containment as essential for the development of the individual. Both Winnicott and Bion stressed the necessity for the mother to be 'good enough' in responding to her infant's distressed cries. This relates directly to a shared concept between Jungians and Kleinian analysts that in an adult couple relationship, the capacity of both to contain each other's anxieties and projections will depend on whether they experienced containment by a good enough caregiver during their early years.

The idea of the role of the marriage itself as a container for the couple's anxieties (Colman, 1993a; Morgan 2005) owes much to the marriage of these two strands (Jung and Bion) in the history of the Tavistock.

Marriage as a psychological container

Colman (ibid.) suggests that in a flexible relationship, the couple invests in the marriage as a 'container', a third entity to which both contribute. Together they create what we might call a 'shared internal couple' on which each can draw. It is as if the relationship is a symbolic third entity which is the result of their creative intercourse. Thus, the relationship needs to be continually nurtured if it is to both survive and develop.

In addition, it is necessary for the couple to believe in the robustness and continuity of this relationship and to be able to receive projections from each other and process them. In all marriages there will be projective and introjective mechanisms going back and forth. A good marriage can deal with these projective processes and stay on track.

Since we are thinking about the dynamics of couples in this chapter, we also need to acknowledge the challenges or tensions faced by every couple in an intimate relationship (Colman, 1993b).

Normal tensions in marriage

These normal tensions that are encountered in everyday life can be thought about as a series of dichotomous experiences, namely:

Autonomy and intimacy

Evelyn Cleavely (1993) in discussing close relationships, points out that 'at the very core of every emotional conflict lies the longing for a close intimate relationship with a significant other and of a self-sufficient "I", independent, autonomous, certain of being able to survive alone' (p. 59).

These longings are associated with the anxiety of being either dominated and taken over by the other, or of being abandoned by the other. This idea was first cited by Michael Balint and later Rey (1994) introduced this concept of the claustro-agoraphobic dilemma that he witnessed in his work with borderline patients. In claustrophobic anxieties, the individual fears engulfment in being too close to the other. In agoraphobic anxieties, there is a fear of being too far away and being rejected, lost or falling into pieces. This is a common dilemma in couples seeking psychotherapy and to some extent part of the struggle in any marriage. The affects of separateness and clinging can be split between the partners with each carrying one aspect. For instance, a husband might pursue separate activities while his wife complains that she wants to do more things together. This results in conflict within the relationship. If each is not secure in their own separate identity, they will find it difficult to achieve real intimacy.

Dependence and independence

At the time when individuals commit to a close relationship, they may struggle with anxieties about losing the independence and autonomy which they have worked hard to achieve. In order to balance the dependent/independent dichotomy, a secure sense of self is required. Dependence can be threatening and therefore vulnerability may be defended against intrapsychically by being projected into a partner or child. This might mean that in the consulting room, a family may present a child as the problem. Alternatively, partners can be stuck in an excessively dependent relationship which imposes a limitation on independent action and autonomy. This dependence/independence dichotomy is never fully resolved. With each stage of the life cycle, such as birth of a child, illness or retirement, this tension is revisited.

Defence and development

Individuals need to develop outside the marriage as well as inside and this creates a tension of opposites: a tension between growth and stability. Real marriage requires the capacity for opposites, for split-off parts to come together inside the self and the inner world of the couple. Marital difficulties could be seen in a positive way, that is, they could be seen as the couple's struggle to make an internal couple.

Love and hate

It is only when ambivalence is acknowledged that the marriage is able to afford the couple a sense of security and safety. Aggression needs to be integrated before the couple can enjoy an ongoing sexually satisfying relationship, where they feel safe enough for erotic exploration.

A history of sexual abuse will interfere with this integration and the trauma may remain as a barrier to the development of a mature sexual relationship.

If a couple can manage these tensions, then they have achieved the mature developmental state that could be thought of as mutual interdependence (Fairbairn, 1958; Winnicott, 1960b), where they can both come together and be intimate and also separate and function as secure individuals. Of course all these things are reflected in the sexual relationship of the couple. It is unlikely that a couple will function effectively and be able to achieve a satisfying level of emotional intimacy unless they have also achieved a satisfying level of sexual intimacy. Negotiating the latter requires considerable effort on the part of the partners particularly when over time a variety of changes occur.

Good marriages are where partners can be themselves, and are not forced to conform to the other's projective identifications. If each partner is aware that they each have needs, rights and responsibilities in the relationship, there will be the opportunity to grow both individually and together. In addition, a good marriage is stable enough to allow scope for negotiating the inevitable transitions while minimising anxiety. This combination of flexibility and robustness is a hallmark of health, something good marriages are founded on, and that is an outcome by which to measure a successful relationship.

To quote Henry Dicks: 'This flexibility is, of course an aspect of the capacity to tolerate ambivalence – perhaps the key to the secret of all human relations. It is the ability to contain hate in a framework of love' (Dicks, 1967, p. 3).

We will now consider some of the relevant theories relating to couple psychotherapy, beginning with Henry Dicks.

Dynamics of marital pairings

Henry Dicks' *Marital Tensions* (1967) is now regarded by object relations couple therapists as something of a classic, as in this publication he draws on concepts such as Klein's defensive mechanisms of projective identification and splitting (associated with the Paranoid-Schizoid Position) and Fairbairn's model of psychic structure and internal objects, incorporating them into his ideas about the dynamics of couples.

His central thesis is that past family experiences, real or fantasised, are incorporated into our inner unconscious worlds and are replayed and/or transformed in our present relationships. That is, our inner worlds influence the way we perceive people in our external lives. Nowhere is this more evident than in the intimate sexual partnership.

From his work with couples, Dicks was able to describe two common marital pairings. First, *Identification with parents*. In this marital pairing, there is a simple displacement of the original object onto the marriage partner, involving identification with parental roles and expectations. We are all familiar with the comment, 'He married his mother'.

The second common marital pairing he described as *Counter-identification with parent*. Partners often consciously do not want to be like their parents or to marry someone resembling their parents. In this pairing, the parental models are repressed. For example, a wife might choose a passive husband because she does not want an aggressive man like her abusive father. Because the choice of partner is unconscious, the repressed aspects of the family of origin may be re-enacted. Therefore, after the marriage, she herself might become the bully and behave like her father.

We would now like to introduce you to a couple, Martin and Frances. Vignettes from couple psychotherapy with them will be used to illustrate the various theoretical ideas that we will elaborate in the rest of this chapter.

Martin and Frances

Frances, aged 36, and Martin, aged 37, met while completing their medical training. Martin was now employed as a general practitioner while Frances had specialised in surgery. The couple had married soon after graduation and now had two children aged 6 and 7 years. They presented with marital difficulties, apparently precipitated by Martin discovering that Frances was having an affair. It was Martin's distress about this that brought them to therapy.

When the couple first met, Frances said she was attracted to Martin's confident manner, but also by the way he admired her and supported her in her ambition to become a surgeon. She commented that 'He was the kindest, most caring man I had ever met'. Martin said he had found Frances very attractive, but added: 'I was impressed with the way she approached her specialist training in such a determined way. I saw her as very strong and capable.'

Frances was the oldest of three children, with two younger sisters. Her mother was frequently overwhelmed and would then enlist Frances' help with the younger children, but then criticise her. Frances said: 'I always felt that in my mother's eyes, I was never good enough.' Her father, who was a busy doctor in a general practice, worked long hours. However, when he was at home, he encouraged Frances in her academic achievements, but also in her musical pursuits in playing the violin. The father himself played the cello, and as Frances grew older and became more accomplished, father and daughter would often play duets together.

Martin was the older of two children, with a younger sister. The father left the family when Martin was 11 years old. He described his father as an 'exacting man, with high standards both for himself and for his wife and children'. Martin added that 'as the oldest child, I always felt that more was expected of me'. After the father remarried and moved interstate, contact with him became infrequent. Martin became his mother's support and confidante. She depended on him to be responsible for his sister until she returned home from work in the evenings.

If we follow Dicks' ideas about common marital pairings, it would seem that Martin and Frances had chosen each other based on an identification with the parent: 'a displacement of the original object onto the marital partner' (Dicks, 1967, p. 55), where each carried fantasies about and had a strong identification with the parent of the opposite sex. They both wanted to have a partner with whom they had a special, 'idealised' place. Martin married someone like his mother who made him feel important and who looked to him for support. Frances was looking for a partner who would admire her, and encourage her in her achievements, as her father had done. It could be speculated that they shared unresolved Oedipal issues that affected their ability to make an adult, intimate relationship. This issue of Oedipal anxieties in couple relationships is associated with difficulties in arriving at a depressive position level of functioning. We will refer to Oedipal anxieties later in this chapter.

Idealisation

In describing this first common marital pairing, the identification with the parent, Dicks pointed out that there is a danger of idealising the partner (trying to make the partner conform to the internal idealised parent). The impact on the marriage of this denial of the reality of the actual partner with his or her strengths and weaknesses results in an inevitable disillusionment when the reality of living together impinges.

Like Martin and Frances, who described their initial mutual attraction in very positive terms, most intimate relationships begin with a fair amount of idealisation, the rosy glow we call 'falling in love'. In the early stages, there is a sense of fusion whereby the partner becomes the most important person in the world (mirroring the mother–infant dyad) and the separate development of the individual is on hold. Indeed the separate development of the partner is seen as threatening to the fantasy of the ideal couple. In Fairbairn's model of endopsychic functioning this would equate to an exciting object relationship, where there is a yearning to be together, a desperate longing for the other which has taken over the ego's capacity to function in a reality-based good enough way. The experience is of a feeling of perfect satisfaction, but this only extends to times when in the other's company.

This is reminiscent of the *Romeo and Juliet* scene from Shakespeare where the lovers are so closely united against a hostile world that their independent existence is denied.

Juliet: *Yet I would kill thee with much cherishing,*
          Good-night, good-night! Parting is such sweet sorrow
          That I shall say goodnight till it be morrow.
Romeo: *Sleep dwell upon thine eyes, peace in thy breast!*
          Would I were sleep and peace so sweet to rest!

Ultimately and tragically in the case of Romeo and Juliet, in their merged adolescent state each felt that they could not survive without the other, and their suicides are an ultimate expression of this.

With most couples, as contact grows, there is a breakdown in idealisation and an increase in reality-testing, so that soon the 'honeymoon' is over and the denied aspects of the self and other can no longer be ignored. When the partner fails as an idealised object, then the split-off repressed aspects emerge. The idealised object can become the disappointing, denigrated object. The previously cherished and loving partner may become hated and persecuting. Dicks expresses this idea in his first 'Hypothesis': 'Many tensions and misunderstandings between partners seem to result from the disappointment which one or both feel and resent, when the other fails to play the role of spouse after the manner of a preconceived model in their fantasy world' (Dicks, 1967, p. 62).

Dicks is hypothesising here that idealisation will inevitably result in difficulties in the relationship. Many couples are able to navigate these treacherous waters and find ways of moving on from idealisation, dealing with disillusionment, disappointment and ambivalence, and arriving at a more realistic perception of each other, resulting in a strengthening of the relationship. However, others may become stuck to the extent that the relationship is prevented from developing and deepening.

The second pairing, *Counter-identification* as mentioned above, also has its problems. Here Dicks refers to 'complementariness' or 'the pull of opposites'. He explains that initially, an individual might be attracted to another because they are perceived as totally unlike themselves. After marriage, this may change and the very characteristics which were initially attractive are then attacked and criticised. 'Even in the marriage "by contrast" (to the hated parent figure), there is the fashioning of an idealised object . . . the same love-object with its "badness" removed by splitting or denial' (Dicks, 1967, p. 62).

The reason for the strength of this attack is that these characteristics represent denied aspects of the self. These denied, split-off parts have been projected onto the partner, and this 'oppositeness' which had been an important part of the initial attraction is now despised in the other. This is one form of projective identification. A fairly common example of such a pairing would be an obsessional introverted man who marries a woman who is overly emotional. He is attracted to her emotionality and she is attracted to his stability. Over time she ends up feeling he is withholding, staid and uptight and he in turn feels overwhelmed and intolerant of her emotionality, where everything is a drama.

This concept of complementariness led Dicks to the construction of a second hypothesis: 'Subjects may persecute in their spouses tendencies which originally caused attraction, the partner having been unconsciously perceived as a symbol of "lost", because repressed, aspects of the individual's own personality' (Dicks, 1967, p. 63).

Examples might be a passive woman being attracted to an assertive, aggressive man (or vice versa – a passive man attracted to a vibrant woman) or the emotionally labile and the obsessional pairing as mentioned above. Dicks explains that: 'When, by the continual reality test of married proximity, the partner fails as an idealised object, then, like a glove turning inside out, the "other half" of the polarised ambivalence comes uppermost, the idealised relationship becomes the hated, persecuting object-relation' (ibid., p. 66).

This is an aspect of projective identification that we often see in couples who seek help. Each is in battle with the repressed and projected parts of themselves, identified in the partner.

In the case of Martin and Frances, idealisation broke down, probably after the birth of the children, when Frances struggled to adjust to motherhood. She found breastfeeding difficult, and then chose to have a second child close to the first as she was anxious to return to work as soon as possible. Unfortunately, the second child suffered from reflux, and would regularly scream for hours and fail to respond to Frances' attempts to comfort him. She commented: 'I felt like such a failure. I was a doctor; I was supposed to know what to do.'

Like her mother, who had not coped well with the physical and emotional demands of motherhood, Frances found being a mother difficult and turned to Martin for help. However, although he wanted to be helpful, as he had been to his mother, he also felt overwhelmed and did not know what to do. In his eyes, Frances became the exacting father who made him feel he was not good enough. He therefore withdrew into his work, justifying it to himself by arguing that until Frances returned to work, he was the sole provider. Frances resented the fact that Martin did not help her with the children; she felt abandoned by him just as she had at times felt abandoned by her own absent father when she was left to meet the unreasonable demands and criticisms of her mother. Both became disillusioned. In Dicks' words, 'the glove had turned inside out'. What had been split off and repressed by both of them in their shared idealisation of the relationship now emerged in the reality of their difficulties.

Frances returned to work and Martin cut back on his work hours for a time until both children were old enough to start school. From that point, both struggled to cope with the dual tasks of parenting and careers. Martin was then devastated to learn that Frances was having an affair with a musician who played with her in a string quartet. In her disappointment with Martin's inability to provide the level of support she needed from him, she had turned to someone else who would admire and encourage her, as her father had done. Martin was deeply hurt and angry at her rejection of him. Through projective identification, Frances' affair left him feeling abandoned and unloved, the same feelings Frances had experienced some years previously, when she felt rejected and unsupported by him after the birth of the children.

In working with Martin and Frances, the therapist found herself dreading the sessions. She began to wonder whether she was in the thrall of a strong counter-transference. Being with the couple seemed to contain all the horrors of a war zone. With each rejecting the other and potentially rejecting the therapist as well, she wondered whether the therapy would survive. She thought that perhaps each had to blame the other rather than accept some responsibility for the marriage's difficulties. They shared an internal critical parent from their experience of the parent of the same sex. When the mutual idealisation could no longer be maintained, they were left with the split-off unacceptable parts of themselves. Consequently, there was a tendency to tenaciously cling to the ideal, rather than consider what was of value in the relationship that could be built on.

The narcissistic dynamics of idealisation and devaluation implicit in Fairbairn's endopsychic structure

Fairbairn's model for ego functioning describes a tri-partite split in the individual's ego. Consciously, there is an 'ideal' or 'good enough' object relationship which implies a capacity for stable and flexible relating. In the unconscious part of the self, Fairbairn suggested there are the frustrating object relationships, which he called 'the exciting and rejecting object relationships'. These frustrating object relationships are the traces of our infantile experiences of being overwhelmed with feelings that were unmanageable, and which are defended against by splitting and repressing the feelings. Both of these ways of splitting are defences against the feeling of rejection that the infant experiences and also a way of preserving the ideal mother.

The rejecting object is associated with feelings of anger, frustration and sadness, the exciting object with feelings of craving and longing. It is not a great leap of imagination to see how helpful this can be in understanding the internal world of the couple. Adults who have not resolved their own internal object relationships to a stable (good enough) degree, in their intimate couple relationship, may resort to the infantile strategy of splitting the internal world to defend against a perceived rejection. Even an ordinary rejection entailed in the struggle between dependence and independence that occurs in every couple relationship, such as a partner having to go away for work, may prove to be very provocative for some couples.

Fairbairn can provide another level of understanding of Martin and Frances' marital predicament. Neither had experienced a 'good enough' relationship with their mothers. Martin was a support for his mother after his parents separated. He was thus denied the reality testing of being an 'ordinary' child. Further, as an adolescent, his role with his mother could well have ignited Oedipal anxieties in him, now that his father was absent. His mother 'excited' his anxiety, but was not containing of his feelings about this. However, he idealised his mother, which prevented him from accepting her limitations. He may at some level have felt he had to satisfy his mother's longing for her absent husband, and to have always felt inadequate to meet her unrealistic expectations. Perhaps he was also always insecure about whether he could ever really meet Frances' expectations. Thus when she became overwhelmed in her mothering role, Martin may well have felt not only like a man who did not have an admiring partner but also like a little boy who could not satisfy his mother. To his mind this was confirmed by the affair.

Frances, like her mother, did not find mothering satisfying. It seems that both had an internalised rejecting mother that affected their ability to mother. Frances had felt criticised and rejected by her mother and had turned to her father who made her feel special on the occasions when he was available. When she was overwhelmed in her mothering and turned to Martin for help, his failure to fill this role was experienced by her as another rejection that left her craving attention and care. This turmoil of emotions was exacerbated by the disjunction between her competence and sense of worth as a surgeon, and her lack of confidence and pleasure in being a mother.

Conjoint personality: early conceptualisation of narcissistic object relations in couples

With the extensive use of projective identification in a couple, a conjoint personality can be created with blurred ego boundaries (Dicks, 1967). This can create a sense of belonging for the couple as the partner is now unconsciously perceived as part of the self. This seemed to reflect the way that Martin and Frances were at the beginning of their marriage, before the birth of their two children.

In order to maintain this blurring of boundaries, a high level of collusion is required between the partners. The therapist will find the collusive marriage is difficult to work with, as it is maintained by a system of shared internal phantasies and rigid defences which restrict the growth of the relationship as well as the growth of the individuals concerned. In the words of Dicks: 'the mutual collusive interacting of two partners is powerful and inescapable in a disturbed marriage' (Dicks, 1967, p. 73).

This is why when working with troubled couples we can appreciate that these deeper unconscious bonds form a unit, or joint entity. As couple therapists, this helps us understand what keeps some couples together in spite of the observed level of conflict and the unfulfilling nature of the relationship. For instance, it is common in these marriages that one or other partner has difficulty in attending therapy, a reluctance that is in fact being expressed for both of them. At a deeper level this reluctance may reflect a shared fear that subjecting their relationship to scrutiny will bring about disastrous change, perhaps even the loss of the relationship. It is likely that some of the counter-transference dread that the therapist experienced in working with Martin and Frances was a projected fear of what might be discovered and disturbed in their marriage. They were no doubt worried that uncovering the roots of the shared projective system described above and the intense feelings that are associated with it would be too much to bear, and would lead to the end of the relationship and the terrible grief and loss involved. This is a very common anxiety that needs to be addressed with couples who are attending couple therapy. There is a reality to these fears as a change to the defensive structure will disrupt the balance in their relationship and more conflict may occur. Both partners may then attack the therapist for changing things for the worse.

This idea of a conjoint personality seems to anticipate later ideas about narcissistic ways of relating in couples developed at the Tavistock in the 1990s.

Narcissistic defences

As indicated earlier, Dicks' ideas, in particular the role of projective identification, underpinned the later work of couple and family therapists at the Tavistock. The idea of the 'conjoint personality' was further explored with a particular focus on narcissistic defences as one of the main difficulties for a couple in creating their 'marriage as a psychological container' (Colman, 1993a). Here projective identification is used less as a way of projecting aspects of the self into the other and more as a way of maintaining a particular state of mind, dominated by the phantasy of being with or residing in the other. Projective identification is used defensively in an attempt to either control the other or to merge with her/him. In this case, the phantasy of merging is often reinforced when the couple come together in a sexual union. This can be understood as the reawakening of the infant's phantasy of a blissful union with the mother.

James Fisher (1999), who has written with erudition on the subject, defines narcissistic object relating as a relationship where there is 'an intolerance of the reality, the independent existence of the other. Narcissism in this sense is in fact a longing for an other who is perfectly attuned and responsive and thus not a genuine other at all' (pp. 1–2).

Later, he says: 'It is not the state of identification or oneness that is problematic, but the rigidity that cannot allow for the reality of difference and thus it attacks and undermines that reality in a variety of ways' (p. 220).

In a narcissistic partner choice, the couple will share a phantasy of fusion. Aggression and hostility is projected onto the outside world which is then seen as a dangerous place for both of them. Consequently, any expression of individuality or attempts at autonomy will threaten the other and will be totally rejected. If the phantasy of fusion cannot be maintained, a sense of absolute isolation of the individual will result, because separation will be experienced as abandonment (cf. Romeo and Juliet). These couples may react to the sense of abandonment by withdrawing from each other into their own bleak, empty world. The loss of the idealised, merged other is experienced as a deep sense of betrayal.

This fused state might suggest a level of paranoid-schizoid functioning in the couple, but our view, as outlined in Chapter 2, is that the narcissistic relationship generally carries aspects of both the Autistic-Contiguous Phase (Ogden, 1989) and paranoid-schizoid ways of relating. Frances, experiencing the loss of the sensuality of the merged sexual relationship (because of the birth of a child and her perceived loss of an admiring, supportive partner), sought that sensory contact elsewhere. We contend that the emergence from the fused early stage of relating produces the sort of conflict typical of paranoid schizoid ways of relating. What appears as attempts to control the other and a kind of terror about their separate existence can be seen as a desire to return to a more merged and superficially harmonious relationship.

When Martin and Frances came for therapy, Frances was in such a fused, narcissistic state that she was genuinely baffled as to what went wrong. When the phantasised, idealised state of fusion could no longer be maintained with

Martin because of the arrival of their children and her need for support in being a mother, Frances sought a new idealised other in an affair. During one early session, she announced that as she had terminated the relationship with the musician, she could not see why Martin could not put it behind him and resume the marriage. She was trying hard to rediscover the lost, idealised fused state with Martin, pleading: 'We used to be so happy together. You used to be so sweet and loving. How can we get back to us?'

Other conceptualisations of narcissistic object relations

The projective gridlock

Continuing the theme of the role of projective identification in narcissistic ways of relating, when projective identification is used to excess, Morgan (1995) suggests that a projective gridlock might result. The ensuing confusion about ego boundaries will mean the capacity to be a separate entity within the relationship will be restricted. Here the therapist will struggle with a counter-transference in which there is pressure to be fused with the couple. In that state, it will be impossible to have one's own mind and to make useful interpretations. This may also partly explain the strong negative counter-transference felt by the therapist working with Martin and Frances. The therapist struggled to find space in her mind to think about what was happening. This is similar to the counter-transference experience of the therapist as described below in discussing the 'false self couple'.

The false self couple

When the mother is unable to contain and respond appropriately to the gestures of communication of her infant, but responds with something from herself, the infant may experience this as an intrusion into his own nascent individuality, and feel a compulsion to fit in or comply with the mother. This can result in a compliant 'false self' as described by Winnicott (1960a), the 'true self' remaining unrecognised and indeed perhaps denied.

Therefore, the term 'false self couple' describes a couple relationship where the partners share a particular history of lack of parental containment. In this kind of couple dyad, there will be 'a tyrannical self and a compliant object' (Fisher, 1993, p. 164) and the dominating partner pressures the other to fit in. It is important to note that this is a dynamic, and within each compliant partner there is a tyrant waiting in the wings for an opportunity to be on stage. As we described earlier, there will always be a tension in couples between a need for togetherness and a need for space. However, in these couples, one of the partners will experience the other who is pressing for closeness as being intrusive. This is intolerable and he withdraws, feeling that the integrity of the self is being threatened. Unfortunately, when the partner withdraws, he/she is then experienced as an 'impenetrable other' (Fisher, 1993) and this spurs the first partner into more forceful attempts to connect. Inevitably, this can prove to be destructive to the couple relationship. Colman (2005) refers to this dynamic as an 'anti-relating' cycle.

In the therapy room, forceful verbal interactions escalate as one endeavours to get through to the other, while the therapist finds she is the subject of intense projective identifications which make it difficult to maintain independent thought. Common to these narcissistic couplings is a pressure on the therapist to join with the shared defence against difference, thus rendering him or her impotent.

There are degrees of narcissistic collusion in all couples, and many will continue to struggle to emerge from this in order to achieve a more mature relationship.

The significance of introjective identification

Jill Scharff, from her experience of the inner world of the infant, brought a particularly helpful understanding to the projective processes in couple relationships. Introjective identification is less discussed than projective identification, but Jill Scharff maintains that it is vital in understanding the way in which the mother's success or failure with the infant's projections are re-incorporated into the infant's view of themselves. She says of a maternal failure to metabolise infantile anxieties:

> [T]he infant then fears that feelings that might have overwhelmed the infant self had they remained within will now return in the haunting form of a mother who has been infused with these frightening feelings. The mother is then seen as a retaliatory object. This is the second phase of the projective identification process. Now the infant takes in this view of the mother through introjective identification, which is the third phase of the projective process. The infant now becomes more like the frightening mother and has even more fearsome feelings to get rid of.
>
> (Scharff and Scharff, 2005, p. 38)

When we think about these processes in a troubled couple relationship, it becomes clearer how couples come to grief when there has not been sufficient containment of infantile states of aggression and envy in the primary relationship. If one (or other) in the couple cannot sustain the projections of the partner and return them in a more benign form to the other, then not only does the partner become a 'retaliatory figure', but the other partner, who is left uncontained, becomes filled with overwhelming feelings of badness.

Shared unconscious phantasy

We frequently find that a couple will demonstrate shared internal phantasies and shared defences. These could be seen as the consequences of mutual projection and introjective identification.

This presupposes that the couple will have complementary internal objects associated with these phantasies. For example: the couple may share an unconscious collusion that maintains their initial illusory expectations of each other rather than deal with disappointment and potential conflict. Conflict would imply evidence of difference from the narcissistic fantasy of merging, and this cannot be tolerated for fear of disastrous consequences.

It seems that when Martin and Frances chose each other, they shared an unconscious agreement that he would fit in with her, support her and protect her from the harsh realities of life.

Colman (2005) described such a shared unconscious phantasy as 'a relationship between a needy and dependent child and a parent who is invalidating the child's needs by replacing them with their own' (p. 68).

In attempting to fulfil his own and his wife's expectations that he would rescue her and protect her from harsh reality, Martin was doomed to fail. Inevitably, reality impinged, leading to disillusionment. Through projective identification, he was trying to rescue in his partner his own disavowed vulnerability.

Colman suggests this is a form of narcissistic relating where the couple share an aspiration to find perfection both in themselves and their partner. He goes on to say:

> In this state of mind, the primary relationship is to the perfectionistic ideal rather than to the actual other. Indeed the real other may be experienced as an obstructive obstacle to the fulfilment of the ideal. In these circumstances, what passes for relating is thus revealed as anti-relating.
>
> (Colman, 2005, p. 70)

So in reality the partners are not there for each other at all, and the marriage is a source of tension, a weight, not a resource which allows replenishment.

With other couples, the shared unconscious phantasy may involve a mutual anxiety that maintains their defence, thus preventing them from being open to an intimate relationship. There may be a shared fear of a calamity if there is a real coming together and this will result in a lack of any real intimacy. The couple may then exist in a relationship more like that of siblings, their sexual relationship non-existent, rather than as a mature, creative couple. This shared fear may be traced back to unresolved Oedipal anxieties where the child phantasised that the coming together of the parents was a violent coupling that was destructive, and resulted in a catastrophe.

This sense of a calamity might also originate in quite profound anxieties around damage that can be enacted during sex, and childbirth, particularly to the woman, but of course also the man (the common fear of the vagina dentata). Many of the above examples are at the extreme end of the continuum but some aspects of these defensive patterns will of course be found in many close relationships that function reasonably well most of the time.

Oedipal issues

Another fundamental area of consideration is a reawakening of interest in Oedipal anxieties and the threat of the third for the couple. Since the publication of *The Oedipus Complex Today* (Britton *et al.*, 1989), the impact of early and late Oedipal anxieties has been highlighted in more recent publications (Fisher, 1999; Grier, 2005; Jools, 2012) to name but a few. The implications of these Oedipal anxieties have been included in our developmental model and are touched on in the two earlier chapters. Of particular relevance is the idea that the capacity to tolerate a 'third' in the relationship, often a child, comes from a resolution of Oedipal anxieties, which in turn allows for the capacity to be witness to as well as to be part of a couple or family relationship.

Attachment

Of all psychoanalytic ideas, attachment has been the concept most assimilated into contemporary discourse about parent–child relationships. *Circle of Security*, a form of attachment-based intervention for parents and children experiencing difficulties, is widely used in Australia. This research-based model has also been used to describe adult couple relationships and had been one important direction that Tavistock Relationships has taken, derived in part from the need to provide an evidence-based model for research purposes (Clulow, 2001). We make greater reference to attachment research in a later chapter.

The creative couple

Earlier we commented on the flexibility and robustness of a healthy marital relationship. What ingredients are required to form what is known as 'the creative couple'?

Morgan (2005) says that: 'In the creative state of mind, the couple feels they have something to which they both relate, something they can turn to that can contain each of them as individuals' (p. 29).

This means that the relationship needs to be seen by the couple as a separate entity and that the relationship itself has the potential to provide containment and security for them both.

In mature relating, there is an acceptance of ambivalence towards the other as well as an appreciation of difference. This coming together of opposites can be enriching as it allows the relationship to be both creative and containing. In achieving what we might call a true psychological marriage, there is also a capacity to observe both oneself and one's partner from a 'third position' (Britton, 1989). This reflects a movement from the narcissistic, paranoid-schizoid form of relating to the achievement of the depressive position where the individual is able to perceive the partner as a separate entity and to feel concern for and gratitude towards the partner. With this recognition of separateness also comes a genuine curiosity about the other. Thus, when the depressive position has been achieved, individuals in a relationship experience a freedom to be themselves and in turn offer the same freedom to their partner. With the achievement of this third position, Oedipal anxieties are at least partly resolved and the parental combined object is allowed to exist as a separate entity, resulting in an introjective identification with the parental couple. This involves the internalisation of a benign (as opposed to a destructive) parental relationship and allows for a mature intimacy in the couple relationship, something to which we can all aspire.

Conclusion

After eighteen months of therapy, Martin and Frances were still together. They were both able to express a sense of loss and mourning for the close relationship they had enjoyed when they were first married. They were also able to acknowledge how inadequate and worthless they both felt after the birth of the children. It was painful for Frances to confront the fact that she had deeply hurt Martin by her affair and to begin to explore the motivation behind it. There was much work to do, but both commented on the safety of the therapeutic space that had been provided and how they were now much better able to talk about things themselves. 'We imagine that we are in the room with you', said Martin. Thus, they could be describing the beginning within themselves of a triangular space, or the capacity for a third position as described by Britton (1989).

This chapter has brought into our model later insights and influences from both the Tavistock and from Jill and David Scharff in the United States.

Dicks laid the groundwork for the application to couple psychotherapy of both Fairbairn's and Klein's ideas about psychological development and the splitting and projection involved. In his ideas about the conjoint personality he anticipated the later work on narcissistic relating in couples, a theme strongly developed at the Tavistock (Ruszczynski, 1995; Fisher, 1999). Ideas were also incorporated from Britton et al. (1989) about the importance of early Oedipal anxieties in a couple's difficulty in relinquishing some narcissistic aspects of their relationship.

Jill and David Scharff applied their knowledge of Fairbairn and his ideas about splitting to advance understanding about some of the projective processes in couples. Jill Scharff's focus on introjective processes in couples helps us to understand the strength of anxieties about annihilation in couples (Scharff and Scharff, 2005).

Perhaps on a more benign note, the 'marriage' between Jungian and Kleinian ideas at the Tavistock has given a strong focus to containment in marriage, including a discussion of the normal tensions involved in any intimate relationship. Building on this notion of containment, recent thinking has focused on the idea of the 'creative couple', a phenomenon that we sometimes, hopefully often enough, witness developing in our consulting rooms.

References

Box, S., Copley, B., Magagna, J. and Moustaki, E. (Eds.) (1981). *Psychotherapy with Families: An Analytic Approach*. London: Routledge & Kegan Paul.

Britton, R. (1989). The missing link: parental sexuality. In R. Britton, M. Feldman and E. O'Shaughnessy (Eds.) *The Oedipus Complex Today*. London: Karnac.

Britton, R., Feldman, M., and O'Shaughnessy, E. (Eds.) (1989). *The Oedipus Complex Today*. London: Karnac.

Cleavely, E. (1993). Relationships: interaction, defences, and transformation. In S. Ruszczynski (Ed.) *Psychotherapy with Couples: Theory and Practice at the Tavistock Institute of Marital Studies* (pp. 55–69). London: Karnac.

Clulow, C. (Ed.) (2001). *Adult Attachment and Couple Psychotherapy*. East Sussex: Brunner-Routledge.

Colman, W. (1993a). Marriage as a psychological container. In S. Ruszczynski (Ed.) *Psychotherapy with Couples: Theory and Practice at the Tavistock Institute of Marital Studies*. London: Karnac.

Colman, W. (1993b). The individual and the couple. In S. Ruszczynski (Ed.) *Psychotherapy with Couples: Theory and Practice at the Tavistock Institute of Marital Studies*. London: Karnac.

Colman, W. (2005). The intolerable other. In *Psychoanalytic Perspectives on Couple Work*. London: Society of Couple Psychoanalytic Psychotherapists, Issue 1.

Dicks, H.V. (1967). *Marital Tensions: Clinical Studies towards a Psychological Theory of Interaction*. London: Routledge & Kegan Paul [Reprinted London: Karnac, 1993].

Fairbairn, W.R.D. (1958). On the nature and aims of psychoanalytic treatment. *International Journal of Psycho-Analysis*, *39*, pp. 374–385.

Fisher, J. (1993). The impenetrable other: ambivalence and Oedipal conflict in work with couples. In S. Ruszczynski (Ed.) *Psychotherapy with Couples: Theory and Practice at the Tavistock Institute of Marital Studies*. London: Karnac.

Fisher, J. (1999). *The Uninvited Guest: Emerging from Narcissism towards Marriage*. London: Karnac.

Freud, S. (1916/1917). Introductory Lectures on Psycho-Analysis. Lecture XXXVIII: Analytic Therapy. S.E. Vol.16 (pp. 448–463). London: Hogarth Press.

Grier, F. (Ed.) (2005). *Oedipus and the Couple*. London: Karnac.

Jools, P. (2012). Children of Oedipus. *Couple and Family Psychoanalysis*, *2(2)*. London: Karnac.

Morgan, M. (1995). The projective gridlock: a form of projective identification in couple relationships. In S. Ruszczynski and J. Fisher (Eds.) *Intrusiveness and Intimacy in the Couple*. London: Karnac.

Morgan, M. (2005). On being able to be a couple: the importance of a 'creative couple' in psychic life. In F. Grier (Ed.) *Oedipus and the Couple*. London: Karnac.

Ogden, T. (1989). *The Primitive Edge of Experience*. North vale, NJ: Jason Aronson.

Rey, H. (1994). Schizoid phenomena in the borderline. In J. Magagna (Ed.) *Universals of Psychoanalysis in the Treatment of Psychotic and Borderline States*. London: Free Association Books.

Ruszczynski, S. (1995). Narcissistic object relating. In S. Ruszczynski and J. Fisher (Eds.) *Intrusiveness and Intimacy in the Couple*. London: Karnac.

Scharff, J.S. and Scharff, D.E. (2005). *A Primer of Object Relations Therapy*, Second Edition. New York: Jason Aronson.

Shakespeare, W. (1592). *Romeo and Juliet*, Act 11, Scene 11. In *The complete works of William Shakespeare*, Vol.1. New York: Nelson Doubleday.

Winnicott, D. (1960a). Ego distortions in terms of true and false self. In *The Maturational Processes and the Facilitating Environment*. London: Hogarth Press (1965).

Winnicott, D. (1960b). The theory of the parent-infant relationship. In *The Maturational Processes and the Facilitating Environment* (pp. 37–55). New York: International Universities Press, 1965.

Chapter 4

Containment and its challenges

Jenny Berg and Penny Jools

In this book so far, we have worked to develop a theoretical framework for understanding the unconscious anxieties and internal object relationships that underlie those emotional problems that may bring a couple or family to our attention. We call these internal patterns *the family within*.

This chapter takes a more practical approach. We will outline the ways that this theory is embodied in the way we work, with a focus on how this framework helps us to make sense of our patients' lives, and how hard it is for them to change these internal patterns.

The idea of *containment* is fundamental to this work of therapy. Containment, in this context, examines how we use ourselves as the agents of therapeutic change – and how we encounter and respond to the anxieties our patients bring into our consulting rooms. In essence, this use of the self as the agent of change is the fundamental idea at the heart of all psychoanalytically-based therapies.

This chapter will begin by expanding on the concept of containment, illustrating it with clinical vignettes of some of the typical situations we may face in our work.

What do we mean by containment?

In this chapter, the term refers to Bion's idea of containment: the provision of a containing function. This occurs when the overwhelming terrors and anxieties an infant experiences are metabolised by a 'normal' mother and a more benign, habitable worldview is transferred back to the infant. The infant projects his overwhelming experiences outside; they have to be received by another, processed, and handed back in a more tolerable form in order for psychological growth to occur. The relationship between the infant and his mother is integral, as it provides the containing function. Bion (1962) suggests that this experience of containment in infancy provides the groundwork for the growth of the mind, and that there can be no growth of one mind without another. By extrapolation, this experience of containment is also what a good therapist is able to provide for their patient.

Martha Harris (1975, p. 35) describes Bion's ideas as follows:

> Bion .... talks of the infant's need for a mother who will receive the evacua-
> tion of his distress, consider it, and respond appropriately. If this happens, the
> infant has an experience of being understood as well as of being comforted.
> He receives back the evacuated part of his personality in an improved condi-
> tion, together with an experience of an object which has been able to tolerate
> and to think about it. Thus, introjecting what Bion called the mother's capac-
> ity for 'reverie', the infant begins to be more able to tolerate himself and to
> begin to apprehend himself and the world in terms of the meaning of things.
> The mother's failure to respond to his distress results in the introjection of an
> object that is hostile to understanding, together with that frightened part of
> himself which is divested of meaning through not eliciting a response. This is
> then experienced as a 'nameless dread'.

Containment and developmental anxieties

Can Bion's ideas about containment be related directly to the capacity of the couple
in a family to contain each other's anxieties and projections? You will have noted
that this idea of a 'containing function' seemingly applies only to the relationship
between a mother and a baby, rather than to the relationship between two adult
individuals. However, we believe that there is a similar function of containment
that members of a couple can provide for each other, or which parents together can
provide for their children, that is beneficial to psychological well-being.

Often, the difficulties faced by couples that we meet are rooted in very early
experiences of being un-responded to or uncontained in their infancies. The couple may then struggle to find a way to cope when these feelings reoccur in intimate relationships – particularly when a baby, a rival for care, is introduced into
the situation.

In couples work it can often feel like there are two babies in the room, both
in competition for an understanding mother, and that to understand one means
to abandon the other. The anxieties we deal with in this situation are very primitive, the transference and counter-transference of an autistic-contiguous nature.
Holding and containing both of the couple can be difficult work.

A more common way couples come into our consulting room is in overt conflict, which distresses them but motivates them to seek help. In this state, the
dynamics of the couple are in the open and we witness their strongest feelings –
raw, painful and humiliating, but expressing something real, the truth of what
they feel. This way of relating is typical of couples functioning largely in the
Paranoid-Schizoid position, characterised by splitting and projection. There are
often accusations and counteraccusations; a great deal of anger and disappointment can be expressed. It can be difficult to experience this without feeling per-
sonally affected, and not be drawn into the split and take a side.

There can also be a sense of the loss of what was good in the relationship – that earlier period of happiness, the sense of trust. Often, it is felt as a betrayal that the 'good' has been taken away. There are examples of this in the case histories of Chapters 2 and 3.

Sometimes we also see couples who are usually quite able to manage the good and bad aspects of each other and their relationship – people who are perfectly capable of depressive position functioning, but who have been overwhelmed by a particular crisis or tragedy, and who need help to process their feelings.

The work of containing: what to try to keep in mind when starting the work

Like the mother receiving her infant's distress, the first principle of containment is to receive what needs to be conveyed – to sit and listen. As therapists we often find ourselves wanting to 'do' something to alleviate the obvious distress we see. But most couples have had experience of well-intentioned friends and families who offer advice that does not help. Their most pressing need is just to be listened to and understood. This is often what couples fail to do for each other – and what we should try to model, as psychotherapists.

Naming the unnamable fear: nameless dread

At the start, it may be difficult to assess the couple or family's capacity to create a reflective space and thus learn from experience. The therapist must be able to name what the couple or family is most fearful of – maybe a fear of separating, or that they have damaged their child. By naming this shared fear, and continuing to discuss and be sensitive to what it is that the couple dread, the therapist demonstrates that the present distress can be addressed and faced – that there is a possibility the future will be different from the past, that there is hope. The therapist's mind has not been destroyed. Because the therapist's mind has not been destroyed, s/he provides from the start a reflective space, where frightening and destructive thoughts can be openly discussed – like a mother receiving and metabolising unbearable thoughts for her infant.

Transference issues

A specific containment issue, related to family of origin history, is how the couple is able to use their therapist in the transference. Harris, in her 1975 paper, suggests that a failure of maternal containment results in a hostile internal maternal object, that is wanting to reject the therapist. Couples who have had bad experiences with their families of origin, or with previous therapists, expect failure – and may, as result, actively and unconsciously undermine the therapeutic relationship (cf. Chapter 1 and Fairbairn's idea of the 'internal saboteur').

This *use of the self* in the therapeutic encounter is central to psychoanalytic psychotherapy. Writing this chapter, one of the authors was struck by the fact that she will often say to her couples: 'I have been thinking about you since our last meeting'. This is an expression of containment – being in someone's mind, being thought about – and it is essential for therapy. It is their relationship that is in her mind. Her curiosity and interest in them is something they may have lost in each other, and something they perhaps have never experienced. This may be the first time that the couple have been genuinely listened to. This listening is not just about empathy, but about being mindful of what has been expressed previously, the unconscious elements (Bion's beta elements) – as well as tolerating the over-whelming intensity of what is occurring in the couple or family's relationship. This can take many forms, but is usually less about what is actually said and more about how it is expressed, or what happens in the room.

Affect: conscious and present: strong feelings and the negative transference

One of the first challenges we encounter is that couples and families who come to therapy are often overwhelmed with strong feelings. There is almost always unhappiness, often to the point of bitterness. Sometimes individuals are as angry with themselves as with their partner. Affects of anger and blame are common, and in couples there can be accusations like 'You've changed; you're not the person I married', or 'It's all your fault, you had the affair!' This is an example of splitting, of paranoid-schizoid functioning being enacted in the consultation.

Acknowledging these strong affects is important – this in itself is containing, as it demonstrates that the therapist is not damaged by these feelings, will not shy away from them, and is willing to allow space to understand them. The impact of these emotions as they are projected back and forth is an important source of information about the couple's emotional functioning.

Often, these strong feelings are projected onto the therapist; it is easier to blame the therapist, just as they have been blaming one another, than to face the truth. Negative transference from individuals in therapy is challenging; in couples it is, we argue, even more difficult. A warring couple can suddenly unite and direct their hatred towards you with the same intensity they have been hating each other. This intensity is hard to bear. They may now threaten to abort the therapy instead of the marriage, as was demonstrated in the case of Wendy and Hilton in Chapter 3.

It is often hard to think in a situation like this, and there may be a temp-tation to strike back. It is important to manage your counter-transference feel-ings, to acknowledge the couple's anger with you, and, if possible, interpret their attempts to 'shoot the messenger' as a way of avoiding understanding the hateful feelings between them. It is also important to maintain the frame – which we will discuss shortly.

Bion (1959) has discussed attacks on thinking in the analytic session. It is often difficult, if not impossible, to take notes after a session with a warring couple: perhaps this is concrete evidence of Bion's notion of attacks on the therapist's mind by disturbed patients.

Affect: unconscious and missing: strong feelings in the counter-transference

When overwhelming feelings are present but unacknowledged, the therapist may be affected by this too, either because the therapist notes that affect is missing from the story, or the affects or experiences appear in the counter-transference, projected there unconsciously.

The following case vignette demonstrates the impact of primitive annihilatory anxieties that had not previously been contained in the family of origin.

Five-year-old Isobel, a precocious, lively child, was referred for 'oppositionality', which turned out to be difficulties in getting to sleep and out of the door on time for school. Her father had chronic, treatment-resistant depression and had attempted suicide earlier in the year. Since then he had not worked, so Isobel's mother, who had been a stay-at-home mum, had been forced to resume full-time work. As the history unfolded in the initial session, the father became increasingly withdrawn and disconnected, as did the therapist in the counter-transference. After some time the therapist managed to shake off the torpor that had overcome her. She realised she had become inert in the session as the mother increasingly focused on Isobel's behaviour. The mother wanted help to manage Isobel's non-compliance, to avoid the fights. The therapist suggested that perhaps Isobel was distressed about what had been troubling the family, and her non-compliance might be because she did not want to have her father out of her sight. The mother dismissed the impact of her husband's depression on Isobel's behaviour, saying Isobel didn't know about it, and that she had always been a difficult child. The therapist then found herself wondering about Isobel's conception. The mother became tearful and revealed that Isobel was conceived after ten cycles of IVF, of which three had taken and miscarried. Moreover, there were a number of further attempts to have another child after Isobel, which had all failed. The therapist also found out that the couple had delayed having a family until they had paid off their mortgage, by which time the mother's reproductive chances were seriously reduced, as she was over 40.

It seemed that Isobel had to be full of life to counteract the dead feelings in the family, particularly feelings about her father's depression. In the consulting room, the 'deadness' in the family, relating to a shared sense of devastating and unmourned grief, had been projected into the therapist. Her 'reverie' allowed for the beginning of a capacity for thinking about these terrible feelings and the possibility that they might be able to be explored in a safe, containing space. As the focus shifted from Isobel to her parents' shared grief at their losses, Isobel settled down.

We have just described a situation where the therapist carries the projected split-off overwhelming feelings for the family, and previously a situation where the therapist is attacked by the hostile feelings of both of the couple. This mechanism of splitting off feelings can happen even at the time of referral, even the first phone call, when one of the couple initiates the contact. What does this mean for the other member of the couple? Is the non-initiating member reluctant to be in therapy, or carrying reluctance for both of them?

A similar split can occur with a couple referred by the therapist of one partner. The tenor of the referral may be that the problems reside in the partner who does not see the referring therapist. Clearly, when the couple or family is reluctant to attend a session together, it alerts the therapist to the possibility that splitting may be in action in this family.

These are important issues to bear in mind for the first meeting with the couple. Remember, splitting such as this is a characteristic defence of the paranoid-schizoid stage of development.

Intergenerational issues

We will have all worked with families where there have been traumas or tragedies that have left their painful legacies. And this may go back for generations. The impact of the Holocaust is clear, as is that of the 'Stolen Generation' here in Australia. Our current refugee crisis worldwide will be reaping its malign influence on the child survivors. These circumstances are horrific and have an impact which will take generations to undo.

On an individual scale what happens to the children in families is what is most salient.

Couples that seek psychotherapy, like individuals who seek psychotherapy, have all probably suffered a failure of containment in their families of origin. This is one reason why it is important to establish the family's history, including intergenerational issues. Is there a history of loss, trauma or psychological difficulty in the family? Many of the case histories in this book attest to this. The case of Paul in Chapter 5 comes particularly to mind. We do not mean an exhaustive chronology of the family, but, as in the example with Isobel, it is helpful to follow the affect: she was burdened with the need to make up for the many losses her parents had not dealt with.

A mother's, or indeed father's, capacity to contain her infant depends to a large degree on how she feels 'held' by her partner, and by her relationship to an 'internalised parental couple'. Parents are limited in this by the extent to which they were cared for in their own childhoods. There is often a transgenerational aspect to parenting – both good and bad aspects are transmitted. We all know families where a talent for sport or art is passed on from one generation to the next and is valued and cared for, or families where the opposite occurs, and this capacity is enviously attacked. In other families, this transgenerational transmission works in more ambivalent and complex ways, with both exciting and rejecting object relationship aspects being enacted simultaneously. Isobel's mother described her parents as educationally focused but emotionally cold and quite harsh. There were suggestions of more overt abuse which she was unwilling to discuss. So Isobel, at age 5, was given much time and attention for her studies, not the attention she necessarily wanted, and had to meet rigid expectations regarding homework and household routines. Isobel's father modulated her mother's irritability around Isobel's non-compliance with these routines, prior to his depression becoming too severe. Isobel became more resistant as the father withdrew, and her mother's irritability increased without his emotional support.

The work of containing: how we keep the couple or family in mind

The couple or family is the patient

Here, the notion of the couple as the 'patient' is important. This concept is central. We are not treating one or the other; we are treating the relationship – the marriage, or the family. This focus serves many functions – it establishes a secure boundary, it provides containment, it mitigates scapegoating. This focus on the relationship rather than the symptoms is a particular aspect of the frame of the therapy that needs to be maintained, that we will elaborate below.

While one partner may contribute more to the problems in a marriage, e.g. alcoholism, abuse or depression, and this needs to be clearly identified, it is the impact of these issues on the marriage or family that is the focus of the couple or family therapist. We are not doing individual therapy with a couple in the room. It is crucial to understand how the intersecting internal worlds of the couple may perpetuate the problem, without permitting the abdication of individual responsibility.

The frame

Like all psychoanalytically-based therapy, work with couples and families needs a secure frame to hold them, and the therapist. The therapist's capacity to maintain this frame highlights the importance of the relationship to the couple – that the relationship is the patient and needs to be respected even if the couple are devaluing it.

The therapeutic contract requires a regular commitment from both partners, reinforcing the idea that their relationship is worth investing in. Arrangements regarding such issues as times, fees, who attends, and what happens around missed sessions need to be clarified, so the meaning of acting out around these can be interpreted. Additionally, starting when both arrive and not continuing after one leaves makes the point that the work is very clearly for the couple.

Contextual and focused holding

Jill Savege-Scharff and David Scharff (2005) helpfully distinguish between what they call *contextual* and *focused* '*holding*' of the patient. Contextual holding pertains to the 'frame' of therapy, and to conscious feelings about therapy. Focused holding refers to the unconscious aspects of the relationship with the therapist, i.e. the transference and counter-transference. They suggest moving from contextual to focused interpretations over time as the work deepens.

'Holding' is a term Winnicott (1960) introduced to refer to the physical aspects of care for the infant, and it has been extrapolated to refer to the physical aspects of the therapy: the arrangements at a practical level. These physical arrangements, the 'frame' of therapy, are containing in themselves, as they indicate that we are reserving space for the couple, physically, and in our minds. However, it is also often important to deal with some aspects of the unconscious transference relationship early in the work (focused holding), particularly if there have been previous (particularly unsuccessful) experiences with other therapists.

Anna and Stephen had been together for twenty years, and have three children. Five years ago, Anna found out about a relationship Stephen had before they met, and she has not felt the same towards him since. She felt it was silly that she could not get over it, but she could not. They had been to a number of therapists, but had never felt they had reached the heart of the matter. The therapist also learnt a great deal about Anna's very disturbed mother, who was critical and constantly demeaning of her daughter. As the session progressed, Anna became increasingly critical of herself. The therapist noted that Anna seemed to blame herself for the difficulty in the marriage. Stephen offered that they had not continued with other therapists as Anna always felt blamed.

The therapist was able to interpret the transference in an early session. She said to Anna: 'So perhaps you think that here, too, you will be found to be the problem.'

This early 'focused' interpretation allowed the work to continue. A space was created to understand the significance of what seemed like an irrational feeling on Anna's part. Her focus on her husband's pre-marital sexual relationship meshed with the degree to which her relationship with her mother had created an internal 'bad object', and she felt blamed and at fault even for things beyond her control.

Seeing the couple separately

Colleen and David, in therapy for several years, agreed that David could come alone next time. Colleen was unable to attend, but positively encouraged David to do so. After David's solo session they had a fight, where Colleen angrily accused him of taking it for himself, as if she had not agreed. When the therapist confronted Colleen with her prior agreement to the change in the frame, she relented and said she knew she was distorting the facts, and had used it as ammunition against David because she was so upset at having been left out.

Although ostensibly about a change in the frame, the therapist's holding firm to the agreed arrangement reaffirmed the boundary and challenged the wife's anger at the changed arrangement. The therapist then explored the meaning of the feeling of being 'left out' which the wife had enacted. Colleen tearfully related her feelings of being 'left out' of her parents' relationship as a child. This case illustrates the point that contextual holding, while ostensibly about conscious processes, can also be a way of accessing unconscious aspects of the relationship. But the meaning of a change in the frame can only be understood if there is a clear agreement regarding the frame and the therapist is vigilant in thinking about the meaning of violations to the boundaries of the therapy.

Splitting: encountering ambivalence

All intimate relationships exist in a balance between loving and hateful feelings, and can tip in the negative direction in the course of therapy. Hateful feelings towards a child or partner can be distressing and difficult to face, and to deal with when they persist.

It is necessary to acknowledge this ambivalence, but to point out that it is shared; both halves of the couple feel hopeless and despairing about getting what they need or want from each other, or that they both have hateful feelings towards their child, but also love and want to help the child. Stating this in itself can be helpful, as the couple can see themselves as partners in facing a difficult situation.

Sometimes the ambivalence is projected powerfully into the therapist, who then feels despairing about the couple's future (see Chapter 5, Julia and Daniel). Supervision can be helpful for the therapist to withstand these powerful projections that can also undermine his or her competence.

Acting out of Oedipal rivalry

We mostly work on our own with a couple, without a co-therapist; this means we are likely to be positioned as taking sides with one of the couple. Often one or both are worried that they will be blamed – that the therapist will not see what the other is contributing. This issue of feeling excluded needs to be kept in mind and addressed, as it can cause splitting to occur; the therapist may be drawn into an unconscious rivalry, resulting in the therapy ending prematurely.

The work of containing: narcissistic relating in couples

Dealing with ongoing conflict

In couples and families with entrenched problems, the therapist's task of understanding and unravelling the complex projective processes is difficult (Fisher, 1995). Sometimes couples who start therapy quite civilly seem to deteriorate into using the consulting room as a battleground. Things can get worse before they get better. This is difficult for a beginning therapist, as they may feel they have failed. It is also distressing for the couple, who will accuse the therapist of making the situation worse. Threats to leave the therapy follow. How do we understand this apparent devolution?

Couples in a merged relationship, who do not cope with separateness and are intolerant of difference, may have experienced little overt conflict in the past, although they have come to therapy expressing their mutual unhappiness. In some cases (Chapter 3) their child expresses the difficulty for them. Once therapy is established and individuation starts to take place, more overt conflict may emerge as paranoid-schizoid functioning develops. This can be unnerving for both therapist and the couple, but is actually evidence of a developmental progression towards separateness. However, one should not underestimate the disturbing impact of a highly charged couple battling with each other in the consulting room. It is as if their uncontained annihilatory anxieties have attacked you and your capacity to think. As Fisher says: 'Until one has experienced the power of this psychotic process to lock two people together in what feels like hell to both, it is, I acknowledge, difficult to credit' (Fisher, 1999, p. 456).

Emma and Joe are in their early forties. She is a scientist, he is an accountant. They are trying to have a baby, and have been on IVF for a year. Emma is angry because she had wanted to try to fall pregnant six years ago (they have been together twelve years) but he was not ready. Now she is about to turn 40, and conceiving has become problematic.

Emma: *We had a big fight last night, and it's still going on.*
Joe: *I don't know what she was so upset about.*
Emma: *You were the one who was upset. I feel I can't say anything about your mother without you flying off the handle – I just feel I have to shut up.*
Joe: *You never shut up about anything. Why can't you just get on with her? She's just an old woman, she doesn't mean any harm.*
Emma: *But I didn't say anything bad about her, I just said that she and your sister are in each other's pockets . . . they are just close, there's no judgement in it.*
Joe: *But you overreact – you just can't let things go.*
Emma: *You're the one who overreacts. I kept on saying that I wasn't upset, and you got so angry that you said you wanted to end the marriage – and that's what happens every time. That's what upsets me so much.*
Joe: *Why can't we just be a happy family?*
Emma: *Well, the fact that you were drinking last night didn't help. You know I want you to stop drinking so we have a better chance of conceiving. You promised me . . . .. (reproachfully)*
Joe: *I just hate this whole thing, I hate that our sex life is tied to getting pregnant, there's no fun in it. Everything is programmed.*
Emma: *I just feel that you don't want to have this baby. It isn't easy for me, going through month after month of disappointment.*
Joe: *Well, maybe we should just forget the whole thing!*

The above vignette is a good introduction to a difficult aspect of the work of a couple psychotherapist: dealing with narcissistic ways of relating. Couples who can only see things from their own point of view will not welcome the therapist's attempts to show a different perspective. These couples will often appear to be having the same fight every time they are in conflict.

This shift in feelings to the negative, even to hating one another, can lead to despair and threats to leave the relationship – usually in the heat of the moment when the frustration is felt acutely. Here the unbearable fear (of loss/rejection) is projected into the other as a way of coping, or is used in an attempt to manipulate the other into a place where they are too vulnerable to leave. This is the case with Joe and Emma. Other examples of this kind of stuck dynamic would be: 'Why don't you go just go, then?' which is met with 'Okay, I will then', or 'That's it, I'm leaving', to which the reply is 'Well, go then'. This can become an entrenched sadomasochistic cycle.

When these cycles are going on in front of the therapist, there will be a projection of the hopelessness onto the therapist, and a questioning of the point in bothering to pursue therapy.

The understanding of the destructive effects of these narcissistic ways of relating, increasingly a focus of work at the Tavistock Centre for Couple Relationships (later Tavistock Relationships) in the 1990s, owes much to Dicks' earlier work (1967) elaborated in the previous chapter.

In general, narcissistic relating in couples has been seen to involve a conflict over allowing separateness of the other. This is solved either through attempts to dominate the other, and in doing so, merge with them, perhaps through the use of massive projective identification (Morgan, 1995), or in living side by side with the other in a kind of adhesive way, not really relating, but using the other as 'psychic skin' to be held together by.

The need for such a merger or sameness in the relationship is to avoid the pain of separateness, which is felt as abandonment. Attempts at real relating (i.e. being a different person with one's own position and needs) rupture this control over separateness, and threaten the integrity of the self, through abandonment or annihilation.

Our own clinical experience has led us to understand that there are several aspects to narcissistic relationships at a theoretical level, as outlined in the last chapter. We see narcissistic relating as inhabiting a borderline zone/state between autistic-contiguous and paranoid-schizoid anxieties. In the early phase of a narcissistic relationship, there is a denial of difference, leading to a sense of impoverishment in the relationship – a clinging together in a hostile or empty world. There is a blurring of the couple boundaries due to lack of individual ego development, an unhealthy prolongation of the narcissistic state of being in love. There is confusion and lack of resolution of issues, often conflict over even simple decision making, and an absence of a sense of shared responsibility. Usually neither one of the couple feels their needs are being met. This is because, to negotiate all of these issues, there must be an acknowledgement of the other as a person, with a position which is not the same as one's own.

We also see resistance to change from this stuck position as couples unconsciously, but realistically, believe that acknowledgment of difference could lead to the dissolution of the relationship. In our view it often takes some holding and containment before 'the work' can begin. Both partners cling to an idealised phantasy of what the relationship should be like.

Duncan and Margot, who had been together for thirty years, have made a regular commitment to spend time together. They decide to go to the movies. They arrive twenty minutes before time and, after buying the tickets, Duncan says he'd like to browse the record shop. Margot goes along with him, but is quietly unhappy about it, later admitting that she would have rather gone to the book-shop, but did not as she felt they should spend the time being together. After the movie their afternoon degenerates, as Margot behaves in a 'frosty' manner and resists Duncan's suggestions for further activities. He gets angry and accuses her of doing what she always does, of spoiling what for him was a perfectly good time. She retreats further, and does not say anything about her hurt feelings, as her ideal version of their together time crashes to pieces. Her retreat enrages him. In reaction he threatens separation, which is exactly what she is most afraid of.

Margot's phantasy of togetherness with Duncan failed when he wanted some-thing different to her, and her subsequent 'frostiness' later caused the same phantasy to fail for him. Both felt intruded upon by the reality of the other, and abandoned when the other reacted to this. This of course replays earlier family relationships: Margot is used to exclusion as her parents did everything together, excluding her from their exciting lifestyle, and Duncan is uncomfortably used to inclusion; he split the family as he was doted on by mother, but cruelly rejected by father.

This vignette illustrates what Colman (2005) calls the anti-relating cycle in nar-cissistic relationships, where one partner presses for togetherness, which the other experiences as intrusion and a threat to their personal integrity. Their defensive reaction (withdrawal/anger) causes the first to feel abandoned, and so a circular narcissistic stand-off ensues, where a 'couple state of mind' (Morgan, 2005) is lost.

We have already made the point that it is fundamental to the work to clearly establish a safe base, a frame that is able to hold the patient. This is so that attacks on the frame, such as missed appointments, can be interpreted. Similarly, attacks on the marriage, or threats to leave it, disturb the containing function of the mar-riage (e.g. Margot and Duncan) and these should be identified as such: destabilis-ing attacks on the capacity of the marriage to be a safe place.

Part of keeping the frame is to limit the amount of fighting in the consulting room, and we believe it is necessary to be directive about this at times: 'Look, we have been here before – can we stop and think about what has happened that provoked this same old fight.'

It is often hard to listen when a couple are fighting, and we have already com-mented on how difficult it is to take notes after a session with a warring couple or family. If it is possible to think, it is helpful to consider what lies underneath, what the fight might really be about.

It may be there is an event early in the relationship that they have not recov-ered from, an early abortion or the experience of postnatal depression. This may repeat feelings from the past, a sense of being the failure in the family, or of being neglected as a child. Repressed internal object relationships return. From our theoretical viewpoint, narcissistic relating may arise in the very early mother–child relationship, from uncontained autistic-contiguous anxieties. So in narcis-sistic couples, we would hypothesise that neither of the partners has been able to separate from their mother in a satisfactory way, leading to a shared desire for merger, and a shared fear of separation.

A possible link between these repetitive conflicts and early family experiences can be a shared unconscious internal phantasy – for example, a belief that they are both unlovable. It can be helpful to interpret this in a way that the couple can both relate to. In the cinema vignette above both could be seen to share a sense of hopelessness about getting what they wanted, and a shared fear of abandonment. A reframing of shared anxieties can lead to an understanding of what they share, which paradoxically is one of the reasons the couple came together in the first place.

It is also important to consider the issue of unconscious destructiveness in these cycles, but to name this slowly, and only after attempts to tap their shared vulnerability fails. It is likely that the defences people create against vulnerability are largely self-protective in the first instance. To name hostility too early will risk intensifying their defences.

Linking

As previously mentioned, links between what is happening for the couple now and what has happened in their families of origin may be brought into consciousness, so that they can recognise how their entrenched difficulties are shaped by intergenerational issues.

> Susan and Peter have three children. Susan is 'controlling and driven', like her own mother. Her father was an unpredictably violent alcoholic. Peter is 'laid back' – he is the oldest of five and his father was a travelling salesman. This meant Peter helped out quite a bit and his mother had little time for him individually, though the atmosphere was generally loving. Susan goes away for a girls' weekend, with his encouragement. She comes home to a house with happy children, but with washing drying in the lounge room, kids' toys lying around and the recycling not put out. Susan thinks Peter is really saying that he is cross that she has gone away and has not done things to her standard, on purpose to upset her. Peter then feels angry and asks why she cannot appreciate that he has looked after the kids and done the washing and give him credit for that, not grief for the 'mess' as she perceives it.

In this way, they recreated a cycle where she saw him as angry like her father and he saw her as unavailable like his mother. This had happened many times before. They were locked into negative views of each other, and felt like giving up on the relationship, and the therapy. The session following Susan's weekend away revealed Susan's need for control (of things and people), particularly anger/mess which is linked to the anxiety of her childhood and the mess created by a violent alcoholic father. The couple came to understand that this anxiety about anger clouded Susan's ability to see past the physical mess, to acknowledge the effort her husband had made to look after her. She misinterpreted Peter's 'mess' as his being angry with her. The overwhelmed little girl part of her felt bad for not looking after things – she always looked after her father in his drunken rage. Her interpretation completely missed Peter's loving gesture, and repeated his history of lack of acknowledgment from his own overburdened mother. A recognition by both Peter and Susan of the role of their families of origin issues in the current conflict allowed Susan to express her gratitude to Peter for looking after the children while she was away, acknowledging her issues with 'mess'. Peter was then able to admit how much he wanted her approval, something he had never really felt from his harried mother. The therapist's capacity to help link their emotional reactions to their 'internal family' helped the couple to move on by rein-tegrating the split-off, uncared for, unacknowledged parts of themselves as a couple.

It can be argued that different developmental stages of the couple invite differ-ent couple interpretations as illustrated in Table 2.1 in Chapter 2 (see also Keogh and Enfield, 2013). So in the early stages of therapy, in the grip of disintegrative anxieties, couples need holding – whereas those functioning in a more paranoid-schizoid way need interpretations that highlight shared anxieties, hopefully lead-ing to more depressive position functioning where awareness of split-off and projected parts of the couple can be acknowledged, as in the case above.

Therapists working with narcissistic couples can find the work hard and frus-trating, and usually benefit from the support of a supervision group to hold them. In our experience, this may be necessary in order to hold the couple. The supervi-sion group functions to try to understand and metabolise different feelings that the couple have projected into the transference and counter-transference relation-ships. Group members pick up different aspects of the split-off and projected material, and so provide a clearer idea of the dynamics.

Termination in couple and family psychotherapy

Our experience, both in our own work and also from supervising other therapists, is that it is not easy to have a good ending in psychotherapy with couples. So before describing a 'good' termination it is important to think about why couple or family therapy might end prematurely.

Premature endings

Some couples come for counselling when in fact the relationship is already over. For example, a couple may come to therapy because of an affair, but it quickly becomes clear that the 'affair' is not able to be relinquished. Or, one member of the couple may have decided that they no longer want the marriage to continue, and they bring their partner along so that the therapist can help them to end the relationship.

Another reason therapy may end prematurely is because feelings of rivalry and exclusion were not addressed early enough; we believe this to be a common, undisclosed reason why one partner wants to leave therapy. This transference issue, particular to couple work, is exacerbated by the fact that the couple is seen by a single therapist. A family history of unresolved Oedipal issues, such as a sib-ling who was favoured, or a marked sense of exclusion from the parents' narcis-sistically exclusive relationship, and the re-enactment of this in the transference, are signals to watch out for.

Couples may also end therapy prematurely because they cannot let go of their shared narcissistic defences. This can happen at a crucial moment in a therapy.

One member of a couple may want to continue to identify the other partner as the problem, as in the example below.

Jack, the husband, was a successful car salesman. He was often absent, leaving his wife to look after their three children. His wife Marion had had a series of 'fits' that looked like epileptic seizures, but neurological consultation found no organic cause. They were referred to a therapist, and Jack made it clear that the therapist was to find out what was wrong with Marion so that they could get on with things. In the second session the therapist asked them how they got together. Jack said that Marion had become pregnant, and they got married as a result. He had not wanted to get married. The therapist said: 'So it seems that there were problems in your marriage right at the beginning.' Jack cancelled further sessions and did not reply to a follow-up letter.

Successful endings

Our aim as therapists is to help couples find more mature ways of psychological functioning; in our schema this is termed depressive position functioning. This means the capacity to develop a reflective space to which the couple can bring their difficulties. It is a space to think about each other and their relationship – what they need from each other, would like from each other, can and cannot expect of each other – a capacity to think about the pluses and minuses, realistically and without excessive expectation. This involves acknowledging the reality of *ambivalence*, being able to balance feelings of hate with love.

A successful end to the therapy can only be achieved if such a reflective space has been created within the therapy room. As Mary Morgan (2005) makes clear, problems in the marriage will not disappear but the couple will have developed a space in which these problems can be discussed and worked through, just as has happened in the therapy. The couple or family has been able to use the experience of working in therapy as a temporary container for their anxieties. Over time this containing function is internalised. Warren Colman (1993) similarly refers to the possibility of marriage as a third entity to which both of the couple can turn for emotional support and security. The creation of this third space marks the beginning of the end of the need for therapy.

So what signals that this is happening? First and most obviously, couples (and families) start to talk about how things feel much better, and they are entertaining the idea of ending therapy. This gives the therapist an opportunity to reflect on what is happening – is this a sign of resistance, or is there evidence of achieving the 'depressive position' and the creation of a 'reflective space'?

Morgan (2005) notes that curiosity, an interest in the 'other', in his or her ideas, feelings, difficulties, is a sign that the relationship has changed. This is something that the therapist has modelled in their work with the couple. Curiosity, Colman (1993a) says, is the opposite of narcissism.

In our work, the idea of the 'third' is important, (Britton, 1989) as our aim is to create a space in which there is room for a third. This third space can be demonstrated when a child, like Isobel, settles into a normal childhood after some couple or family therapy. The third space can also be a space for a baby. Joe and Emma conceived a child and finished therapy. They brought a beautiful boy in to meet the therapist, proud and happy about this shared achievement. The third can also be a capacity to be together in an intimate way which was not previously possible.

Perhaps the final sign that the therapy is at an end is the mourning of the relationship with the therapist. As we know from Freud's classic work *Mourning and Melancholia* (1917), the work of mourning is vital to the internalisation of the lost object. In order to be mourned, the therapist has to be seen as a 'good enough' therapist – attempts to split the therapist have stopped and he/she is seen as an ally to the third entity, the creative marriage the couple are now in the process of bringing into being.

References

Bion, W.R. (1959). Attacks on Linking. *International Journal of Psychoanalysis*, 40, 308–315.
Bion, W.R. (1962). *Learning from Experience*. Northvale, NJ: Jason Aronson.
Britton, R. (1989). The missing link: parental sexuality in the Oedipus complex. In J. Steiner (Ed.) *The Oedipus Complex Today: Clinical Implications* (pp. 83–101). London: Karnac.
Colman, W. (1993). Marriage as a psychological container. In S. Ruszczynski (Ed.) *Psychotherapy with Couples: Theory and Practice at the Tavistock Institute of Marital Studies*. London: Karnac.
Colman, W. (2005). The intolerable other. In *Psychoanalytic Perspectives on Couple Work*. London: Society of Couple Psychoanalytic Psychotherapists, Issue 1.
Dicks, H.V. (1967). *Marital Tensions: Clinical Studies towards a Psychological Theory of Marital Interaction*. London: Routledge & Kegan Paul [Reprinted London: Karnac, 1993].
Fisher, J. (1995). The impenetrable other: ambivalence and the oedipal conflict in work with couples (pp. 142–166). In S. Ruszczynski (Ed.) *Psychotherapy with Couples*. London: Karnac.
Fisher, J.V. (1999). *The Uninvited Guest: Emerging from Narcissism toward Marriage*. Tavistock Institute of Marital Studies. London: Karnac.
Freud, S. (1917). *Mourning and Melancholia*. S.E. Vol. 14 (pp. 237–258). London: Hogarth Press.
Harris, M. (1975). Some notes on maternal containment in 'good enough' mothering. *Journal of Child Psychotherapy*, *4(1)*, 35–51.
Keogh, T. and Enfield, S. (2013). From regression to recovery: Tracking developmental anxieties in couple therapy. *Couple and Family Psychoanalysis*. *3(1)*, 28–46. London: Karnac.
Morgan, M. (1995). The projective gridlock: a form of projective identification in couple relationships. In S. Ruszczynski and J. Fisher (Eds.) *Intrusiveness and Intimacy in the Couple*. London: Karnac.
Morgan, M. (2005). On being able to be a couple: the importance of a 'creative couple' in psychic life. In F. Grier (Ed.) *Oedipus and the Couple* (pp. 9–30). London: Karnac.
Savege-Scharff, J. and Scharff, D.E. (2005). *A Primer of Object Relations Therapy*. Lanham, MD: Jason Aronson.
Winnicott, D.W. (1960). The theory of the parent-infant relationship. In *The Maturational Processes and the Facilitating Environment* (pp. 37–55). New York: International Universities Press, 1965.

Chapter 5

Finding the patient in couple and family psychotherapy

George Haralambous and Penny Jools

Transference, counter-transference and the use of the self

The use of the self is the hallmark of therapeutic work with couples and families that is based on a psychoanalytic understanding. We believe that the understanding of transference and counter-transference phenomena, aspects of projective identification, is the way in to deepening an understanding of the psychological functioning of a couple or family. These processes have been touched on in the case material of preceding chapters. This chapter focuses, however, in more detail on what goes on in the mind of the therapist when working with couples and families and how the therapist with an awareness of his or her own internal experience can bring about change.

Transference in couples and families refers first to the ways in which each individual in the family views the therapist as standing for someone in their own inner world, with the affect that belongs with that relationship. For example, the therapist might remind one member of the family of a loved grandmother, while she was viewed by another member as a cantankerous old woman. More importantly we find it useful to think in terms of what the family might share in terms of the transference relationship to the therapist. While one partner may find the therapist cold and dismissive for example, the other partner may see him or her as warm and thoughtful, but they may both, in their own individual ways, be expressing a longing to be heard and understood.

An acknowledgment of the importance of the communicative function of counter-transference has a long history (Heimann, 1950; Bion, 1962a; Segal, 1977). Although initially viewed as something the therapist should not bring to the therapeutic relationship, later thinking suggests that counter-transference forms an important part of the patient's communication with the therapist. The family or couple communicate repressed feelings with the therapist via the mechanism of projective identification. It is the therapist's capacity to contain and understand these projections that becomes an important conduit to metabolising these feelings. As Moustaki points out:

In working with couples and families in trouble, projective and projective identification processes are inevitably operating so that members of the family are carrying feelings that the parent or the parental couple cannot bear. Other members of the family may have been assigned the role of carrying some of these for the whole family, and projections that they have carried hitherto may now be experienced by the therapist in the countertransference and made available for understanding.

(Moustaki, 1981, p. 169)

Finding the patient

Donald Winnicott famously said that 'there is no such thing as an infant', meaning of course that 'whenever one finds an infant one finds maternal care, and without maternal care there would be no infant' (Winnicott, 1960). The idea here is that the infant develops in the context of the relationship with the mother. In a similar way, many troubled couples or families can only develop and discover their real problems, needs and potential in the context of the relationship with the therapist. At first reading, Winnicott's idea may appear to refer to the ordinary attention to physical needs that all infants require for survival. However, as a psychoanalyst, Winnicott was also talking about the way in which maternal care is informed by the unconscious exchanges that occur between the mother and infant that form an essential part of the mother–infant relationship. In a similar way, the relationship between the couple or family and the therapist develops through the gradual shared understanding of the unconscious processes at work in the consulting room.

This is reflected in Winnicott's observation of a young child he saw as a paediatrician who said to him, 'Please doctor, mother complains of a pain in my stomach' (Winnicott, 1948). In this example, Winnicott illustrates how a child may be drawn in to becoming an integral component of the mother's organised defence against her own depression and how the mother's real concern for her child may be confused with her own unprocessed internal experiences. Similarly, at times the therapist may act out experiences in the consulting room rather than reflecting on what is happening as a potential source of insight.

The purpose of this chapter is to illustrate some of the ways in which these unconscious processes are represented in both couples or families and in the mind of the therapist. It might be surprising for those who think in terms of a formal assessment that these complex and largely unconscious processes are in play right from the first contact with the family, even from the first phone call, as is illustrated in the following case.

Cecilia and her family

Marge phones to arrange an appointment for her 17-year-old daughter, Cecilia, who is described as 'bright and beautiful' but 'causing havoc in the home', with a

---

'total disrespect for anybody or anything in her orb'. During the initial telephone conversation, Marge tells me that Cecilia is a very talented musician, but that she doesn't put in the effort, is smoking, drinking and probably using drugs, and that she has been failing in her studies.

I start to wonder about frustrated creative desires and what these represent for the family, an issue that seems especially relevant as I later learn that Marge is a music teacher and that her husband, Tony, worked in an arts-related field.

Returning to the initial phone call, Marge, who seemed to be presenting Cecilia as the patient, says, in response to my invitation for the whole family to attend, that there is no way that Cecilia's elder brother, Philip, in his final year of university studies (and doing very well with this by the way), will be able to come to an appointment.

I find myself thinking about the split good and bad projections and who is carrying what on behalf of whom for this family. Is Philip, the firstborn and only son, the good one and Cecilia the bad? I also find myself feeling repelled by Marge's loud and abrasive telephone voice and thinking that maybe it would be easier to simply see Cecilia alone as then I wouldn't have to deal with Marge. I recognise that this is a counter-transference reaction but only later, after presenting the family at a peer consultation, become aware of a deeper level of shame that this communication contained. I was feeling ashamed of my feelings of repulsion and recognised that this was part of the communication that was evident in the brief initial exchange with Marge and that I would need to sit with for a while until it could be further understood. Even so, at the time of the initial telephone contact, I also find myself wondering how much Cecilia has been reacting angrily to a loud, dominating and controlling mother or perhaps openly expressing hostility on her behalf.

Marge then asks how experienced I am with such matters, adding that 'it's just that you sound so young'.

Although irritated I begin to wonder what this means in terms of projected feelings of inadequacy.

As the telephone conversation continues, Marge tells me that her husband, Tony, is also very busy, that he will find it difficult to find the time to attend, and that he may not be able to attend at all.

I hence find myself, still recoiling from feelings of impotence and inadequacy, invited to collude with the exclusion of all male family members, which I resist, by asking that everyone in the family attend. I later also wonder, in line with my thoughts about the failure of the creative impulse, how much Cecilia has been made to carry the parents' unrequited hopes and dreams, and how much she has

been expected to become, through their shared unfulfilled desires, the creative
object that has in essence been lost for the parental couple.

During the first session, attended by Cecilia and her parents but not the brother,
the parents take turns in complaining about Cecilia's 'bad attitude' and scorn-
ful, 'rude' retorts to anything they ask of her. In response, Cecilia sits sullenly
and silently until she eventually indignantly says that this is no different from
how they, the parents, treat each other. Marge replies, 'We're not here to talk
about us', and Tony goes on to talk of how Cecilia seemed to lose interest with
music and began to fail at school when she became involved with an older boy.
Tony says that Cecilia is a talented musician who only needs to try harder. To my
complete surprise, Cecilia, with a sudden outburst of tears, and clearly distressed,
emphatically exclaims, 'You built me up to think I was the best! But I wasn't!',
in response to which Tony, with the first compassionate expression that I experi-
enced from him, replied, 'But we believed in you!'

I notice that, from the outset of this first session, the parents seem to avoid
looking at their relationship while they remain instead focused on Cecilia, dis-
paraging in their criticisms to an extent that I am left feeling very uncomfortable
and drawn to defend their daughter. Cecilia is, by the way, very adept at defend-
ing herself and at launching strikingly effective counter-assaults. I resist the
urge to act in defence of Cecilia. When Cecilia makes reference to the couple's
difficulties, they quickly return to talking about their daughter as the problem.
They seem to be reluctant to acknowledge the marital difficulties. I also note
that Cecilia seems to be the one most in touch with emotional issues as it is she
who expresses distress at how much has been expected of her. Moreover, I note
that the most significant emotional connection in this first session, in terms of
hopes and desires, is between Cecilia and her father.

From the first point of contact with the family we wonder about who is really
the patient. Is it Cecilia or are there problems in the couple relationship and/or
deeper problems in the way in which the family functions as a unit? Is it easier for
the couple to focus on Cecilia than to acknowledge their own struggles? We are
already thinking about what has been *projected* into Cecilia and what Cecilia carries on behalf of the family. Why is there such concern about her creativity? What
does this mean about the creative part of her parents and perhaps their own unfulfilled creative desires? Is it possible that they have split off the creative parts of
themselves and located them in Cecilia? The creative parts of Cecilia are treated
with high expectations and criticism. It is not too difficult to imagine that perhaps
Marge and Tony were also treated like that as children. However, as Dicks has
pointed out, it is not just that parts of the self are split off, the other important issue
is how these parts are treated in the person they are projected into (Dicks, 1967).

From the initial telephone contact, there is already information at a potentially
deeper level that needs to be processed; the therapist has experienced negative

feelings towards Marge in the *counter-transference*. He has been repulsed by her loud and dominating voice. Marge has told him that he sounds very young and that her husband, like her son, may not be able to attend the session. Feelings of impotence, inadequacy and shame are felt by the therapist. These feelings, potentially felt by the therapist on behalf of the family, can be easily defended against and negated. If thought about, however, these feelings can be a potential source of insight.

In the first session, Cecilia points out how badly the parents treat each other, yet they remain focused on their daughter. The parental collusion in denigrating her makes the therapist uncomfortable and defensive on her behalf. Hence, there appears to be *projective identification* between the therapist and Cecilia, both feeling demeaned by Marge.

This brings us back to the issue of 'finding the patient'. From the first session with this family, it seems reasonably clear that there are difficulties in the marriage. The focus on Cecilia perhaps expresses the parents'/couple's disappointment in their own creative capacity, not only as 'artists' but in creating a happy family. The feelings of impotence and inadequacy, projected into the therapist, are a powerful communication about Marge and Tony's own sense of failure.

This first session with a family demonstrates how the therapist experiences and thinks about the *projections* that are flying around within the family. Cecilia is presented by her parents as the problem: however, an understanding of the role of projection and projective identification allows the therapist to understand some of what Cecilia is carrying for the family. At times the therapist is in *projective identification* with Cecilia in his dislike of Marge's dominating role in the family. The strong *counter-transference* feelings he experiences, once reflected on, start to give him an idea of how unhappy the parents are with each other, a shared sense of failure and shame about themselves and their family. Cecilia can be seen to be the one most in touch with emotional issues in the family, although as a child, she is also unable to resolve them. Subsequent sessions confirmed long-standing marital dissatisfaction, where both parents seemed to have given up hope in their relationship and invested all hope in Cecilia. After some months of work, the parents agree to come as a couple, but more of this later.

The value of the frame

The provision of a regular time and a predictable space provides a holding environment for the couple or family. The importance of this 'frame', as we keep stressing, is that, like the holding capacity of the mother, it allows for the family to build enough trust in the therapist to understand and relinquish their defences. Then a therapeutic alliance can be made and the real work of therapy can begin.

Deviations from the frame may hence reflect unconscious acting-out that begs to be understood. For example, Marge did not want her husband or son to attend sessions. That injunction from Marge could be colluded with or challenged, as indeed the therapist did, by stating, in terms of the frame, 'The whole family needs to attend if I am to understand what is going on'. Despite this challenge, the son, a university student, did not attend, confirming the therapist's sense of the split in the family along gender lines but also between the 'good' and 'bad' child. The father did attend, however, and was a valuable source of information about family dynamics and how he was implicated. That is not to say that the frame is to be rigid or never modified. A more flexible frame may be required, for example, to accommodate the needs of families with very young children.

A later session with Marge and Tony

After enduring Marge's 'stony silence' for what seemed like an eternity, I found myself amidst what felt like a war scene, with a barrage of anger from Marge to Tony who, according to her, was the reason why Cecilia was failing in her studies and abusing substances, the reason why she herself was not an accomplished artist, and the reason why she had never enjoyed holidays or social events. In short, he was the sole cause of her deep unhappiness and the family's problems.

As this continued, I began to experience Tony as more like a helpless child at the centre of abuse and found myself feeling increasingly helpless and power-less, as I understood Marge would have felt in the face of her own mother's angry and violent outbursts towards herself.

Marge's mother became depressed when her father was away on business, as he was frequently, and had made Marge the butt of her anger. Marge idealised her father and had no siblings to buffer the intense anger she experienced from her mother.

On Tony's part, such angry outbursts from Marge seemed somehow (not so consciously) preferable to the emotional disconnection he mostly experienced in relation to her. Tony's experience of Marge's disconnection resonated with his own similar early experiences of an absent father, two older sisters who treated him with disdain, and a depressed mother who was experienced as detached and emotionless and with whom he excessively complied and never challenged. It seems that, as part of Tony and Marge's shared dynamic, there was little room for (non-idealised) effective males but, at the same time, a shared wish that they could find someone to save them from abuse and neglect.

As part of my counter-transference experience, I found myself feeling increasingly paralysed to talk, as I had felt impotent and inadequate during my initial telephone contact with Marge.

When I eventually understood this, however, and found the courage to talk, through the angry barrage, and said something about their shared underlying wish for a pre-sent, available and connected father who could save them from the depression they both felt in his absence, the emotional tone of the session changed. In response Marge became tearful and spoke more, with sad rather than angry affect, about what she had once more clearly hoped for and thought she had found in her relationship with Tony.

Here the therapist, after some months of working with the couple, is able to make a link between Marge and Tony's experience in their families of origin and what they are projecting into their relationship. His capacity to hold and think about these experiences allowed Marge to feel contained enough to get in touch with the longing that was behind the rage that she projected onto her husband and the therapist.

From the outset, what is happening in the therapist's mind can inform us of deeper levels of conflict in the couple or family relationship: these counter-transference experiences are also an important form of communication and insight. This is well illustrated in the therapist's experience with Cecilia's parents, Marge and Tony, where the therapist found himself feeling impotent and inadequate – feelings that later came to be seen as the very feelings that Marge and Tony were experiencing themselves about their couple relationship and their family. The therapist, in the example above, was able to use his counter-transference experience to understand the couple's shared fear of their own inadequacy and their longing to find a good father/therapist to help them. Marge's rage could also be seen as her 'internal saboteur' (Fairbairn, 1952), the part of the self that can destroy the very support and love she most longs for.

A counter-transference experience can also manifest in a sense of disconnection from the emotion in the family as was expressed in the case of Isobel in the previous chapter. The therapist may notice that he is feeling disconnected or bored in the session, but may need to sit with these feelings until they begin to make sense. It may then become apparent that something is split off from consciousness in the family or couple. The split-off feeling may relate to previously unthinkable emotional experiences, such as murderous rage towards a loved one or a child who was not wanted.

Following the affect in taking a history

Formal history taking is common practice, and may provide important information, but may interrupt the flow of unconscious thoughts and associations. It is often better to explore the historical resonance of current experiences at moments when the history seems alive in the room, for example, at a moment of heightened affect as is demonstrated in the above vignette with Marge and Tony. The history we obtain is then gradually gathered at moments of affective intensity in the course of therapy, rather than in a strictly chronological sequence. Once again as demonstrated above, history taken in this way gives better insight into the internal object relations in the couple or family.

As work with the couple progressed, the therapist noticed that tensions and conflict within the family escalated when there was greater, albeit unacknowledged, experiences of exclusion, rejection or abandonment by the other, even in momentary exchanges. When the therapist drew this to Marge and Tony's attention, pointing once again to how they both shared an experience of rejection by their mothers and abandonment by their fathers, they were surprised. But in a later session Tony said:

I noticed that I got really upset the other day when Marge said she really wanted to go away for the weekend with her girlfriends; I was surprised at how cross I felt, because I go away for conferences quite often, and I usually enjoy myself. I thought about what you had said about abandonment, and I realised Marge's wish to go away felt like she was abandoning me, even though rationally I knew she wasn't.

Dreams

Dream and phantasy material may also give access to unconscious phantasies and internal object constellations that are not directly observable. Dreams and phantasies can provide a different language for the expression of unconscious processes in the dynamics between couples or within families. While dreams are not always available from partners in couple psychotherapy, when they are provided they seem to give a different level of information about the internal unconscious worlds of the couple that is once removed from the usual conflicted discourse in couple therapy. One advantage of dreams is that they invite the other party to reflect and share in the meaning of the dream, thus making them a partner rather than an adversary in the process.

Marge's dreams

With considerable obvious distress, Marge described a dream where she and a friend from school, with the similar sounding name as her husband, Tony, were ordered by an unrecognisable and enigmatic figure to bludgeon ponies to death. As our understanding evolved, the dream came to be understood as a metaphor for the destructive and indeed cruel way in which they often dealt with one another and Cecilia, and the destructive way in which they attacked the more vulnerable aspects of their experience, including understanding in therapy.

In contrast, later in the couple therapy, Marge had a dream of sharks becoming two yachts playfully and joyfully bumping together in a harbour. This dream provided a metaphor for a different kind of emerging relationship where their differences could be seen as a way of relating where it was possible to enjoy these differences, rather than a reason to 'bludgeon' each other. The changes in these two dreams represent a movement in the couple from destructive, paranoid-schizoid ways of relating to more depressive level acceptance of difference as potentially pleasurable.

It is obvious here how much Marge has been able to use the therapy to access her difficult internal relationships. In the second dream, of sharks transformed into yachts, she reveals the possibility of her bad internal objects being transformed in the therapy relationship.

Paul and his family

Paul, aged 12, was referred by the school counsellor at his private school because she was concerned he might be depressed. She said he was a bright boy who had always achieved well at school, but lately his grades had dropped. She said when she rang 'frankly he looks depressed, he seems more isolated from the other boys and I haven't seen him smile in a long time, whereas he was much more cheerful at the beginning of the year.'

I rang the home and Paul's mother answered the call. She said that she too was worried as she had been tidying her son's room and found that he had left a folder on his desk labelled 'suicides'. When she opened it she found a collection of printouts of internet and Facebook material about people who had killed themselves: Kurt Cobain, Amy Winehouse and others. I found myself feeling anxious about this boy and wondering why the mother had not sought some help herself after discovering the contents of the folder on Paul's desk.

The family were in the waiting room when I went to collect them; his father John was a vet and his mother Julia a teacher. Paul had two younger sisters, Jane, aged 10, and Jenny, aged 8. As they came into my room, John took the lead, I pointed out the chair that I usually sat in and invited the family to the couch and chairs distributed around a coffee table. I had made sure there were enough seats for the whole family. Despite my statement about where I sat John went straight to the seat I normally occupied and sat down.

I found myself irritated by this, and experienced a sense of loss of control. I also felt humiliated and heard an internal voice muttering the words of a barrister friend of mine who always, teasingly but disparagingly, asked me how work was going 'with all you shrinks and basket weavers'. I wondered if I should choose another seat, but decided that I would assert my role as the therapist and said, quietly, 'Sorry John, that is where I like to sit'. I thought about my irritation, my own sense of loss of control and humiliation, and I wondered to myself what this meant, and why John might feel he had to be in control.

John moved to the couch to sit next to his wife, the two girls squeezed themselves onto the couch next to the parents and Paul sat in a chair on his own.

As the first interview progressed I became aware of a sense of loss in the room, and a feeling of sadness.

As I was asking about the history of the family I could see that John was becoming agitated as we talked about his own family. He said that his father had died when he was 13. As he spoke, Julia put her hand on his arm and the children became very quiet. Paul in particular looked very sad. John said he would rather not talk about this in front of the children.

I decided to talk to Paul on his own next, since he was identified as the problem. I found myself anxious because of what his mother had revealed about the 'suicide' folder and felt he might well be at risk. I had a sense already that John, his father, was a troubled man. Paul said he was being bullied at school, he had loved primary school, a small local public school, but he had found the move away to boarding school at a large private school difficult, (the school was one that his father and his grandfather had attended). The older boys gave him a hard time and he had no friends from primary school at this school. His drawing of the family revealed his mother and his sisters on one side of the page and his father and himself on the other side, both separated from the girls and from each other. Both he and his father had downturned mouths.

He said 'I am worried about Dad, he gets angry a lot, and he is worried about me which makes me feel worse, he was really good at rugby, but I don't like it, I like swimming, I'm good at that, but Dad sort of doesn't think it counts . . .'.

At the next session I saw the parents by themselves. As we came into the room, John said 'I had better not take your seat again', and looked anxious. Julia, his wife, said that she thought that Paul had seemed happier that week, but he didn't want to talk about what he had said to me in the session.

I was aware of anxiety in the room, despite the initial smile, John was restless, he kept shifting position on the couch and once again Julia put her hand on his arm.

Therapist: *I was aware last week that it was difficult to talk about your father and his death and I felt of a great deal of sadness in the room. I observed that Julia looked at her husband, there was quite a long pause, she seemed to take a deep breath and said . . .*

Julia: *John hates talking about it, his father was a vet like him and he shot himself when John was 12 and John found him. It was hushed up in the family and John was not allowed to go to the funeral. His Dad was depressed and I think the family just ignored his depression, it was sort of unmanly, and he never got any help, he was living in the country . . . John doesn't want to talk about it in front of the children.*

John: *I really hate talking about this . . .* (wipes away tears). *It was terrible, I don't know if my Mum ever recovered and I had to be the man in the family, with this terrible secret . . .. I never told anyone at school, really Julia is the first person I spoke to about it . . .. I don't want to burden the children like I felt.*

Therapist: *I am thinking about the fact that Paul is the same age that you were when your father suicided.*

(John looks surprised.)

Julia: *I hadn't thought about that, but I know that John is terribly worried that Paul might be depressed, that mental illness runs in the family and Paul is suffering from it.*

In this session the therapist's counter-transference, her irritation at the way in which the father in the family 'took control' and her sense of humiliation were valuable clues to the internal world of the family. But her capacity to be curious, at the same time as asserting a frame for the session (the therapist has created a space, for the family and herself), allowed for some reflection about what this might mean. The sadness in the room and the father's reluctance to talk about his own father's death suggested that something had been split off and was being projected into the therapist . . . her experience of sadness and loss. The strong experience of humiliation the therapist experienced suggested another aspect to the experience of loss. In the same way that that grandfather's depression was seen as a sign of weakness, and therefore a source of humiliation rather than sympathy, both the father and his son are experiencing humiliation in the face of the possibility of the son's depression. Hence perhaps the father's need to take the therapist's seat, he was ashamed of admitting his vulnerability. This may be because of the father's fear of the stigma of mental illness (as well as his own fear for his own genetic contribution). The therapist also wondered about what had been projected into Paul. Was his depression a projective identification with the father? What exactly was the father trying to control?

As in the first example of Cecilia and her family, the therapist's capacity to reflect on her counter-transference experience allowed for the unresolved grief in the father to become expressed. In addition, the space created by the therapy for a discussion of Paul's grandfather's depression and suicide in the context of contemporary understanding and treatment began to relieve the father of his sense of humiliation and his son from carrying his projections. After some family sessions, the father sought some therapy for himself and Paul got on with being a normal 12-year-old boy.

This family was able to use the experience of therapy to move on relatively quickly from the initial presentation of Paul's depression. As the work with the couple proceeded, John revealed that his relationship with his mother, before his father killed himself, was warm and loving. His father's death coincided with a separation from home and his mother as he had been sent to boarding school just six months before his father killed himself. John could see that his mother was too devastated by the loss of her husband, her own humiliation at losing a husband to suicide, and perhaps her own guilt about not insisting that he got help, to be able to help her son.

In Julia, Paul had chosen a wife who was sympathetic to his grief, he had a mother who had provided a 'good enough' internal maternal object: it was as though the split-off parts of himself, his grief and humiliation, were placed in her for safe-keeping. She was understanding, but as a country woman, like his mother, she shared her husband's ethic of stoicism and a suspicion of psychiatric help. It was therefore Paul, in his projective identification with his father, who was able to express and bring into the family the fear of suicide which John had split off, ostensibly in an attempt to protect his children from what he had suffered.

Projective identification and linking

Transference and counter-transference experiences are important ways for the psychoanalytically-trained psychotherapist to understand the unconscious currents in family functioning. Curiosity is important as it allows for the linking of external to internal events, leading to the capacity to learn from experience as Bion (1959) has suggested:

Projective identification makes it possible for him to investigate his own feelings in a personality powerful enough to contain them. Denial of the use of this mechanism, either by the refusal of the mother to serve as a repository for the infant's feelings, or by the hatred and envy of the patient who cannot allow the mother to exercise this function, leads to a destruction of the link between infant and breast and consequently to a severe disorder of the impulse to be curious on which all learning depends.

(p. 313)

It is possible to think about John, Paul's father's dilemma in this context. His mother's shame and inability to deal with her son's distress about his father's suicide made it impossible for John to be able to think about his father's suicide in a way that ascribed it meaning. Instead it became a source of *'nameless dread'*, unprocessed anxiety and distress (Bion, 1962 b). Although he had been able to tell his wife, she was not able to process and metabolise the complex web of feelings John had experienced, so although loving and supportive, Julia was not able to offer a real 'containing function'.

When there has been a failure to provide this sort of linking in the family of origin, it can also manifest as a difficulty in making sense of emotionally significant events in the family or couple's history, resulting in families who may be unable to create their own history or narrative. This is another important role for the couple or family therapist, to provide the linking between these significant events so that the couple and family begin to create a more coherent 'family within'. Parents who are able to offer this to their children are helping them to understand not only their family's history, but are linking them to their own emotional life and future.

This difficulty with linking may also manifest in a couple or family who seem unable to link one session to the next: often it is ambivalent feelings that are split off and are unable to be integrated. Here the therapist may need to make the links for the couple or family. This is illustrated in the following vignette.

Julia and Daniel

Julia and Daniel first presented for couple therapy seven years into their relationship. They seemed to be in conflict over many issues but spent a considerable part of the second assessment session arguing over whether they could afford to move from being renters to buyers of their home. Daniel had done the sums and could not seem to understand Julia's reservations. Julia acknowledged that 'all else being equal', they could afford the purchase and acknowledged that her reservations were not simply about finances. She recognised that the issue reflected her ambivalence about commitment, with devoted but passive and dependent Daniel, who always seemed to get his own way. From the history obtained, I could therefore point out to Daniel that he had no reservations about purchasing the home as he adores Julia and is committed to her, just as he felt, as the youngest of five siblings, adored (at least on one level!) by his four elder sisters and parents. I suggested that, in Julia, he had found a lost part of his earlier experiences, a projected lost part of his ego, and that, while he was positive and the one expressing hope on behalf of them both, there is anger and ambivalence located somewhere else, albeit still in the relationship.

The argument about buying or renting a house, when explored by the therapist, revealed deeper anxieties about commitment, caused in part by projections from each of them from their families of origin. Daniel wanted Julia to be an adoring parent that gave him favoured status as a youngest child. Julia wanted to be a part-ner not a mother, and Daniel's assumption of her easy indulgence of him brought up her rage towards her younger brother who was her mother's favourite.

The therapeutic work continued for some months, the ambivalence manifest-ing in the relationship often seeming 'on and off' from one session to the next.

Julia and Daniel, after a session where it seemed that their relationship was over and that they would separate, commented despairingly that they seemed to be struggling with the same unresolved issues over and over again They arrived for the next session looking very pleased and unexpectedly began talking about a new-found commitment to their relationship. This commitment apparently followed from Daniel arriving home from work one evening with a bunch of roses, followed by what they described as 'the best' conversation they had ever had and then mutu-ally enjoyable sex.

Prior to this session, I was convinced that their relationship was over and was entertaining the fantasy of an evening appointment time becoming free to offer to someone new. Maybe, I thought, I wouldn't offer the time to anyone else; maybe I'd finish earlier and just use the time for other leisurely pursuits. I was thinking of moving on, that the couple and I would be moving on, and, while feeling some sadness, was not feeling crushed or defeated. Rather, it seemed right that we had reached this point, right that they separate, and that they and we would indeed be better off apart, with each of us getting on with our separate lives. I was convinced that this was a shared reality and was hence surprised with Julia and Daniel's new-found commitment to one another.

It seemed that, while confusing, I was meant to feel pleased along with them, and there seemed to be pressure to agree with them. I was also curiously, from previously feeling alert, albeit a little sad, finding myself feeling increasingly tired, unable to think clearly, hopelessly disengaged from them in the session, and like I was spoiling their party. I began to think that I was perhaps carry-ing split-off, projected and unacknowledged despair and hopelessness that had threatened to blow their relationship apart only one week previously, and that I was carrying this on their behalf. Realising this, I made the link to the last ses-sion, to the striking difference in mood states, and wondered where the despair about their relationship had gone. In a later session, we came to understand that the despair I carried on their behalf in part related to a struggle with fertility, a stillbirth, and all that this meant for them. The more immediate shared manic

defence of the couple and the despair held exclusively by the therapist suggested that we would have to wait before any sense of these underlying dynamics could be tolerated and understood by the couple.

The importance of the therapist's linking from one session to another allowed for the acknowledgment of their ambivalence, which had been split off in the session where Julia and Daniel flaunted their new-found commitment to one another. Some weeks later the therapist was able to bring their despair into the session, to create a space to talk together about their losses – the struggle with fertility, a stillbirth, and help the couple to begin to integrate the good and bad in their relationship, creating a more realistic and robust relationship for the couple.

Conclusions

From the first moment the therapist meets a family or couple they may be plunged into a confusing and overwhelming sea of emotions, as happened at the therapist's first encounter with Marge and her family. This is often what happens when a family comes into a consulting room for the first time. In our view it is essential that the process of 'assessment' and the therapy itself acknowledge the role of projective processes present from the first encounter and the force of the transference and counter-transference feelings that are both a way of understanding what is going on and a way of resolving them.

These feelings, like those projected into the two therapists in this chapter, strong feelings of humiliation and sadness, reveal not only the presence of these feelings in the couple or family, but the degree to which they have not been contained in their families of origin. Both Klein's (1946) and Fairbairn's ideas (1952) are helpful here. Fairbairn helps us understand the longing for connection that underlies Marge's rage, which can be seen as a rage against herself. She expected the therapist to reject her because she had internalised the rejecting object relationship with her mother. In Kleinian terms she had internalised a 'bad' sense of herself and she expected the therapist, like her daughter, to find her unlovable.

The therapist's feeling of sadness and humiliation in the case of Paul's family brought into consciousness the split-off feelings in Paul's father. Not only his great sadness about the loss of his father, but the sense of rejection from his mother at a time when he most needed her. Additionally, he was fearful that his son might inherit some form of depressive illness and his humiliation at the idea of mental illness in the family prevented him from being able to be compassionate towards his son

Projective identification puts the therapist in touch with the families' difficulties with split-off parts of their experience, as was demonstrated in the case of Isobel in the previous chapter. The therapist's capacity to 'link' the couple or family with these split-off parts helps the couple or family to create a coherent history for themselves, including from one session to the next, in order to understand their own 'family within'.

The therapist's task in this situation is aided by his own therapy or analysis and the help provided by supervision.

This chapter started with Winnicott's idea that 'there is no such thing as an infant', that the infant has to be seen in the context of the relationship with the mother, without whom he would not exist. The 'patient' in the family, often the couple itself, we believe, begins to emerge through the therapist's use of themselves, their own mind, in making sense of transference, counter-transference and projective identifications in the consulting room.

References

Bion, W.R. (1959). Attacks on linking. *International Journal of Psycho-Analysis, 40,* 308–315.

Bion, W.R. (1962a). The psycho-analytic study of thinking. *International Journal of Psycho-Analysis, 43,* 306–310.

Bion, W.R. (1962b). *Learning from Experience.* London: Heinemann.

Dicks, H. (1967). *Marital Tensions: Clinical Studies Towards a Psychoanalytic Theory of Interaction.* London: Routledge & Kegan Paul.

Fairbairn, W.R.D. (1952). *Psychological Studies of the Personality.* London: Routledge & Kegan Paul.

Heimann, P. (1950). On Countertransference. *International Journal of Psycho-Analysis, V(31),* 81–84.

Klein, M. (1946). Notes on some schizoid mechanisms. *International Journal of Psycho-Analysis, 27,* 99–110 [Reprinted in M. Klein, *Envy and Gratitude and Other Works 1946–1963.* London: Hogarth Press, 1980].

Moustaki, E. (1981). Glossary: A discussion and application of terms. In S. Box. *et al.* (Eds.) *Psychotherapy with Families: An Analytic Approach.* London: Routledge & Kegan Paul.

Segal, H. (1977). Countertransference. *International Journal of Psychoanalytic Psychotherapy, 6,* 31–37.

Winnicott, D.W. (1948). Reparation in respect of mother's organised defence against depression. In *Through Paediatrics to Psychoanalysis: Collected Papers* (Ch. 8). London: Tavistock.

Winnicott, D.W. (1960). The theory of the parent-infant relationship. In *The Maturational Processes and the Facilitating Environment* (pp. 37–55). New York: International Universities Press, 1965.

Case studies in developmental anxieties

Introduction to Part II

Penny Jools

In the first part of this book we described our ideas about couple psychotherapy from an object relations perspective. Both Klein (1946) and Fairbairn (1952) offer helpful perspectives to think about the impact of the early splitting of the object in response to a failure of (constant) maternal care and the impact of this splitting on the inner world of the infant: this model is useful in thinking about the 'mind' of the family and couple. Chapter 2 outlines a hierarchy of developmental anxieties that provides a way of thinking about the couple or family's functioning in a developmental sense – how mature, flexible and robust are their ways of thinking about themselves and each other? Case studies in Chapters 1 and 2 illustrate how these ideas can be applied to the dilemmas that couples and families bring to therapy. Chapter 3 describes how ideas about couple psychotherapy have changed in the last fifty years, particularly with the impact of Dick's ideas, as well as the later contributions from Tavistock Relationships and the Scharffs (2005) in Washington DC.

The last two chapters of this section provide a more 'hands-on' description of what can be done to help a couple or family move on. Chapter 4 focuses on the important idea of 'containment', how as therapists we are able to contain, i.e. understand and metabolise our patients' anxieties so they learn from experience and make better decisions. Chapter 5 focuses on another important aspect of object relations work with couples and families, the 'use of the self' as an instrument of therapeutic change through transference, counter-transference and projective identification.

So where does Part II of the book take us?

Four detailed case studies form the next part of this book. Each case demonstrates and enriches our understanding of the developmental aspects of the particular couple or family's functioning. In Chapter 6, Jenny Berg utilises Thomas Ogden's (1989) concept of an autistic-contiguous phase of development, and a lack of 'good enough' holding (Winnicott, 1956) that together leave the infant with an inadequately internalised ego.

This results in a lack of capacity for self-containment, and an ongoing vulnerability to overwhelming experiences of fragmentation. In the case of Sue and

Dean, this fragmentation is explored from the perspective of the couple's sexual difficulties, where each partner, because of traumatic early experiences of separation, neglect and abuse, experienced sexual intercourse as a threat to their psychic integration. The dream that is included in this case study well illustrates this dilemma for both of them.

Sue volunteered a dream of being chased by a 'predator'. In the dream she is running through a large building, locking doors after her as she goes, attempting to escape from a male pursuer. The dream ends with Sue panicking because she realises she is locked into a room that she cannot escape from, as the predator is on one side, and there is another male person, a 'creepy caretaker' on the other side of her, the exit door.

Sue's associations revealed that the predator represented disowned parts of her (sexual) self, which she could see she had projected into her husband, to avoid. She knew that she had been prey, and was disturbed by the idea she might also be the predator.

Dean's associations to this dream confirmed his unconscious rejection of his sexual self and needs and how being sexual made him feel.

In Chapter 7 Julia Meyerowitz-Katz also examines the sense of fragmentation in a couple's relationship. The couple described in this chapter had suffered early abuse, loss and neglect. Julia uses a Jungian framework to understand the 'psychoid' processes, an unconscious mind/body process that contributed to the couple's fragmented relationship. The therapist's patient work of containment using the transcendent function (the bringing of apparent opposites together) helped bring about a more integrated and co-created couple.

In Chapter 8, Lissy Abrahams shows how a couple's difficulties are related to issues from the family of origin, in particular the lack of containment for feelings of vulnerability aroused by anger. For both Mitch and Helen, this resulted in a splitting and projection of the vulnerable feelings into the children in the relationship, who were looked after at the expense of the couple (paranoid-schizoid functioning). Unable to bring their vulnerability into their own relationship, the couple dealt with this by denying their sexuality and becoming a 'no-sex' couple. Some progress towards an understanding and re-integration of their vulnerability occurred in the therapy, but Helen's terror re-emerged after a therapeutic break and resulted in a 'separation under the same roof', which offered, perhaps, some future possibility of rapprochement.

A marked feeling of exclusion is the hallmark of the Oedipal issues that the two families bring to therapy in the last chapter in this section written by Penny Jools. In the first case, a child, Crystal, was struggling to be included in a family that denied her a proper place as a child. In the second case a husband excluded his wife of sixteen years from a legacy inherited from the husband's mother. The husband, recruited as a child to be his mother's protector because of the traumatic death of his father, could not relinquish his sense of responsibility towards his (now dead) mother to the exclusion of his wife. In both cases therapy provided some resolution of these Oedipal anxieties and the families were able to move on.

These four case studies give the reader a more detailed understanding of the enactment of the developmental anxieties outlined in Chapter 2: a movement from autistic-contiguous anxieties through paranoid-schizoid to depressive level functioning, with Oedipal issues emerging at a number of points.

Another theme in these four chapters is the impact on a couple's sexual relationship of early somatic disturbance, leading to a shared fear that intercourse is destructive to psychic integrity. Chapter 8 highlights the role of splitting and projection that protect the couple from their shared vulnerability which is essential for real sexual intimacy.

The experience of a containing therapeutic mind functions to metabolise some of the couple's anxieties, to render these fears understandable and thus able to be viewed with compassion. In Julia Meyerowitz-Katz' chapter, the process of therapeutic containment is poignantly illustrated by a couple who adopt a wounded puppy, a concrete representation of their shared damage:

- They worried about how much damage the healthy puppy was going to cause.
- The wounded and damaged puppy, who turned out to be healthy, perhaps represented something for them of the hopeful possibility that they too, wounded as they were, could co-construct a healthy and creative relationship.

References

Fairbairn, R. (1952). *Psychoanalytic Studies of the Personality*. London: Routledge.

Klein, M. (1946). Notes on some schizoid mechanisms. *International Journal of Psycho-Analysis*, *27*, 99–110 [Reprinted in M. Klein, *Envy and Gratitude and Other Works 1946–1963*. London: Hogarth Press, 1980].

Ogden, T. (1989). *The Primitive Edge of Experience*. New York: Aronson.

Savege-Scharff, J.S. and Scharff, D.E. (2005) *A Primer of Object Relations Therapy*, Second Edition. New York: Jason Aronson.

Winnicott, D.W. (1956). Primary maternal preoccupation. In Collected Papers: *Through Paediatrics to Psychoanalysis* (1975), pp. 145–156. London: Hogarth Press.

Chapter 6

A bad moment with the light[1]

Considering the impact of autistic-contiguous anxieties in couples' sexual difficulties

Jenny Berg

Introduction

This book describes a way of thinking about couple and families from a developmental perspective. By that we mean that many anxieties in couples and families stem from difficulties experienced growing up in their families of origin. We all have difficulties in our early development, but often, as Dicks (1967) pointed out more than fifty years ago, our choice of partner can bring us face to face with our early unmet needs. Some couples and families sort this out through the process of 'growing up'. Others need help to do so.

This chapter gives a clinical example of the impact on a couple's relationship, particularly their sexual relationship, of unresolved traumatic early experiences that affected their sense of containment, both a sensory and a psychic level, resulting in shared primitive anxieties. Both husband and wife, because of their early deprivation and abuse, had not internalised a sense of the capacity of the skin to hold them together. This led to a fear of fragmentation and terror precipitated by the mutual inter-penetration involved in sexual and emotional intimacy.

A mature adult sexual relationship provides a space for the couple to rework the psychological and physical tensions that occur between the positions of loving and hating, and merging and individuating. Individuals in a couple benefit from having an ongoing space to continue to feel replenished and integrated, or whole. As such, the sexual relationship functions as the embodiment of the continuing ability of the couple to move between these positions of P/S>>D, which facilitates the development of K, knowledge of self and other (Bion 1962a). Many couples coming for therapy have been unable to achieve this capacity for depressive position functioning, or whole object relating, and mature sexual relating. As such they have difficulty helping each other to grow, face challenges in life and adapt to change.

Sexual problems are often thought about in terms of unresolved Oedipal situations – relationships tinged with incestuous inhibitions. This requires a capacity for part object relating, where there is an awareness of a self and other, even if the attributions or qualities of the self or other are distorted. While this has bearing on much sexual difficulty, in this chapter we explore the impact of traumatic pre-Oedipal experiences on the adult sexual relationship. These earlier impingements interfere with psychic development, precluding a stable sense of self, and impact directly on the capacity for intimacy to be established.

In particular, we examine the intensely psychosomatic nature of the difficulties experienced by a couple who have deeply dissociated, traumatic internal object relationships, as they struggle to find an adequate way of connecting. They share histories of severe early neglect and later childhood abuse. As a consequence, their experience of sexual intercourse, and the therapy that explores the lack of sex in their relationship, unleashes overwhelming feelings that disrupt the couple's capacity to 'go on being', a term Winnicott applied to mother–infant dyads (1956, p. 303).

These overwhelming feelings emanate from a self prone to fragmenting, consequent upon an earlier flawed 'holding environment' (Winnicott, 1960), which did not provide a 'potential space' (Winnicott, 1951) within which the infant could begin to develop psychic structure. If the infant does not internalise ego structures there is an inadequate development of a sense of self, a lack of differentiation between internal and external experiential realms, and an ongoing threat of falling to pieces, psychically and physically. Consequently, there is a propensity to decompensate to the very early primitive anxieties that characterise what Ogden has called the Autistic-Contiguous phase of development (1989).

Theoretical overview

Freud states that the ego is 'first and foremost a body ego' (1923, p. 26). In a footnote dated 1927 he adds, 'The ego is ultimately derived from bodily sensations, chiefly those springing from the surface of the body'. Here it is clear Freud is thinking about what constitutes the nucleus of ego development and he locates this in perceptual awareness of our physical selves; 'sensations springing from the surface of the body'.

This idea eloquently introduces us to the area of psychic functioning we will focus on, called the Autistic-Contiguous Position (Ogden, 1989). Ogden synthesised and extended the work of Esther Bick (1968), her supervisees Donald Meltzer (1974) and Frances Tustin (1984) among others, and described a phase of psychic development, which precedes the more well-recognised Kleinian Paranoid-schizoid and Depressive phases.

According to Ogden, the 'Autistic-Contiguous' phase of psychic development is 'a sensory-dominated mode in which the most inchoate sense of self is built upon the rhythm of sensation' (1989, p. 31).[2] Moreover, he maintains that experience in this phase occurs in 'a pre-symbolic, sensory mode and is therefore very difficult to capture in words' (ibid., p. 32). We will return to the subject of how this very early experience is encoded in the psyche, and how it is accessed later in life.

It is not a new idea that the earliest phase of psychological experience is one where the infant is not differentiated from his environment, and does not have the capacity to discriminate me from not-me experiences (Winnicott, 1951). Nor is the idea that the infant learns about himself and others perceptually, through his senses. Ogden, however, focuses particularly on sensations perceived by the skin, both externally and internally, as experiences that provide information about the infant's physical 'limits', the boundary between himself and the world, including others. According to Bick (1968), the internalisation of this function of the skin gives one of the earliest experiences of being passively held together, and contained. Without this there would be an experience of something unboundaried, like a deadly falling to pieces. Additionally she maintains this experience of being held together by the skin provides the infant with a primitive notion of spaces that exist both inside and outside the self, and therefore of an interior to the self, and of somewhere that can serve as a container for what is inside oneself. This understanding is a prerequisite for the development of the splitting, projective and introjective mechanisms that are fundamental to Klein's Paranoid-schizoid and Depressive positions.

So what this means is that the sense of touch on skin lies at the heart of our earliest comprehension of self as separate to other, and that skin is the primary vehicle for the experience of bounded relationships with others. Having a boundary to the self allows one to enter and leave relationships; coming together and separation are possible. Without such a boundary there are great difficulties in approaching and leaving another; the psychic danger is of annihilation either through merger or abandonment, both of which involve the experience of losing oneself, or of being lost. This 'claustro-agrophobic dilemma' (Rey, 1994) represents a marked difficulty with creating a shared psychic space. A couple without such a boundary experience the sharing of psychic space as leading to what Britton describes as 'catastrophic consequences', the threat of psychic annihilation (Britton, 1998).

This internalisation of sensory experiences in the service of boundary formation that is central to a developing sense of self is further complicated by the fact that touch on the skin is also an erotogenic experience: 'very definite erotogenic effects are to be ascribed to certain kinds of general stimulation of the skin' (Freud, 1905, p. 200).

The experience of containment, which is first obtained through sensations at the level of the skin, is infused with diffuse erotogenic sensations. It follows, therefore, that the erotic aspects of touch may be compromised and even made aversive or hypersensitive by an earlier lack of containment.

So how does this early sense of self develop? In infancy the ordinary 'good enough' mother (Winnicott, 1956) gives herself over to meeting the needs of the infant so well that the infant has a brief experience of omnipotence. She shields her infant from the initially overwhelming impacts of sensory experiences, allowing only as much reality (not-me) as he is able to bear. She acts as an auxiliary ego, and through appropriate holding and handling, spares her infant the experience of unmanageable amounts of 'unthinkable anxiety' (Winnicott, 1962), thus facilitating the development of ego maturation and integration. It is the physical aspect of the care, which is of course influenced by the mother's capacity for containment (Bion, 1962b), that modulates this early sensory experience.

This 'unthinkable anxiety' is related to an awareness in the infant of the experience of separateness, and therefore of absolute helplessness and dependency. Winnicott describes this as manifesting as 'going to pieces, falling forever, having no relationship to the body, having no orientation' (1962, p. 57). We want to highlight 'having no relationship to the body' . . . which brings us back to Freud's 'the ego is first and foremost a body ego', a proposition Ogden (1989) agrees with.

So what happens if a psychic representation of one's physical sense of self is not reliably developed during infancy; if adequate psychosomatic boundaries to the self are not formed? Ogden suggests this leaves the individual afflicted by a core anxiety: 'the experience of impending disintegration of one's sensory surfaces, or one's "rhythm of safety" (Tustin, 1986), resulting in feelings of leaking, dissolving, disappearing or falling into shapeless, boundless space' (Ogden, 1989, p. 68). There is a fear of disintegration, of falling apart, both physically and psychically. There is no sense of internal psychic space, there are no boundaries, and the distinction between one's self and another collapses. This core anxiety threatens to reoccur and is readily reactivated within the skin-to-skin context of the adult sexual relationship.

Ogden describes the defences generated in this position to ward off these extreme anxieties as having obsessive-compulsive qualities, involving attempts to re-establish the sense of boundedness and rhythm upon which early integration depends. This is often through the use of physical activity or sensory stimulation. In the therapy session defences may manifest as repetitive physical actions, for example foot tapping, self stroking, muscle clenching, focusing on symmetrical patterns of objects, self soothing repetitious mental activity, e.g. counting. Outside the therapy room they may include a vast range of repetitive actions; exercising, eating rituals (putting things into and expelling them from the digestive tract), rocking, self harming, e.g. cutting, keeping (physically or intellectually) busy, compulsive masturbating.

Interpersonally, defensive manoeuvres against these primitive anxieties manifest through 'faulty second skin' formation (Bick, 1968), or as Meltzer described it 'adhesive identification' (1975); absolute dependence on an external object in order to maintain integration. The infant attempts to adhere to their object for a rudimentary sense of safety, to combat catastrophic anxieties about ruptures in the integrity of the self that could result in the experience of disintegration.

This idea is highly relevant in work with couples. This absolute dependence on the other to maintain a sense of self has been described as narcissistic object relating in the couple (Fisher, 1999; Ruszczynski, 1993). The other is not allowed an independent existence, but is required to be perfectly attuned and responsive to the self with no room for, or possibility of, difference. A dynamic of omnipotent control exists between the couple, which Fisher (1993) has graphically conceptualised as resulting in a 'false-self couple' extending to the couple relationship the type of infant–mother dynamic that forecloses on the development of a true self.

To return to the question posed previously, how are these early pre-verbal sensory experiences accessed in later life? It has become increasingly established that very early experiences with objects, and also later memories of a traumatic nature, are stored in non-declarative memory as 'implicit' or 'procedural' memory and cannot be consciously accessed. However, these memory traces influence current experience and behaviour and re-emerge in relationships, and in the transference, as acted out implicit relational schemas (Process of Change Study Group (PCSG), 1998).

This accords with Fairbairn's views (1954); he presciently hypothesised that severe situations of neglect, or of abuse in later childhood, could overwhelm the developing ego's capacity to repress. He thought that splits in the ego could become so severe that some experiences, and their associated states of being, may evade the integrating capacity of his 'central' organised ego. Fairbairn thus maintained that these catastrophic experiences are dealt with by dissociation, not repression. That is to say they are stored in a different memory system, out of conscious access.

Moreover, Fairbairn suggested that these dissociated parts of the ego become closed off from contact, not open to change, 'frozen in an unchanging state' (1958). The idea of an infant or child freezing in response to trauma is suggestive of an experience of dissociation, and the memory of instances of the self falling to pieces becomes frozen as well. Hopper (1991), who worked with children of Holocaust survivors, has a similar concept of 'encapsulation' as a defence against the experience of annihilatory anxiety, complete helplessness and utter dependence.

This type of defence against severe neglect or trauma is deeply resistant to conscious awareness, and is something the therapist has to infer from observed behaviour in the transference and counter-transference, from silences and gestures, or the lack of them. When working with couples these implicit relational schemas are acted out between the partners, as well as with the therapist. Due to the highly sensory nature of the early traumatic experiences, these schema are more likely to be played out in the arena of the sexual relationship of the couple, or where the sexual relationship is explored in couple therapy.

With these thoughts in mind we now present some clinical material where these very primitive anxieties underlie the difficulties for both of the couple in their sexual relationship. How to access these frozen experiences, and then contain, metabolise and integrate these terrifying feelings becomes the major therapeutic dilemma.

Clinical material

The couple gave permission to use their material for academic purposes. Their identities have been disguised.

They initially presented functioning at a paranoid-schizoid level. There was a split with one carrying the burden of blame for all that was wrong with the relationship. As the therapy progressed, it became clear that the regression point was at the earlier level of primitive sensory anxieties. These anxieties were expressed in powerful bodily ways, which were hard to put into words. We will focus on these phenomena selectively as they are difficult to see clearly due to interpenetrating, superimposed elements from paranoid-schizoid and depressive modes. Ogden describes a continuous dynamic interaction between the primitive autistic-contiguous stage and the other stages of psychic development, that is to say they operate simultaneously, in a dialectical fashion.

Sue and Dean were both in their early forties. They had been together fourteen years and had three children, a girl aged 11, and boys aged 8 and 4.

He was a tradesman who worked long hours, she was a part-time librarian and the main child-carer, though this was changing, as the children grew older.

The referral was from Sue's twice weekly psychotherapist, who felt unable to get to Sue's internal world, because she felt Sue projected all that was wrong into her husband. Sue's therapist hoped that some couple work might help to address this.

Sue presented full of complaints about her husband; Dean was emotionally disconnected from her, and did not talk about things that really mattered. In sessions Dean was silent and offered no response. He needed encouragement to describe his version of the relationship, which was that Sue was negative, critical and complaining, and that he felt he was always in the wrong. Dean, however, admitted that he handed over responsibility and relied on Sue to run their family life. Sue agreed Dean rarely did things to her liking (not even cooking pizza with the kids) and acknowledged that she had, at some level, agreed to be the decision maker for the family, creating a rod for her own back.

The problem in this fused dynamic was that Sue's dependent needs were not met, nor was Dean's independence fostered. Intermittently Sue would explode with the frustration of these unmet needs and blame Dean for their marital difficulties. She would then feel guilty, and become depressed. Dean would become fearful and confused by these emotional storms and not knowing what to do, he would keep his distance until Sue returned to 'normal'.

They both felt unhappy, and had thoughts of separating, but did not feel able to act on these. Instead they had come to avoid intimacy: he by withdrawing through being busy at work or with the children's sporting activities, and she by her repetitive complaining, talking at Dean in a haranguing way that left him feeling criticised, wounded and unable to reply, thus perpetuating her complaint.

This version of the couple's shared dynamics had Sue in charge, trying to manage her own internal sense of disconnection, of falling to pieces, through controlling intrusive projections into Dean. This mechanism failed and Sue spilled out in an angry and incontinent fashion. Dean, psychologically overwhelmed by these projections, was rendered passive and compliant, unable to manage Sue's internal distress because it triggered his own similar uncontained experiences. So Dean defensively withdrew when Sue erupted into destructive angry tirades, adding further to her fears that no one was there.

This is a common couple presentation with couples functioning at the level of narcissistic object relations (Ruszczynski, 1993).

According to the developmental schema we are elaborating in this book this type of object relating exists in a border zone between autistic-contiguous and paranoid-schizoid anxieties. What we see in the couple's clinical presentation is a cycle where parts of the self, including multiple un-integrated experiences, are unconsciously split off from the self, projected into and then identified with in the other. This is an omnipotent use of the other, as it involves domination and denies the other's separateness, thereby blurring personal boundaries. In such a couple it can be hard to know where one ends and the other begins.

The mutual intrusive projective identificatory processes employed are desperate attempts at 'adhesive identification' with the other (Meltzer, 1975). Meltzer called this a 'folie-à-deux relationship', and suggested it often gave rise to sado-masochistic aspects in the couple (Meltzer, 1995). An ongoing interaction, described by Fisher's 'false-self couple' (1993), exists based on the pre-verbal nature of gestures which if not perfectly attuned to in a way that creates the delusion of omnipotence can trigger the 'unthinkable anxiety' of separateness. The partners collude in a dynamic where one needs to tyrannically control the other into being compliant in a very rigid way, to prevent this occurring.

This dynamic was reflected in their therapy sessions; she spoke continuously in angry monologues, as he would stare fixedly out of the window. Her constant stream of criticism was like a wall of sound, keeping her shut in, and him shut out. His lack of response only intensified her anger. She would often leave sessions crying but continuing with her litany of complaints because they had not achieved her longed for sense of connection.

I tried to intervene in this dynamic, which overwhelmingly drew my attention to her and away from him, and ask Dean what he was experiencing while Sue spoke. Once he replied he was 'just looking at the pattern of bricks on the wall', a self-soothing use of 'autistic shapes' (Tustin, 1984). At other times he would hold himself so tightly that his muscles cramped up, as if he was trying to construct a protective shell to prevent himself from being overwhelmed. He would then have difficulty leaving sessions and was reduced to limping out the door.

It is likely that this intensely physical nature of their interaction functioned at a deeper level, and could be thought of as ways of creating 'autistic objects' (Tustin, 1980), 'edges' of sensory experience to butt up against, an attempt to resist being overwhelmed by an annihilatory experience and to create a boundaried sense of self, with a sense of internal space.

In the counter-transference, I felt intruded upon by her as she spilled out in an uncontained way, and identified with him as the passive recipient of this. Initially I felt pulled towards soothing her and as if I needed to be pursuing him in his retreat. Later I felt like limiting her outpourings, and like protecting him from them. I felt that I was doing a very bad job of being a sensitive attuned therapist with each of them. However, the process that went on between them made them feel 'impenetrable' or perhaps even 'untouchable' as a couple, and I was aware of a sense of despair about getting through to them. This seemed to reflect a shared experience of the couple; they could not get through to each other, to touch or be touched by the other.

Background history

Dean's history

Dean's mother, who had lost her own mother, left home at 15 and was pregnant at 16. When he was born they were destitute, cold and hungry. So infant Dean was placed in an orphanage. His mother saved enough money to reclaim him at 2 years of age. When Dean was aged 3 she married, and he was 6 when the first of his three half-siblings was born. Around this time he developed a marked stutter that can still trouble him today. His mother and stepfather did not obtain help for his stutter, though he was teased mercilessly by both his teachers and classmates, which was profoundly humiliating. As conversation was difficult for him, he became quite involved in sport, at which he excelled. He denied emotional difficulties at home. His mother and stepfather were always busy, and his child-hood was spent outdoors being physical.

He tried to go to university after school, but dropped out and began travelling, eventually ending up in the company of a group of tradesmen who set him on his career. Sue was his first long-term relationship.

Dean idealises his mother, he 'won't hear a bad word about her'. She left Dean's stepfather around the time Dean left home. Dean knows nothing of his biological father nor is he in contact with his stepfather or half-siblings.

Dean and his mother, alone and destitute, were exposed to terrible anxiety in his early days, then huge loss and abandonment when he was placed in the orphanage. There he would not have had the normal holding and handling that allows an adequate sense of self to develop. When he was reunited with his mother he was taken into a house where his mother cared for other children, so would not have gotten much individual attention. The dramatic development of his stutter after the birth of his first sibling was another physically traumatic experience that fractured his nascent sense of self, and any internal sense of containment.

In telling his story, Dean focuses on his mother's reclaiming him as evidence of her care, and follows her lead in using manic denial regarding the consequences of his early abandonment, which he literally cannot think about. In this he displays his default position: that of being compliant with another, rather than defining his own position. At times in sessions when his anxiety is provoked by the threat of separation he describes a sensation of falling, like in a dream, and of nothingness; inchoate sense memories, which he finds terrifying.

Sue's history

Sue's mother survived the Second World War in Germany, but endured many traumas during this time.

Sue's father, the youngest from an upper-class British family, and his mother's favourite, slept in his mother's bed. He suffered recurrent severe depressions and had a lifelong compulsion to cross-dress.

Her parents met in Germany, fell in love, married and moved to London. There they faced considerable anti-German sentiment, which rendered them quite isolated.

Sue is the second child; she has a brother five years older. Her mother had postnatal depression after she was born, and her brother clearly resented her arrival and bullied and abused her from infancy, initially physically and later sexually.

Her parents, who did not seem to notice her, did not protect her from the physical abuse, and Sue did not disclose the sexual abuse, apparently putting a stop to it herself in her early teens. The sexual abuse was overtly stimulating. It involved tickling, hurting and led onto masturbation and eventually digital penetration.

Sue describes her mother as a cold woman, whom she could never please despite being compliant. She downplayed the injuries she received from her brother, for fear of being rebuked. The lack of parental care and concern left Sue with very mixed feelings about the abuse from her brother, the only attention she got.

Occasionally Sue would have 'huge rages' and be sent to her room to calm down. Her mother would then say, 'There, there it's over now', which Sue felt invalidated her feelings. These outbursts earned her the status of the difficult one in her family.

Furthermore, in a role reversal, Sue was a confidante for her mother's anxieties; she was aware that her father was not sexually interested in, nor potent with, her mother, and that he was a cross-dresser. Sue's father is largely absent from her memories of childhood. One memory that remains is of being thrown across the room by him as quite a small child.

Sue behaved in a seductive way towards men from her early adolescence, but usually did not have sex with them.

Sue keeps in touch with all her family hoping that they will acknowledge her, but is repeatedly disappointed by them, and then suffers protracted depressive episodes.

Sue's mother had postnatal depression and was unattuned to Sue as a child. In response, Sue became compliant and developed a good and capable false self. Her older abusive brother, the only one giving her attention, has left her highly ambivalent and controlling about intimacy, particularly sexual contact. She was neglected, abused and sadistically intruded upon, which doubly impacted upon the development of a true sense of self. She rigidly blocks out awareness of her inner confusion, projecting any sense of this into Dean, and by being efficient and competent, she controls her awareness of dependency in her relationships.

As a couple it seemed they shared histories of failed containment due to inadequate parenting. Though not deliberate, their parents abandoned them both in infancy, and were not able to protect them as children when faced with physical insults or abuse.

Sexual relationship issues

Six months into therapy, after many sessions of Sue repeatedly criticising Dean, he revealed his dissatisfaction with the lack of sex in their marriage. This was a huge step for Dean to reverse their shared dynamic, where Sue complained and Dean carried their shared feelings of inadequacy. By speaking up Dean was risking being separate, and having a point of view of his own.

Sue became immediately defensive, saying she had confused being sexual with being cared for, which was not the case. She thought what they both really needed was mothering, and did not acknowledge Dean's separate view on his sexual needs.

She said she had come to avoid sex to avoid the experience of becoming dissociated from herself, that she hated the feeling of 'something being taken away' from her, of being lost to herself. Being touched filled her full of unbearable feelings, which left her 'frozen', in a terrified space. She hated it.

Sue went on to describe the first time the couple had sex. She and Dean were friends, and Dean had helped her with some trouble she was in. Afterwards they had slept together 'for comfort' with an explicit understanding that there would be no sex. The next morning they had been cuddling and, because of his erection, Sue felt Dean had wanted sex, so she 'did not resist'. Sue later came to regard this sexualisation of her need for comfort as a major betrayal of trust.

Fifteen years later in a therapy session, Dean heard this interpretation of these events for the first time, and he was horrified. He protested that he had not forced her, that she seemed keen. Sue agreed, but said from now she would only have sex when she felt like it, implying that she had been compliant with Dean's sexual needs all their marriage.

Dean then admitted to feeling 'sneaky' about having his sexual needs met, as if this was not a legitimate need. He described his desire for touch as 'excessive' and his capacity to achieve erections as 'perverse' and 'immature', saying that a real man would be able to control himself. However, Dean stressed that it was not only sex he wanted, he also longed to be held by Sue, and to hold her.

At this point Sue also revealed her ambivalent feelings about sex, saying that even though she hated what her brother did, 'at least it was some attention'.

Dean's longing for touch can be thought of as in the service of 'second skin formation' (Bick, 1968), as a way of trying to plug the holes in his infantile experience of himself, to quell anxieties that he could not name, the terror of 'formless dread' (Ogden, 1989, p. 39). This may be, in part, why Dean feels his desire is 'excessive', it is as if he is aware that his need stems from a very primitive part of him, and threatens to overwhelm him. This longing for touch is associated with a frustrating object relationship, as his infantile needs for physical comfort went unmet. In line with this idea, Sue did nothing to temper Dean's feeling that his erections were 'perverse', and would not allow Dean to engage in any form of sexual release, whether she was present or not. Dean's obliging this restriction signals his unconscious contribution to a strong rejection of sex by the couple.

Sue is also hypersensitive to touch; but for her touching is aversive, causing her to dissociate, and becoming frozen in a terrifying place. Touch penetrates her tightly controlled self structure and creates 'holes' through which she loses her sense of herself, something is taken away from her. Her sexual difficulties stem from abuse endured at her brother's hands, where she was intruded upon, and also from the infantile abandonment and neglect she experienced at the hands of unattuned parents, leading to a compliant false self aspect. Desire for her is difficult so she projects her longing into Dean, and controls it there. This is the other part that contributes to Dean's 'excessive' load of desire; he carries this for the couple.

Unconscious dream material

In the context of these sexual difficulties being discussed, Sue volunteered a dream of being chased by a 'predator'. In the dream she is running through a large building, locking doors after her as she goes, attempting to escape from a male pursuer. The dream ends with Sue panicking because she realises she is locked into a room that she cannot escape from, as the predator is on one side, and there is another male person, a 'creepy caretaker', on the other side of her, the exit door. Sue's associations revealed that the predator represented disowned parts of her (sexual) self, which she could see she had projected into her husband, to avoid. She knew that she had been prey, and was disturbed by the idea she might also be the predator. She wondered what this meant for the couple.

Dean's associations to this dream confirmed his unconscious rejection of his sexual self, and of how being sexual made him feel. He detested the idea of being seen like the creepy caretaker, but linked this with his previously disclosed 'sneaky' feelings about having sexual needs met. He could not see himself as predatory, and was more identified with the prey. He was aware of how his sexual needs made him feel dependent, little and vulnerable.

Here we see the couple's shared fear of their sexual selves, represented as a predator that could annihilate the other. We argue that it is not sex per se that is annihilatory, but the disintegrative anxieties at the level of the skin.

For Sue and Dean sexual intimacy is terrifying precisely because their original lack of containment is likely to be replicated, threatening to shatter their fragile ego boundaries. In coming together sexually they are vulnerable to these overwhelming primitive anxieties, triggered by the sensory experience of touch that, for them, disrupts rather than contains psychic experience. Sue was afraid to re-expose herself to this frightening experience and so rigidly controlled the couple's sexual contact as a way of defending against these disintegrative anxieties, a stance which Dean was complicit with.

Sex therapy

After this dream material had been revealed Sue broached the issue of sex therapy. She had been feeling bad about excluding sex from the marriage, and suggested that maybe they had to find a way to begin to 'de-sensitise' to what was so scary for them. After some sessions discussing this idea, and its potential difficulties, we negotiated some modified sex therapy exercises (Schnarch, 1998) aiming to explore their difficulty. It was clear that this was an information-gathering exercise, not an attempt to graft mature sexual relating into the relationship. They proceeded slowly for one month, bringing quite a lot of nervous comment about what it felt like to be held. Then the restraint that the routine prescribed was ignored. Sue, angry with Dean for being absent, initiated 'mad, passionate sex'. However she could not stay present, dissociated from the experience, and then became quite angry. Dean, initially pleased, went along with the approach, but was unhappy with the outcome.

Shortly after this Sue watched a TV documentary about 'footie chicks', predatory women who have promiscuous sex with football players. Sue identified with this predatory sexuality, saw these women as 'in control' of their sexual feelings, and was excited by the idea. The next morning she again deliberately initiated sex. On this second occasion Sue was flirtatiously showing off her naked body, thinking she was in pretty good shape for a woman of her age, and even enjoying the idea of her body being 'admired'. Then suddenly she froze again, and could not proceed. Dean had touched her breast and broken her sense of being in control. She had been acting out a narcissistic phantasy, which didn't include the reality of Dean. Dean, who had no idea what he had done to break the moment, felt shattered himself.

In the session after this traumatic encounter Sue said: 'I don't want to have a sexual relationship with you. I know it's hurtful to hear, but if I'm honest, that's what I want to say. Where does that leave us? I don't want to do this anymore.'

Long silence . . . Dean is clearly distressed.

Dean: 'I had a bad moment with the light when you said that. I didn't know whether the room was getting smaller and darker or if it was me . . . just a panic attack.'

Discussion of the use of modified sex therapy in psychoanalytic couples work

It could be argued that my agreement to proceed with modified sex therapy exercises was a counter-transference 'acting in', in the face of these very primitive somato-sensory anxieties. Was I, like my patients, doing something active to avoid facing these feelings rather than holding and containing them? However, it could equally be argued that these 'exercises' precipitated an enactment that revealed the true nature of these anxieties, which otherwise may never have been understood.

The couple both had severe psychosomatic reactions to sexual contact and its repercussions. Sue rejected my advice about proceeding slowly, so we could gather their experiences together and hold them, and acted out by initiating sex. This represents a continuation of her lifelong need for control, with Dean for his part characteristically deferring to her. It is also a sadomasochistic enactment for the couple; the consequence was a repetition of their traumatic anxieties, and of an experience of not being held through these. Sue could not cope with Dean's touch. She dissociated and her body literally froze, as did her mind. She could not think about or describe how she felt in this situation, her capacity to symbolise failed her, and she retreated into denial. She would not countenance that this experience had been so precipitous because of her non-compliance with the technique of slow exploration, and could not see that it could be any other way. She refused categorically to discuss their sexual relationship issues ever again.

On hearing Sue's ultimatum of '*no sexual relationship*', Dean became withdrawn and distressed in the session. Later, when he could, he described an experience of acute anxiety and altered sensory perceptions – physical reality became distorted, his world collapsed.

Work on the couple's sexual difficulties had recreated '*frozen*' or dissociated traumatic experiences for each of them, the experiences they avoided by avoiding sex. Their locked away experiences were similar in nature, and reflected a similar level of difficulty. For Sue this anxiety was that she was not in control, her sense of herself had been intruded upon and emptied out, penetrated by the reality of Dean's separateness. Dean's experience of himself was shattered, and his perceptual capacity fell apart, and he felt abandoned by Sue in the experience.

I felt stuck in a similar way; it felt difficult to work when negative transferences, which repeated these core traumatic experiences for each of the couple, were evoked either by proceeding (intrusive for Sue) or not proceeding (abandoning for Dean) with their sexual problems.

At this point the viability of the therapy was as much in jeopardy as the couple relationship. I felt I had turned into the predator for each of them, with Sue defensive, feeling unsafe and intruded upon in the therapy room, and Dean abandoned, threatening to retaliate by walking out. I felt unsure that the couple would return to face these conflicting feelings towards me. I wondered how I could deal with anxieties of this magnitude in two, not just one, individuals.

They did return for subsequent sessions. Sue resumed her previous complaints about Dean. Dean was unable to take a stand against this, and again became compliant. Sue in particular seemed not to want to hear my point of view: my attempts to discuss the parallels between what had occurred in the therapy, in their sexual relationship and in their early experiences were not taken up. Sue continued to embargo work on their sexual relationship. She also would not permit my contacting her individual therapist about what had happened. This felt controlling, like Dean's not being permitted to engage in any form of sexual release in Sue's presence. Dean however understood how his abandonment issues had been activated and agreed to take up individual work for this. However, Sue had felt Dean needed to develop more emotional capacity to better support her, so he was in part complying with her wishes. I felt controlled and unable to work with them, and wondered why they were continuing to come. Was I being manoeuvred into a situation where I was unable to function, 'frozen' in a way, and that I would eventually repeat the experience of not being able to hold them, as neither of their mothers had been able to do?

The couple had regressed to their earlier fused dynamic and it was unclear whether my maintaining the frame would allow a re-engagement with what was being defended against, and permit a gradual exploration and reworking of the dissociated overwhelming affects for each of them.

Summary and conclusion

Many couples presenting for therapy at some stage reveal that they have difficulties in their sexual relationship. It is often assumed that these problems derive from inadequate Oedipal resolution, but genitally based Oedipal conflicts cannot be properly negotiated until pre-genital Oedipal issues are able to be managed.

We have argued that pre-genital Oedipal conflicts may stem from the very earliest experiences of the skin, from what Ogden calls the Autistic-Contiguous stage of psychic development where experience is largely sensory, through touch. The skin at this early stage during infancy functions as a major vehicle for comprehending a sense of self, a sense of bounded experience, which is a prerequisite for the development of an internal space inside the skin (Bick, 1968), 'a place where one lives' (Winnicott, 1971). Only once this function has been internalised will there be the recognition of external space, outside the skin, inhabited by others, and the recognition of separateness.

Without this capacity, which requires the availability of a 'good enough' experience of being held, there are great difficulties in approaching and leaving another – the psychic danger is of annihilation either through merger or abandonment; the experience of losing one's sense of self, of falling to pieces. These primitive annihilatory anxieties described by Ogden often involve a sense of physical disintegration, and may be defended against with repetitive, physically based actions in an attempt to re-establish a boundary for the self. The impact of physical and sexual trauma and abuse later in childhood will further undermine this fragile sense of self.

Couples who share these core anxieties may utilise narcissistic defences, attempting to merge with the partner, via dynamics of omnipotent control, literally using the partner as a 'second skin' (Bick, 1968). However, the focus of such physically based 'unthinkable anxieties' is likely to become condensed, displaced and projected into psychosomatic symptoms, particularly at the level of the skin. These anxieties are then prone to be re-activated by close skin-to-skin contact, in the couple's sexual relationship. What is then touched here is anxiety about a loss of one's self, psychic annihilation, a void.

How to work with couples when very early experiences at the autistic-contiguous level have affected the couple's sexual relationship is a challenge since the experience of intimacy can feel terrifying, and predatory. Exploring these merged dynamics to try to understand and alleviate the need for these controlling defences inevitably must allow the experiences that have not been able to be thought about to emerge. Attempting to facilitate a capacity for individual development for each the couple while attempting to hold and contain the couple is a difficult balancing act. Further thinking is needed to understand how best to explore and intervene in this complex merged intrapsychic terrain.

For healthy relating the omnipotent need for control or to be controlled will need to be relinquished and be replaced by curiosity and concern about one's own and the other's experience and needs. Hopefully the partner may then be seen as 'an object that can be given its freedom to come and go at will' (Meltzer, 1978). However there are frozen terrors to negotiate on the way.

Notes

1 A modified version of this paper was first published in *Couple and Family Psychoanalysis* Vol.2 No.1 (2012) pp.33–48. It is republished here by kind permission of the editor, Molly Ludlam and the publisher, Karnac.
2 This phase is not universally accepted.

References

Bick, E. (1968). The experience of the skin in early object relations. *International Journal of Psycho-Analysis*, *49*, 484–486.

Bion, W.R. (1962a). A theory on thinking. *International Journal of Psycho-Analysis*, *43*, 306–310.

Bion, W.R. (1962b). *Learning from Experience*. London: Karnac.

Britton, R. (1998). Subjectivity, objectivity and triangular space. In *Belief and Imagination: Explorations in Psychoanalysis*. London: Routledge.

Dicks, H.V. (1967). *Marital Tensions: Clinical Studies towards a Psychoanalytic Theory of Interaction*. London: Routledge & Kegan Paul.

Fairbairn, W.R.D. (1954). Observations on the nature of hysterical states. *British Journal of Medical Psychology*, *27(3)*, 105–125.

Fairbairn, W.R.D. (1958). On the nature and aims of psychoanalytical treatment. *International Journal of Psycho-Analysis*, *39(5)*, 374–385.

Fisher, J.V. (1993). The impenetrable other: ambivalence and the Oedipal conflict in work with couples. In S. Ruszczynski and J. Fisher (Eds.) *Intrusiveness and Intimacy in the Couple*. London: Karnac.

Fisher, J. (1999). *The Uninvited Guest: Emerging from Narcissism to Marriage*. London: Karnac.

Freud, S. (1905). *Infantile Sexuality*. S.E. Vol. 7. (pp. 200–207). London: Hogarth Press and The Institute of Psychoanalysis.

Freud, S. (1923). *The Ego and the Id*. S.E. Vol. 19 (pp. 12–66). London: Hogarth Press.

Hopper, E. (1991). Encapsulation as a defence against the fear of annihilation. *International Journal of Psycho-Analysis*, *72(4)*, 607–624.

Meltzer, D. (1974). Mutism in infantile autism, schizophrenia and manic-depressive-states: the correlation of clinical psychopathology and linguistics. *International Journal of Psycho-Analysis*, *55*, 397–404.

Meltzer, D. (1975). Adhesive identification. *Contemporary Psychoanalysis*, *11*, 289–310.

Meltzer, D. (1978) A note on introjective processes. In A. Hahn (Ed.) *Sincerity and Other Works: The Collected Papers of Donald Meltzer* (pp. 458–468). London: Karnac, 1994.

Meltzer, D. (1995). Donald Meltzer in discussion with James Fisher. In S. Ruszczynski and J. Fisher (Eds.) *Intrusiveness and Intimacy in the Couple*. London: Karnac.

Ogden, T. (1989). *The Primitive Edge of Experience*. Northvale, NJ: Jason Aronson.

Process of Change Study Group (PCSG) (1988). Non-interpretative mechanisms in psychoanalytic therapy: the 'something more' than interpretation. *International Journal of Psycho-Analysis, 79*, 903–921.

Rey, H. (1994). *Universals of Psychoanalysis in the Treatment of Psychotic and Borderline States*. London: Free Association Books.

Ruszczynski, S. (1993). Narcissistic object relating. In S. Ruszczynski and J. Fisher (Eds.) *Intrusiveness and Intimacy in the Couple*. London, Karnac.

Schnarch, D. (1998). *Passionate Marriage: Keeping Love and Intimacy Alive in Committed Relationships*. New York: Holt Paperbacks.

Tustin, F. (1980). Autistic objects. *International Review of Psycho-Analysis, 7*, 27–40.

Tustin, F. (1984). Autistic shapes. *International Review of Psycho-Analysis, 11*, 279–290.

Tustin, F. (1986). *Autistic Barriers in Neurotic Patients*. London: Karnac, p. 272.

Winnicott, D.W. (1951). Transitional objects and transitional phenomena. In Collected Papers: *Through Paediatrics to Psychoanalysis* (1975, pp. 229–242). London: Hogarth Press.

Winnicott, D.W. (1956). Primary maternal preoccupation. In *Collected Papers: Through Paediatrics to Psychoanalysis* (1975, pp. 145–156). London: Hogarth Press.

Winnicott, D.W. (1960). The theory of parent-infant relationship. In *The Maturational Processes and the Facilitating Environment* (1965, pp. 37–55). London. Hogarth Press.

Winnicott, D.W. (1962). Ego integration in child development. In *The Maturational Processes and the Facilitating Environment* (1965, pp. 56–63). London: Hogarth Press.

Winnicott, D.W. (1971). The place where we live (pp. 122–129). In *Playing and Reality*. Harmondsworth: Penguin.

Chapter 7

Gathering fragments
Steps in the evolution of a creative coupling

Julia Meyerowitz-Katz

Introduction: a fragmented not-couple

When I opened my consulting room door to Matthew and Laura at the start of their first session, Laura was standing alone, slightly uncertain, but, paradoxically, with the air of a capable, sensible and precocious child. I experienced intense shock seeing her standing there alone. I had been expecting a couple, I had *seen* a couple: when I had opened my door at the end of the previous session to allow my patients to leave, I had seen Laura and Matthew waiting for their session together. I had seen that there were two, and now, ten minutes later, seemingly, there was one. I had an immediate embodied sense of a tension between the existence of a couple and a fragmented not-couple; the experience of something being shockingly absent and missing. This first interaction with Matthew and Laura, who were both 32 years old, conveyed clues as to what kind of shared unconscious wounds they might have shared.

Awkwardly, Laura said, 'Matthew is being silly'. This felt like a communication from a child feeling responsible for the shameful behaviour of another child whose shame somehow joined with her own. It transpired that Matthew was hiding in an alcove; he hesitantly emerged a few seconds later. I was reminded of mother–infant peek-a-boo games and of young children in therapy who like to hide, hoping to be found but feeling shamed by their need to be found.

I have thought of this communication as a complex psychosomatic enactment. In the context of our work together, it was the first of many concrete communications of unrepresented experience (Freud, 1914) that eloquently conveyed the presence of primitive, infantile, pre-symbolic bodymind states. In those moments on the threshold, Laura and Matthew had cooperated in enacting aspects of a tension between a precocious, parentified child and a young, undeveloped infant; as well as something about the shock of absence, of something missing in the relationship and consequently, a relationship that could fragment shockingly.

Consequently, it was not a surprise to discover that they shared threads in their histories which resonated with their presentation. These were to do with fragmentation, loss and things missing in a relationship; and of children becoming precocious in the absence of appropriate parenting and in the presence of deprivation.

Matthew was the younger of two children, with an older sister. His parents divorced when he was 7 and he went to live with his father, rarely seeing his mother and older sister. He described his childhood experience of being left alone, of becoming a 'latch-key kid', eating microwaved pre-cooked meals alone while his father was at the pub. He conveyed a sense of bleak despair in his account of this time. He became alienated at school and found comfort in being part of a group of adolescents who used cannabis and alcohol extensively. With no encouragement from either parent to continue studying he left school at 16.

Laura was the oldest of three children; she had two younger brothers. Her parents were both alcoholics and there was alcohol-related domestic violence in the family. Laura's role was to protect and care for her younger brothers, particularly after her parents' divorce when she was 11. As a young child she was sexually abused by a male babysitter. Her father touched her inappropriately on her weekend visits to him when she was a teenager, filling her with confused feelings of shameful excitement.

Matthew and Laura were both drunk when they met for the first time at a mutual friend's party. Alcohol remained a central feature of their relationship and they planned their relationship around their drinking. Laura reported that she couldn't have sex unless she was drunk. Matthew used cannabis habitually, gambled and was in debt.

They had had a fraught on-and-off relationship for ten years prior to seeking therapy. Break-ups left Laura suicidal, taking overdoses, and Matthew severely depressed, lying in his bed and not eating. Laura had had a termination during one of their break-ups. There was deep regret and anger with each other about the termination. Unsuccessful attempts to conceive another child over a two-year period had led to anxieties about their fertility.

On the surface, Laura and Matthew seemed startlingly different. Matthew habitually wore grubby riding clothes and was very tanned from his work as a trainer and horse-riding teacher in a stable. Laura was a businesswoman, well groomed and usually dressed in business suits. However, their shared enactment of a fragmented not-couple, in those first few moments on the threshold of therapy, had alerted me to the possible root of their difficulties. It was as if they were saying something like, 'we may appear to be adults but there are parts of us that are in fragmented bits: undeveloped, very young, full of shame and although we are trying to manage these parts of ourselves and each other, we aren't equipped to do this.'

In the account which follows, I describe how, within the containment of the couple therapy, these fragments were gathered up and transformed so that a reliable co-created couple emerged. To begin with, I introduce several key theoretical threads: Jung's (1954/1991) notion of marriage as a problematic bilateral unconscious psychological container. This is an image of a fragmented, pre-symbolic and therefore undeveloped couple state of mind. I compare Jung's notion of the container and the contained within marriage with Bion's container/contained. Following that, I introduce the idea of the development of a co-created third position; a developmental achievement that leads to the beginning of a couple state of mind. I then return to the first session and to the unfolding of the clinical process.

The 'problem of the contained and the container' in couple relationships: some theory

Writing in 1925, Jung (1954/1991) suggested that marriage is a 'psychological container' with a hidden, unconscious and 'highly complex structure'. Within this structure are each partner's nuanced developmental achievements and lacks, inter-generationally transmitted 'unconscious motivations' and expectations deriving from their experiences within their families of origin, and particularly in relation to how they experienced their parents. Jung suggests that there are also unconscious presumptions that the other partner has a similar psychological structure to one's own, and that there is an unconscious agreement between the couple that their wounds are shared. Each partner unconsciously seeks containment in, and therefore healing by, the other as if the other functions as a parent.

Jung seems to be offering an image of a 'couple state of mind' in which what is happening in the couple relationship is a reflection of what is going on in each of them. Jung suggests that each partner longs for the other to be a container for the anxieties, hopes and desires they bring to the relationship, but this is only possible to the extent that the each has negotiated developmental achievements that enable them to contain the other. This means that the degree of the unconsciousness of their choice causes a complex, painful and layered predicament that Jung described as 'the problem of the contained and the container' (Jung, 1954/1991, para. 331c). This predicament has to do with being confronted with the other's alterity; and it also has to do with the vertical dissociation of the psyche resulting in what Jung called 'complexes' and accompanying uneven development.

Complexes can be thought of as internal structures 'focal or nodal points of psychic life' (Jung, 1921, para. 925) which are imbued with powerful affect whose source is hidden from consciousness and by which individuals can be gripped; as Jung writes: 'complexes can **have us**' (Jung, 1960/1969, para. 200, bold original). Consequently, in this kind of 'psychological marriage', the other partner can be experienced consciously as 'an alien other': an unreliable fragmented contained and container with hidden parts.

There are obvious resonances between Jung's idea of the container and contained within a psychological marriage between adults and Bion's notion of container/contained between mother and infant. However, there are significant differences. Using his understanding of the relational processes between therapist and patient, Bion (1962) proposes that the mother–infant relationship functions as a container/contained that enables the development of symbolic thinking, or Alpha Function (Bion 1963). Bion considers that the infant does not have the function for thinking at the beginning of his/her life and that therefore any unpleasant and intolerable feelings are projected into the mother to be converted from overwhelming bodily feelings and sensations into thoughts. Alpha function represents mother's capacity to receive, hold and digest primitive experiences, make sense of them and then return them in a more manageable and digestible form to her infant. It is a metabolising function which simultaneously provides the infant with an 'apparatus for thinking' so that over time, the infant develops the capacity to think independently. The development of this 'apparatus for thinking' between mother and infant, which has to do with linking, with thoughts coming together, can be thought of as an internalised 'creative couple' (Morgan, 2005).

Bion is using the term 'container/contained' to describe how a good enough mother will help her infant to develop trust in her capacity to transform their distress. In this way, infants learn to communicate their needs and thus learn from experience.

Jung, on the other hand, is describing the situation that we so often find in our consulting rooms, the 'problem of the contained and the container' in a couple. Each partner in the couple is seeking the primary maternal containment, as Bion described it, from each other that their original maternal environment failed to provide. Jung is therefore describing the tensions within what I understand to be a bi-directional, pre-symbolic relationship. It represents a shared predicament which is that they each seek something from the other that relies on a developmental achievement that neither has negotiated successfully.

This means that the prerequisite for a creative engagement with another person in a couple relationship, the achievement of a third position represented by an internalised 'creative couple' that signals a capacity to symbolise (Morgan, 2005), has not occurred. Without this developmental achievement, the couple lack the resources to collaborate in establishing their couple relationship as a reliable co-created container in which there is space for them to be individuals and to function as a couple.

This is where the containing function of the therapist can offer an experience that neither partner has experienced in their family of origin. The therapist's capacity to understand and contain the destructive anxieties and create a third space for reflection leads to a greater capacity for symbolic thinking in the couple. There are many references in the literature to the idea of a co-created third (Gerson, 2009) and different views as to how this might be achieved. Colman (1993, 2010) suggests that symbolic communications have to do with the capacity to experience loss, to mourn and to represent absent objects. He views this as a developmental achievement which is essential for the resolution of the Oedipal complex.

In addition, using Jung's idea of the transcendent function, (Jung, 1954/1982) which refers to a psychological process of uniting opposites, Colman suggests that symbolising emerges through the development of a capacity to engage in a process in which opposing elements are linked in such a way that their opposition to each other is transcended in the creation of a third. This represents a process of creative coupling where the tension between the opposites is resolved in a new way: a third position, which combines the two opposing elements in a new level of complexity (Colman, 2007).

In my experience, there are four possible benefits to the adult couple relationship of repeated exposure to the processes of developing new thirds in couple therapy. These may be to decrease the intensity of the emotional tone in the room, the complexes; to heal unconscious wounds; to create a scaffolding of reliable symbolic capacity; and to provide a template of processes for negotiating differences and pressures in the future.

I now return to the first session and to some theory which helps thinking about the *form* of Matthew and Laura's communications and therefore the structure of their relationship.

A confused, fused and fractured internal couple

They sat cosily next to each other in the middle of the couch; Matthew with his arm around Laura's shoulders, Laura snuggling under his arm, with her arm and hand resting on his thigh. In contrast to the first few moments at the door when they seemed fragmented, they presented as one united entity. They remained this way through the session, even through the most bitter, hurtful arguments with Laura telling him that she hated him, didn't want to be with him, and wanted him to leave.

This alerted me to the states of fusion and confusion that I associate with pre-symbolic borderline states and relations. Clark suggests that these occur in shared states where there is a paradoxical experience of intimacy and mutuality in spite of 'non-blissful disharmonious relations, in conditions of attack, fragmentation, chaotic dissociation and incomprehension . . . (they are) necessary metacommunications of disorder which have to be understood and sorted out' (Clark, 1996, p. 355).

Schwartz-Salant (1988, p. 35) describes:

> a fused couple, who are simultaneously in a state of radical disunion, forming a violent and extremely persecutory dyad. Although they violently reject separation, which they experience as abandonment, they are without genuine contact as they are fused into one entity, instead of being two relationally connected people.

In the session I was struck by how Laura and Matthew were physically enacting this confused, simultaneously fractured and fused couple. They seemed to be expressing a traumatic interlocking scene (Pickering 2006, 2008.). Drawing on Jung's concept of complexes, Pickering suggests that couples unconsciously 'audition' each other, selecting a partner with an internalised traumatic family scene that is resonant with theirs. These two individual intrapsychic scenes can become imposed on the relationship. The couple then can become trapped in interlocking traumatic scenes, creating a malignant third (Pickering, ibid.); in this way they unknowingly re-traumatise each other. Through their physical enactments on the threshold of therapy, and in the way they communicated while sitting together on the couch, it seemed to me that Matthew and Laura were communicating interlocking scenes psychosomatically.

Psyche and soma

Psychoanalysis since Freud has attempted to link psyche and soma (Colman, 2009). Winnicott refers to the self as being first a bodily self and says that 'mind is then no more than a special case of the functioning of the psyche-soma' (Winnicott 1949, p. 244). Colman considers that 'Klein effectively introduced an entirely new idea of a sort of liminal area between mind and body, where body is in the process of **becoming** mind' (Colman, 2009, p. 30, bold original).

Grotstein (1997) proposes the idea of an unconscious psychosomatic entity he terms a 'mindbody', or 'bodymind that constitutes a single, holistic entity, one that we can think about and believe that we can imaginatively experience as being separate but that is mockingly non-separate all the while' (Grotstein, 1997, p. 205).

Similarly, Jung says that: 'It is extremely difficult, if not impossible to think of a psychic function as independent of its organ, although in actual fact we experience the psychic process apart from its relation to the organic substrate' (Jung, 1960/1969, para. 368).

Evidence emerging out of contemporary research in neuroscience and psychology seems to support the view, that even though we experience mind as being separate from body, mind only exists as a part of a whole that is a body(brain) mind entity and relational process. Psychic functioning emerges out of these psychosomatic processes (Knox, 2003, 2004; Gerhardt, 2004).

Jung proposed the idea of an unconscious structure and process which he calls 'psychoid' experience (Jung, 1960/1969, para. 368); this experience is both psychic and somatic. The unconscious structure and process underlie and exist in parallel with conscious psychic and somatic experiences. Psychoid processes can be said to be 'a deeply unconscious set of processes that are neither physiological nor psychological but that somehow partake of both' (Addison, 2009, p. 54). It is out of these that the experience of psyche emerges.

The implications are that psychoid experience is fundamental to all psychic experience – its structures and energies – and may therefore be considered its source. Clark (2010) suggests that it is an unconscious, unrealised and unborn mind–body potential, as well as the receptacle of regressed unconscious experiences. It is, in other words, a treasure chest of possibilities of what an individual may become and it also offers clues as to where problems may lie; simultaneously our being and becoming (Meyerowitz-Katz, 2013).

Clark suggests that psychoid experience is experienced interpersonally as well as internally. He proposes that it is signalled and communicated through projective processes, like projective and introjective identification, both intrapsychically, as well as somatically through the autonomic nervous system by an energetic process that he calls 'psychoid substance' (Clark, 1996, p. 354). It seems to me that 'psychoid substance' might be considered to be an embodied form of Jung's (1971) use of Levy Bruhl's term 'participation mystique' (Meyerowitz-Katz, 2016, 2017).

Participation mystique refers to unconscious projective processes which are triggered by projection and identification and have to do with a blurring of psychological boundaries between people (Winborn, 2014).

> This denotes a peculiar kind of connection with objects, and consists in the fact that the subject cannot clearly distinguish himself from the object but is bound to it by a direct relationship which amounts to a partial identity (q.v.). This identity results from an a priori oneness of subject and object.
>
> (Jung, 1971, para.12, cited in Winborn, 2014, p. 3)

Both parties become swept up in a 'shared reality' (Winborn, 2014) that is alive between them and, in the clinical setting, must ultimately be metabolised by both.

This means that through our somatic counter-transference, we are experiencing purposively interpersonal primitive unconscious psychosomatic communications. Clark suggests that they are communicated unconsciously in an embodied form in order to 'painfully unite us in something we unconsciously make together, arising out of an as yet un-met need to share in something undeveloped and uncoordinated' (Clark, 1996, p. 354). These communications are an expression of the hope that something will change and that the wounds acquired through developmental lacks and losses, the experiences of unbearable environmental failure and trauma, will be recognised and attended to. Clark refers to analytic work with individual adult patients, but in the following account I will be exploring how these embodied psychoid communications are a feature of couple relationships and are therefore brought into the couple's therapy (Meyerowitz-Katz, 2016). In Matthew and Laura's case, these were represented in the confused, fused and fractured internal couple that I encountered in the first session.

Slowing down

During this first session, the theme of Laura representing the parentified child, responsible and in control that was referred to earlier, continued. When I wondered if they would like to tell me why they were here, she looked at Matthew and said, 'Do you want me to go first?' When he nodded she said, in a kind of self-satisfied, imperious tone, 'I thought so'. Laura tearfully described how difficult things had been lately. She wanted therapy to either resolve all their difficulties, or help them break up amicably. Matthew described how they keep on going over the same ground; there have been 'so many words' and nothing ever changes.

They communicated a shared sense that Matthew was 'useless'. Laura guiltily said that she had made him feel that way by telling him that he was useless, like her father. Paradoxically, she didn't miss an opportunity to remind him of his uselessness during the session. Matthew described all his failings, including that he was forgetful. In contrast, he believed that she remembered things. I commented that there seemed to be a tension between remembering and forgetting and I wondered if there was a part of him that would like to be like her and remember things.

He said yes, he would. I also wondered whether there was a part of Laura that found the role of being the one who remembered quite onerous. She agreed with that. In this way I was modelling the mechanisms of the transcendent function, linking opposites, thereby planting the seeds of a path towards thirdness.

The session quickly spiralled into a fight. Matthew angrily accused Laura of being a control freak and she angrily accused him of having no boundaries. Things seemed to move very quickly from one topic to the next and I felt myself buffeted around without any thinking space.

I tried to create some space to think, saying, 'Let's slow down and think about what is being represented here'. Informed by my earlier observations of their pre-symbolic communications, I understood that complicated interpretations would not be understood; they might be experienced as bizarre objects, and would be spat out. So in the ensuing pause, I tried to amplify what had been said, and broke it down into manageable bits.

I asked Matthew if he liked it that Laura takes care of things and manages things, but that he also didn't like it. I asked her if she sometimes liked how un-boundaried he can be, and whether she also doesn't like it. We talked about how his relaxed attitude helps her get out of her head. I linked these two positions and wondered if they were representing something for each other, that he can take her out of herself, and she can make him feel organised. As well as modelling the mechanism of the transcendent function, responding to each of them separately while holding them as a couple in my mind could also be considered to be a representation of a kind of meeting (Morgan, 2005), of a coupling; all of which provide containment. This had the effect of lowering the emotional tone in the room temporarily.

Representing the predicament named by Jung of the 'problem of the contained and the container', they expressed the tensions about the ways in which they managed their resources and responsibilities into the session in a series of bitter, angry exchanges. Laura was angry with Matthew, feeling that she was responsible for everything including their finances. He felt that he couldn't control his spending, was full of despair at his debt and wanted her to help him by giving her all his money to take care of while he tried to get to grips with the problems. She refused, angrily saying that that was just more of the same, her being in charge, like a mother. With this he became very angry.

All the while, they were sitting close together, she sometimes stroked his thigh; he stroked her hair. There was a tangible tension in the contrast between the hurt, anger, bitterness and disappointment and the tenderness and physical proximity that they displayed.

Pre-symbolic states were represented through de-symbolised language

Laura angrily said that she didn't want to be his mother, but she found herself mothering him. Matthew became enraged, moving from zero to ten in about as many seconds. He was wired, his whole body taut. I was quite disconcerted by this sudden escalation; we seemed to be on the edge of physical violence. Laura didn't seem to notice. I thought, oh, this must happen all the time, this is so volatile:

Matthew: *I don't want to use that word, 'mother'. Laura is not my mother.*
Therapist: *You are angry because Laura is not your mother, and you don't want to use that word in relation to her.*
Matthew: *Yes, you can't put mother and Laura in the same sentence.*

I mirrored this and linked it back to his previous statement. I said 'You feel you can't put mother in the same sentence, Laura isn't your mother.'

Matthew's response felt like an example of Segal's (1978, 1991) symbolic equation: In the moment when Laura said she found herself 'mothering him', Matthew felt Laura to BE his mother; there was a mix-up in that his real mother, internalised mother, and Laura were all conflated. He responded to his confusion, shame and fear by becoming very angry. I noticed this as a representation of unresolved Oedipal anxieties, and thought again about deficiencies in symbolic functioning, about the lack of an 'as-if' function.

Matthew furiously added, 'And I don't like the word "mothering"', thus alerting me to the prospect of a negative maternal transference.

Thoughts after the first session

It seemed that we had made a good connection and that they had responded well to my moment-to-moment interpretations as ways of providing containment and holding (Bion, 1962; Winnicott, 1971) which appears to have helped them move on in the session.

It seemed that in the face of parental neglect and cruelty and multiple experiences of sexual abuse, Laura had taken on the role of omnipotent carer in order to take care of projected parts of herself with which she identified. She had narcissistically incorporated Matthew's alterity in order to do this and had replaced this with her own projections. But her predicament was that her relationship with those damaged parts of herself was ambivalent; she hated them because of how they were treated by others and thereby hated the parts of herself that she split off and projected into Matthew. She then hated him because he reminded her of her own wounded parts which she feared would never be healed. It seemed that she also hated him because she envied the attention that he was getting. It made her more aware of the deprivation in herself, highlighting that she wasn't being cared for. So she found herself in the excruciating situation of being constantly reminded of her own raw, untended wounds whenever she took care of him.

Matthew, too, suffered from an ambivalent relationship with his own dependency needs and his own wounds. I think that he had experienced internal trauma that resonated with her concrete experiences. He had projected a narcissistic self-persecutory object onto Laura so that her contemptuous and cruel criticism of him mirrored his own internal persecutor.

I was left feeling very full and I noticed during the following week that they were frequently in my thoughts. It seemed that they had got into my bodymind in a powerful way. I understood their penetration of my bodymind to be a psychoid communication (Meyerowitz-Katz, 2016, 2017). The theme of communications through body accompanied by a sense of absence continued.

Cancellation of the second session

Shattering an omnipotent defence

On the day of their scheduled second session Laura called to say that they wouldn't be coming to see me that day as Matthew was in hospital. Matthew had taken a calculated risk at work that day, attempting a high jump on a horse that was new to the stable and that wasn't properly trained. He had fallen, sustaining a serious fracture to his leg. He would be in plaster up to his thigh and unable to work for at least six weeks. I thought about their absence in terms of a vast distance and a seriously wounded, fractured psychosomatic entity. Of course the timing was interesting. In the phone call, Laura questioned whether they were sabotaging their therapy.

I did not think that Matthew deliberately fell in order to injure himself, nor to sabotage their therapy. But I did consider his fall and consequent injuries as reso-nating with existing unconscious psychosomatic structures that they both shared and that underpinned their difficulties; a shared psychoid structure and process. I think there were two central elements to this. One was evidence of an omnipotent narcissistic defence – represented by Matthew choosing to tackle a high jump with an unfamiliar and unschooled horse – and the other was the existence of a broken and wounded psychosomatic entity underlying this defence.

I think that Matthew's fall shattered a collusive narcissistic defence. Laura could not choose how or when she looked after him; she was confronted with his alterity and so he didn't fit into her projections of her own wounded self; caring for him didn't fit her unconscious fantasies about herself or him. Matthew too was freed to some extent by the reality of his position and shocked into shifting in his attitude towards himself.

They were both confronted with Matthew's vulnerabilities and were forced to reposition themselves in relation to each other. To begin with, this was enacted in the sessions in a concrete way. In parallel to this, they were plunged into a shared, painful, desperately angry depression.

When they came to the session following Matthew's fall, in contrast to their first visit, they sat at opposite ends of the couch, both furious and hurt. The gap between them felt huge. Matthew was visibly in a lot of pain. They described how much effort it had taken to come to therapy as Matthew was in so much pain and his mobility was so compromised. I thought, 'But they still came!'

Laura alternated between being responsible and caring, and being furious, persecutory and bitter, adopting a defensive impenetrable narcissistic position.

Matthew was sad, depressed and angry with himself, and with her. He represented their despair saying his injury was the nail in the coffin to their relationship because he was completely dependent on her. They described a terrible week, full of fights.

Over the following weeks leading up to a summer break, a great deal of work was done. Their relationship and their sessions continued to be fraught, with reports of fights and arguments leading to fights and arguments in the sessions. The same intense emotions that had been present during the fights were triggered and so the fights became live in the room. When I could slow them down, these fights provided useful opportunities for thinking about what was going on between them and for slowly unpacking the interlocking scenes that kept them stuck.

Loosening the hold of the traumatic scenes and finding a nascent good object in the form of a relational container

Something had been freed up and this was expressed psychosomatically. They moved around on the couch, sometimes sitting in a fused position, sometimes at opposite ends of the couch in hostile rejection of each other, sometimes facing each other from opposite ends of the couch in a friendly way. Sometimes Matthew reached over gently and lovingly stroking Laura's hair, thus collapsing the space between them.

There was evidence that they were responding well to our work together. A positive transference was represented through discussions that coming for therapy was helpful, as they appreciated talking in an environment without hostility. They reported that when they fought, one or the other would say, 'Tell Julia!' This was a concrete, pre-symbolic way of making a link with our work, but it did suggest that the seeds of a good internal object were becoming planted in each of them at times; and that a sense of a fragile container was developing between them and the therapist.

Our work focused on tensions that existed around their difficulties in recognising either their alterity, or their similarities. We worked out together that they shared experiences of parental abandonment and that they had both found ways of parenting themselves. However, they both tended to easily slip into fixed narcissistic defensive positions, where they could not see each other at all, blaming each other for their own behaviour.

Another indication of the progress they were making was represented by an increasing use of symbolic thought and language. For instance, on an occasion when Matthew referred to Laura's attempt to 'mother him', he caught himself and smiled as he realised that the word 'mother' wasn't a problem anymore. I understood that for him, the term 'mother' had moved from functioning presymbolically, as a symbolic equation, to a symbol. In the context of the therapy, this was an indication of a developmental achievement that was both his and was also a representation that as a couple they were renegotiating important developmental stages together.

Matthew tried to express his love and concern for Laura, and tried to care for her when she was distressed, telling her that everything would be alright; but she was not reachable. We talked about how she could not recognise his attempts to care for her. We opened up a conversation about how complicated being looked after was. Laura felt deep down that she did not deserve to be looked after, and how she therefore felt she always had to do the caring. She took up a lot of space in the sessions; I became aware that she was representing over-fullness, and he represented something very empty, very bleak.

I came to associate this bleak emptiness with Matthew's experiences of his father. This helped me understand his gambling. He described how, when out with his mates, 'when the conversation dies, when no one is talking and there is nothing there, I go to play the pokies'. It seemed that he was describing his need to protect himself from encounters with unbearable overwhelming loss and emptiness – lack of human interaction – through desperately searching for something 'good' by winning money in the machines; although the opposite happened, he lost money. In this way he paradoxically kept himself where he believed he didn't want to be: confronted with loss, emptiness and despair confirming his sense of himself as a failure.

A fragile capacity to hold on to a good object

The fragility of the container and their consequent incapacity to hold on to a good object was demonstrated when they returned after the Easter break. Matthew had a new cast, from his knee instead of his hip, which gave him more mobility. This mobility seemed to reflect something shifting in their relationship. However, at the start of their first session after the break, Laura sadly explained that they were coming to tell me that their relationship was over. They had had a terrible time during the break from therapy, they had been fighting and physical violence had erupted between them. In the session they had positioned themselves at opposite ends of the couch, both lying with their heads resting against the back. Matthew stared at the ceiling with an air of depressed remoteness and distance. Laura lay with her eyes closed. In my counter-transference I felt their despair and pain. I thought: this is desperate, this is hopeless; there is nothing to be done. The relationship is over. I felt helpless. I sat with those thoughts and felt useless for a long time. We remained in a shared depressed silence. But after a time, my counter-transference shifted. I looked at them and had a realisation: they seemed like two needy children who had experienced the break as abandonment. Frightened by their experiences of being abandoned and fearful of not being held in mind while their parent was away, they had turned on each other, and now that the parent had returned, they were expressing their helpless despair at having been abandoned.

I broke the silence. I said, 'It seems to me that in this silence you are letting me know how hard the break has been for you, how you have missed coming here and so you became angry and this led to lots of arguments and fights and even violence and now you are full of despair and feel that the relationship is over.'

After a short silence, Matthew sat up and began filling me in on what had transpired between them during the break. There had been a lot of drinking, huge rows and a violent incident where she had hit him and he had been devastated by what he saw as hatred and contempt in her facial expression. She felt guilty about this and feared that she had been destructive and that she was becoming like her violent father. They were sleeping in separate bedrooms and discussing separating.

I think that through projective processes, they had filled me with their shared despair. I was able to modify this during the session through my capacity to contain and modify my counter-transference experience. This enabled them to talk about the difficulties during the break instead of acting them out.

Losing and finding

Themes of reiterated trauma, loss, and losing and finding unfolded during the subsequent sessions. We tracked and named their compulsion to repeatedly create situations where they disappointed and hurt each other and themselves. Evidence of their capacity to develop insight and a self-reflective capacity emerged.

In one session, we had been talking about how they disappointed each other leading to threats of ending their relationship, as well as the losses from Matthew's gambling. I had said that it seemed to me that they both lived on the edge of loss all the time.

After a thoughtful silence Matthew asked, 'So do you think that I disappoint her so that I can lose her and then find her again?' We talked about the possibility that they both pushed each other away in order to find each other. Their conversation moved to the termination and current fears about their fertility. Matthew had been putting off having a sperm test – frightened to disappoint her yet again, feeling full of shame that his fertility might be the problem. Laura had been diagnosed with a polycystic ovary and worried that she would be unable to conceive.

Of course real medical issues existed. But I also think they were metaphorically representing something about their fears of being so damaged and full of shame that they could never become whole and healthy enough to co-create and nurture a healthy third entity. These fears had been enacted when Laura's pregnancy had been terminated.

Themes of abandonment came up in the form of their parents' neglect of them. These discussions felt like complaints about my abandonment of them during the break. I made interpretations that linked their fights over the break to the interruption in their therapy, that they valued it and missed it when it was missing. I offered a suggestion that we could make good use of this difficult time as it was a communication about how hard it was for them when they felt they weren't being thought about. We talked about the importance of coming regularly and the idea that they were borrowing the containment of the therapy until they could do it themselves.

In spite of the difficulties during the break, Matthew had consulted a gambling counsellor and a financial advisor.

Transformation of a negative transference and amplification of the interlocking traumatic scenes

In the following weeks, a negative transference emerged. They angrily complained that this therapy with me was costing them money and wasn't helping them alleviate their financial pressures, including Matthew's debt. I pointed out that I could see that there was a dilemma, because yes, this therapy did cost, but it was an investment. It had enabled Matthew to go and get help for his gambling and his debt, and it was helping them understand why they became swept up in repeated cycles of coming together and breaking up.

Following that I was aware of a change in my counter-transference to a feeling of sadness which I named. This segued into a conversation about how sad they were that their relationship was such a mess that they needed to come to see me. I noticed a shift in that Laura seemed to be looking at Matthew with curiosity, as if seeing him for the first time. I named this. She said he was constantly surprising her. She mentioned changes at home – they were having more good days, and fights could blow over relatively quickly; Matthew was doing more of the housework. We also discussed how it may have been that Matthew was doing more, but she was letting him and wasn't trying to control him so much.

They subsequently returned to sharing a bedroom. Matthew's cast was removed and he began a programme of physiotherapy and prepared to return to work. In their sessions they continued to use the couch flexibly, sometimes sitting together and sometimes apart. Once, at the start of a session, they began sitting very close together, and then Laura moved away to the other side of the couch, saying 'I like my space' in a confident and humorous way. We all laughed. However, I felt that she was representing something of importance for both of them, which had to do with finding separate space in the relationship, reflecting early small steps towards the emergence of two independent people co-inhabiting a co-created relationship.

It transpired that Laura had precancerous cells on her cervix and she needed to have a medical procedure in order to remove the precancerous cells and scrape and laser her uterus. This brought up an enormous amount of anxiety and distress for them about her capacity to carry a pregnancy. They feared the possibility of her having an 'incompetent' cervix. Ambivalent feelings towards the doctor were also expressed, largely to do with whether she could be trusted.

This was a multilayered communication. On the one hand they were expressing anxiety about the surgery (therapy) about whether the doctor (me) could be trusted; whether the 'cervix' of the therapeutic container was competent, and whether together we could co-construct a competent container in which a symbolic pregnancy could be conceived. They were also signalling their anxiety about whether their couple relationship could conceive and nurture a symbolic pregnancy.

A fight erupted in the session. Laura had been talking about her fears about her approaching gynaecological procedure and Matthew was trying to comfort her saying, 'Everything will be alright'. She furiously and tearfully remonstrated with him for not supporting her. Hurt and frustrated, he angrily retaliated and said he was trying to support her and why wouldn't she let him do that?

When I slowed them down and we unpacked this, we understood another interlocking scene: she explained that she had been told to 'shut up' all her life, and she experienced Matthew's 'everything will be alright' as a dismissal of her feelings and therefore another experience of being told to 'shut up'. We then turned to talking about Matthew's way of trying to comfort her and he gave the example of how if there are two people adrift in a boat on the ocean, and one of them is frightened and crying and saying that he can't continue, then the other one has to be strong, for both of them, otherwise they will both die.

Through our conversation he arrived at an insight about himself that he was just as frightened as she, but he feared allowing his feelings, so in protecting her he was also protecting himself. Later in the session he shifted to being able to say to her 'I know you are frightened, but we will get through this together'.

I think of this statement as a 'we' statement (Meyerowitz-Katz, 2016), in which Matthew was linking pairs of opposites, himself and Laura, and creating a third position (different from you and me). Laura was visibly supported on hearing this from him. It seemed that Matthew was representing something for both of them of a developing capacity for linking and transforming opposites and so moving towards symbolic functioning. This capacity in Matthew and Laura's response signalled the potential for their relationship to function as a container.

Changes over time

Over time I stopped noticing the differences between them. They ceased talking about separating and threats of leaving each other abated. Matthew developed more confidence and became more responsible and successfully tackled his gambling and financial problems. Over time they stopped getting drunk together and socialised differently with their friends.

There was evidence that a couple state of mind was forming. They incorporated me into their relational system: they reported how sometimes one or the other would say, 'Let's slow this down a bit' during their arguments and fights. This would make them laugh and help them diffuse the situation. They told me this during a session and so the next time I said 'Let's slow this down a bit' they burst out laughing. I joined in, happy to be the butt of this joke that signified their introjection of their therapist/therapy in the achievement of a shared third position.

They began to discuss their sexual problems with me. The sexual difficulties that they faced had to do with deep psychosomatic confusions and ambivalences. Discussions about sex in psychoanalytic psychotherapy are a way of metaphorically representing relational problems as well as talking about sex (Colman, 2009; Clulow 2009). It seemed that their bringing sex into their therapy was both a way of trying to get help with a very painful and distressing issue, and a way of trying to represent something about their ambivalence about collaborating in the evolution of a co-created third.

This ambivalence was played out in their relationship with their puppy.

A concrete representation of a co-created third

Typically for them, the next developmental stage was introduced in a concrete way: they adopted an injured, abandoned puppy from a dog rescue shelter. I understood the puppy as a sign of something shifting internally in each and between them. The puppy slept on their bed in between them. This damaged puppy with its wounded body represented something for them about their own unconscious understanding of themselves and their relationship. It was a representation of something that they were trying to negotiate and co-create together.

There was a lot of ambivalence about this possible third. They were expecting the puppy, because of its injury, to be disabled, but it transpired that the puppy could do everything that other puppies did. This was disappointing for them. Communicating their shared fear of their own potential potency and the damage it could cause, they worried about how much damage the healthy puppy was going to cause. The wounded and damaged puppy that turned out to be healthy, perhaps represented something for them of the hopeful possibility that they too, wounded as they were, could co-construct a healthy and creative relationship.

Several months after their adoption of the puppy, Laura discovered that she was pregnant. Her cervix held out and she carried their baby to term. A natural birth followed and Laura and Matthew shared in the ordinary ups and downs of parenting of their healthy son. Their therapy continued until their son was a year old and the three of us felt confident that they had a co-created relationship that they would be able to rely on in the future.

Acknowledgements

I would like to express my gratitude to the individuals who generously gave me permission to refer to the clinical material that is represented in this paper. All identifying information has been changed.

References

Addison, A. (2009). Jung, vitalism and 'the psychoid': An historical reconstruction. *The Journal of Analytical Psychology, 54(1)*, 23–142.
Bion, W.R. (1962). *Learning from Experience*. London: Maresfield Reprints.
Bion, W.R. (1963). *Elements of Psychoanalysis*. London: Maresfield Reprints.

Clark, G. (1996). The animating body: Psychoid substance as a mutual experience of psychosomatic disorder. *The Journal of Analytical Psychology, 41*, 353–368.

Clark, G. (2010). The embodied countertransference and recycling the mad matter of symbolic equivalence. In G. Heuer (Ed.) *Sacral Revolutions: Reflecting on the Work of Andrew Samuels – Cutting Edges in Psychoanalysis and Jungian Analysis* (pp. 88–96). London and New York: Routledge, Taylor & Francis Group.

Clulow, C. (2009). The facts of life: An introduction. In C. Clulow (Ed.) *Sex, Attachment and Couple Psychotherapy: Psychoanalytic Perspectives* (pp. xxv–xli). London: Karnac.

Colman, W. (1993) Marriage as a psychological container. In S. Ruszczynski (Ed.) *Psychotherapy with couples*. London: Karnac Books.

Colman, W. (2007). Symbolic conceptions: the idea of the third. *The Journal of Analytical Psychology, 52*, 565–583.

Colman, W. (2009). What do we mean by sex? In C. Clulow (Ed.) *Sex Attachment and Couple Psychotherapy: Psychoanalytic Perspectives* (pp. 25–44). The library of couple and family psychoanalysis. London: Karnac Books.

Colman, W. (2010). Mourning and the symbolic process. *The Journal of Analytical Psychology, 55*, 275–297.

Freud. S. (1914). *Remembering, Repeating, and Working Through*. S.E. Vol. 12. London: Hogarth Press.

Gerhardt, S. (2004). *Why Love Matters: How Affection Shapes a Baby's Brain*. London and New York: Routledge, Taylor & Francis Group.

Gerson, S. (2009). When the third is dead: Memory, mourning, and witnessing in the aftermath of the Holocaust. *International Journal of Psycho-Analysis, 90*, 1341–1357.

Grotstein, J.S. (1997). 'Mens sana in corpore sano': The mind and body as an 'odd couple' and as an oddly coupled unity. *Psychoanalytic Inquiry, 17(2)*, 204–222.

Jung, C.G. (1921/1971). *The Collected Works, Vol. 6 Psychological Types*. Second Edition, Bollingen Series XX. Princeton: Princeton University Press.

Jung, C.G. (1954/1982). *The Collected Works, Vol. 16 The Practice of Psychotherapy*. Second Edition. Bollingen Series XX. Princeton: Princeton University Press.

Jung, C.G. (1954/1991). Marriage as a psychological relationship. *The Collected Works, Vol. 17 The Development of Personality*. Second Edition. Bollingen Series XX. Princeton: Princeton University Press, para. 324–345.

Jung, C.G. (1960/1969). *The Collected Works, Vol. 8 The Structure and Dynamics of the Psyche*. Second Edition. Bollingen Foundation. Princeton: Princeton University Press.

Knox, J. (2003). *Archetype, Attachment, Analysis: Jungian Psychology and the Emergent Mind*. London and New York: Routledge, Taylor & Francis Group.

Knox, J. (2004). From archetypes to reflective function. *The Journal of Analytical Psychology, 49*, 1–19.

Meyerowitz-Katz, J. (2013). Consciously forgotten, unconsciously remembered relationships made visible: the therapist's use of art making to understand the embodied transference-countertransference relationship. Unpublished paper given at conference 'Kinship ties of creativity', Australian and New Zealand Arts Therapy Association (ANZATA), October 2013, Sydney.

Meyerowitz-Katz, J. (2016). Navigating ambivalent states of bodymind: working with intergenerationally transmitted Holocaust trauma in couple therapy. *Couple and Family Psychoanalysis, 6(1)*, 25–43.

Meyerowitz-Katz, J. (2017) The crisis of the cream cakes. In Meyerowitz-Katz, J., & Reddick, D. (Eds.) *Art Therapy in the Early Years: Therapeutic Interventions with*

Infants, Toddlers and Their Families (pp.118–132). London and New York: Routledge, Taylor & Francis Group.

Morgan, M. (2005). On being able to be a couple: the importance of a 'creative couple' in psychic life. In F. Grier (Ed.) *Oedipus and the Couple* (pp. 9–30). London: Karnac, The Tavistock Clinic Series.

Pickering, J. (2006). Who's afraid of the Wolfe couple: the interlocking traumatic scene. *Journal of Analytical Psychology, 51*, 251–270.

Pickering, J. (2008). *Being in Love: Therapeutic Pathways through Psychological Obstacles to Love*. London and New York: Routledge, Taylor & Francis Group.

Schwartz-Salant, N. (1988). Before the creation: the unconscious couple in borderline states of mind. In N. Schwartz-Salant and M. Stein (Eds.) *The Borderline Personality in Analysis* (pp. 1–40). Wilmette, IL: Chiron Publications.

Segal, H. (1978). On symbolism. *The International Journal of Psycho-Analysis, 59*, 315–319.

Segal, H. (1991). *Dream, Phantasy and Art*. Hove and New York: Brunner-Routledge, Taylor & Francis Group.

Winborn, M. (Ed.) (2014). *Shared Realities: Participation Mystique and Beyond*. Skiatook, OK: Fisher King Press.

Winnicott, D.W. (1949). Mind and its relation to the psyche-soma. In D.W. Winnicott, *Through Paediatrics to Psycho-analysis* (1982). London: The Hogarth Press and the Institute of Psychoanalysis.

Winnicott, D.W. (1971). *Playing and Reality*. Middlesex: Penguin Books.

Chapter 8

Understanding and working with no-sex couples

A developmental perspective

Lissy Abrahams

Sex, whether partners are having it or not, is what makes a couple relationship different from all other relationships. What is able to be negotiated in a couple's sexual relationship is often a reflection of each partner's psychic development and functioning. When thinking about this chapter, I had a moment to reflect on all the different types of sex spoken about by my patients. These include: 'ok' sex, sex with other partners/affairs sex, exciting/great sex, violent and coercive sex, S&M sex, withheld sex, infrequent or too frequent sex, boring sex, I want it/he or she doesn't sex, and the topic of this chapter – no sex. Many couples present to therapy stating that they are a no-sex couple; however, others disclose this later in the work. For most it is a privately shameful and humiliating experience. Being in a no-sex relationship is very common and in my practice well over half of the couples I work with are not having sex.

Grier (2005) wrote about how sexual difficulties arose when the partners share a history of inadequate working through of Oedipal anxieties. In particular, he linked this with Bion's notions of 'catastrophic change' and described how their fear becomes strong enough to induce regression in the couple psyche and joins forces with aspects of the couple that are anti-developmental. Sehgal (2012) linked Glasser's (1979) idea of the 'core complex' to no-sex couples, where the claustro-agoraphobic anxieties in adult relating arise from the infant's earliest relations with its mother. Berg (2012) explored the impact of adverse experiences in infancy on the sexual functioning of a couple, particularly to difficulties at the level of the skin and aversion to touch. She linked this with Thomas Ogden's (1989) concept of an Autistic-Contiguous phase of development, and the idea that a lack of 'good enough' holding (Winnicott, 1956) leaves the infant with an inadequately internalised ego.

While these authors write from a psychoanalytic perspective, my own focus in this paper is on the importance of projective identification (Klein, 1946) and containment (Bion, 1962) in the early experience of the couple I have worked with. Also and importantly, the role of unresolved Oedipal issues that prevented the couple from forming what Britton calls a 'third position' (Britton, 1989). The third position develops when the child relinquishes his sexual claim on his parents and accepts the reality of their unique relationship. This enables, what Britton calls, a 'triangular space' to be created and from this, different object relationships are able to co-exist. According to Morgan (2005), these psychic developments outlined by Britton form a vital part of the individual's psychic structure, which sustains them in a couple relationship. She referred to the crystallisation of these psychic developments as the internalisation of a 'creative couple' (Morgan and Ruszczynski, 1998). Morgan (2005) stated that the 'creative couple' is first a psychic development, where different thoughts and feelings are allowed and able to come together in one's mind, and for something to develop out of them. The above ideas may help to understand why some individuals in relationships are unable to allow the internal co-existence of different thoughts both inside themselves and from their partner. If they are unable to join up in the mind this must affect their capacity to join up as a couple physically.

Introducing the couple

I saw Mitch and Helen weekly for sixteen months. Mitch (53 years old) was tall with short black hair, brown eyes and olive skin. He was quite pleasant looking and wore smart suits to sessions. Helen (41 years) was tall, had thick blonde hair and dark brown eyes. She appeared physically strong and presented neatly dressed. They had three sons – twins aged 14 and an 11-year-old. Mitch had a very high profile in manufacturing as CEO of a multinational company. Prior to having children Helen had worked at a high level in accountancy and was more recently involved in contributing to Mitch's ventures.

Presenting problem

The couple was referred to me by a colleague who had completed a one-session consultation. This was the usual practice at the clinic in London where I worked. In the consultation report the first line of the presenting problem read 'No sex, for which the couple agrees Mitch is responsible'. The report stated that for Helen the problem dated back to the year they married, some sixteen years before, when Mitch seemed to have lost interest in sex. It was reported that Mitch did not entirely agree with this depiction of the timing, feeling that the difficulties had been more acute in recent years – particularly due to his increased focus on work – although he acknowledged he had never had a particularly high sex drive. Mitch indicated that after so many years of very little intimacy 'he did not know how to start to reach out to Helen and close the gap'. By this point in reading the consultation I was already alerted to the possibility that in this couple relationship Mitch might be the one holding a no-sex banner for this couple. Interestingly, both partners agreed more or less with Mitch's position. I was curious about the unilateral ownership of intimacy problems. When working with couples we look for the shared potential difficulties affecting the partners' capacity to have and/or maintain an intimate sexual relationship.

During the consultation Helen voiced her wish to end their marriage in order to salvage aspects of the relationship that she felt were working well. She described them as 'really good friends', sharing an interest in business, and a good capacity to parent their three children. In contrast Mitch voiced his desire to 'keep the relationship and to work on issues so they could create a relationship that would be based on greater understanding'. It seemed that Helen was carrying the more hopeless aspects of their relationship. In addition, she conveyed a feeling that remaining together was potentially damaging to other healthier aspects that they valued, such as being good parents and friends. Any hopefulness was essentially located in Mitch. This report revealed how polarised and entrenched their positions had become and provided rich information for me to think about.

History of the relationship

The report also revealed that Mitch and Helen met at a small dinner party where they were seated side by side. Throughout the evening they conversed easily, from which Helen surmised that 'Mitch must be gay'. Following the party she phoned Mitch and they developed a friendship. However, after several months Helen felt this friendship was not going to develop further. She spoke to Mitch about this at which point he suddenly kissed her and they became sexually intimate. Within nine months they were married and shortly after bought their first home together, one which they had purchased with the hope of raising a family. From this point their sexual relationship deteriorated. They had sex in order to start a family; however, they were unable to conceive. When they explored this with a fertility specialist they received the news that the infertility was 'unexplained'. This led them down the route of IVF which was successful for both pregnancies. Over the years they became more estranged from one another, even sleeping in separate bedrooms. Mitch retreated into work and Helen into the role of caring for the children.

Reading this, I was alerted to how their relationship started non-sexually, with Helen even questioning whether Mitch was attracted to women. There was little to indicate much spark or attraction between them. I wondered why it was left up to Helen to vocalise the difficulties. Also the description of their first kiss and sex seemed to have a manic and defensive quality, rather than one of passionate engagement. Further, what should have been enormously exciting – the purchasing of their first home together – was devastating for their sexual relationship. I wondered why settling down and being a couple who intended to have a family was felt to be so threatening. I was curious to know about their developmental struggles, which would have contributed to the deterioration of their intimate life. Finally, their 'unexplained' infertility must have been felt as a massive blow to this already fragile couple, as they already had a rather sterile beginning and struggled to maintain intimacy.

Mitch's personal history

Mitch was an only child. He described his parents as having a 'good and loving marriage of sixty years', where 'they did everything together'. He was slightly closer to his father, and felt his mother was more distant. He had a few long-term relationships prior to meeting Helen. Once he had even been engaged, however this 'fizzled out' when he moved to Madrid for work. As I read the report I questioned why he took up a role overseas following his recent engagement as his fiancée was not intending to join him there.

Helen's personal history

Helen, in contrast, had a more turbulent family life. Her parents' relationship was tempestuous. Her father had many affairs and was indiscreet about them. The first affair occurred when her mother was pregnant with Helen and these continued throughout her childhood. When Helen was 10, she and her three younger siblings encouraged and helped their mother 'escape' father ('escape' was Helen's word for leaving him) and the five of them moved into a small two-bedroom apartment. They had few financial resources, yet Helen felt 'incredibly happy'. She developed a very close relationship to her mother, and they apparently 'told each other everything'. Her mother died four years prior to therapy commencing and Helen was still grieving the loss. Helen's previous relationships were described as 'not healthy', with men frequently betraying her.

Excerpts from their first session

Helen: *Mitch and I are really good friends and work well together as parents, we don't fight and there are lots of really good parts to our relationship, however there is no intimacy between us. We sleep in separate bedrooms. We don't have sex and haven't for a while. We had sex once in three years. It is just not enough in a marriage. I'm 41 and feel dried up like a plant that has not been watered and now I feel dead. I feel no desire and have given up, no longer hoping Mitch will make an advance.*

Mitch: *I have made advances, however Helen now doesn't want to have sex with me. I'm very attracted to her.*

Helen: *It's too late, I don't feel anyone would be attracted to me. I've put on weight, I eat so much as I am so unhappy.* (As she spoke she did not appear unhappy.)

Mitch: *I feel so guilty I haven't given Helen what she wants and needs. I feel so bad for her.* (He did not sound or appear guilty.) *I am not a very sexual person. I'm attracted to Helen . . . she is lively and full of feelings. I'm not like that, I save all of my energy for work and feel so depleted at the end of the day. I can't even think about being sexual.*

Throughout most of the session they were kind towards each other and appeared careful to be generous and non-wounding. (This is not always the case with couples; some partners can be very cruel and unprotective of the other.)

Therapist: *You both appear very nice towards each other. I wonder about any other feelings you may have that are not necessarily so nice, such as anger, rage, sadness.*

Helen: (Immediately started crying) *I feel humiliated by this relationship. From the outside we are viewed as a happy and lovely couple, yet there is a shameful part that others don't see, and I feel so depressed about it.*

Therapist: *Mitch, are you aware of Helen's feelings of humiliation and shame?*

Mitch: *No. Not really.* (He was quiet for a few seconds then added) *Helen did write this to me in a letter once. When I read it I did not know what to do. It was like there was a big elephant in the room. After a while it became easier to not see the big elephant.*

Helen tearfully described her letter and how she had written years before. It had been a powerful experience for her where she described her distressed emotional state to Mitch. She mentioned that it had taken her a long time to write and that she needed to convey how lonely and distressing their relationship felt to her. (Once again it is Helen raising the concerns about their partnership as she had at the beginning of their relationship.) Like Mitch, Helen also allowed the elephant to sit between them. She had not referred to the letter again until they came into therapy. How had she felt about his non-response? The letter contained all of her unspeakable feelings – the messy, complicated and difficult feelings to navigate between them. They both colluded to ignore them in order to keep functioning. However, the unacknowledged letter never truly disappeared. It just widened the gap between them, as reflected in their only having sex once in three years.

In this session, Mitch also spoke about Helen's mild depression and how at various times in the relationship he had worried about her, particularly around the time of IVF and her first pregnancy when Helen's mother was diagnosed with a degenerative disease.

Therapist   *I can see there have been some very difficult experiences you have*
to Mitch: *both had to deal with, however Mitch I also see how frequently you express your concern for Helen and I wonder if in some way this hides feelings of your own.*

Mitch repeated his concerns about Helen and her depression, almost word for word as he had stated them before.

I remained with my thought and tried again:

Therapist: *I wonder if in this relationship the majority of feelings are expressed*
               by Helen, and for you (Mitch) *all concern is directed towards Helen.*
               However what's less known about for both of you are Mitch's feelings
               about your relationship, his experience of IVF, his anxieties and fears.

Mitch: *I never spoke about how scared I was at that time, it was so hard*
               and a horrible time. I never said anything and I became practiced at
               offering practical business-like solutions.

After two months of working together, I continued to think about their 'niceness'
and the fact they never fought. I must stress that being nice in therapy is not generally considered a problem. However I could not shake a feeling that for this couple
their niceness potentially protected them from something unbearable.

Therapist: *I wonder whether there is something terrifying for both of you about*
               fighting, as if fighting needs to be avoided at all cost.

Helen: (Replied tearfully) *My parents fought all the time. In fact my first*
               ever memory is of my parents fighting. I was little, sitting alone in my
               room, I could hear my parents screaming at each other. My mother
               threw objects. (She paused) *I don't argue, I don't see the point, there*
               is nothing to be gained, I just pull away.

In contrast to Helen's fiery family, Mitch recalled his parents fighting on only two
occasions.

Mitch: *Both times my father left the house to cool down.* (He paused) *My*
               mother fought with her sister twenty-three years ago and they still
               haven't spoken, and when I was younger they fell out for many years.
               I have no relationship with my extended family at all.

I commented that for both of them they avoided fighting as the consequences they
had observed were so extreme – either having relationships brutally cut off for
years on end or having rows that escalated to the point of objects being thrown.
    Helen tearfully replied.

Helen: *That's why I hate Christmas time, I remember all the presents under*
               the tree were kicked around the room, the tree and the decorations
               were ripped apart and everything was broken . . . Mum found out
               dad was having yet another affair.

Mitch's parents appeared very different. They were fused, 'doing everything
together' and Mitch recalled how his mother never appeared to enjoy being with
him as a child. He could not remember her ever laughing with him, only with his

father in another room. I was also starting to understand why Helen needed to put her more complicated feelings about their relationship in a letter and why Mitch ignored it. Neither had a sense that difficult emotional states could be shared, thought about together and resolved. During this session I felt so sad for both the little boy and little girl who had no space to feel special.

In further sessions the themes of independence and being dependent on others dominated. Helen recalled never wanting to get married as she enjoyed being independent. She said 'I had a lot of money, friends, my own house, what more did I need?' She added 'When we met, Mitch really liked the fact that I was so independent.' Mitch responded 'I found it very attractive, as I had been in other relationships and I never really liked the very dependent girls.' Clearly Mitch and Helen each paired with an image of a partner who would not have needs. It was as if neediness, dependency and vulnerability were unacceptable notions that needed to be kept away – like the feelings in Helen's letter. In my mind I was also thinking about these qualities in terms of a sexual relationship, and how impossible it is to have sex in a committed relationship without being able to have needs or be vulnerable.

In sessions we explored dependency in relation to their respective internal parental models and how frightening they were on two accounts. First, they were either dangerous like Helen's where things were 'smashed up' or like Mitch's where his parents seemed fused in a relationship where differences could not be tolerated and from which he was painfully excluded. Despite the partners' parental interactions appearing to be so different externally, internally they both felt unseen by their parents. Helen and Mitch were not able to be children with needs, and they each defensively adopted fully independent personas. This pseudo-independence or over-independence was expressly confirmed by Helen who had always wanted children, yet felt that she could have achieved this on her own. At this moment I saw the extent of her internal struggles and her fear of being dependent on a man who could hurt her, as her father had hurt her and her mother. Helen's way of managing this conflict was to make fathers redundant. She had already removed her father from her family when she helped her mother 'escape' and she clearly had an idea that fathers were even unnecessary when trying to conceive a child. Helen feared and cringed at the thought of being in a merged relationship like Mitch's parents where they 'would do everything together'. For Helen there was no safe position in her mind for coupling, so she unconsciously killed off her sexual desire. If she allowed herself to desire Mitch, what type of couple would they create? It felt as if there were only two options – a destructive one like her parents or a merged one like Mitch's parents. I imagine that Mitch shared Helen's horror at his parents' fused pairing, which left him painfully excluded and affected his capacity to be a sexually potent man desiring Helen.

Interestingly, they both recalled the onset of their sexual problems from the purchase of their first home – one in which they wanted to start a family. However it was not just in the sexual arena the drastic internal struggles were emerging. Mitch started to feel responsible and guilty towards Helen, stating 'I feel terrible, I moved her to a new suburb'. He repeated this several times, not able to take in Helen's view that she was 'willing and happy to go'. He tried to make things 'right' for her even though there was no evidence of anything being wrong. He became narcissistically preoccupied with how Helen viewed him and yet was unconcerned with how he felt about her. I wondered whether young Mitch had been preoccupied with how his mother viewed him and now transferred this preoccupation onto Helen. His feelings for Helen appeared irrelevant to him. Buying the family home appeared to trigger his unconscious fears of being the little boy who was continuously excluded from his parents' coupling. This was terrifying and unconsciously he found an unconscious solution (albeit a temporary one) – to protect his future children by being in a no-sex relationship, ensuring they would not be born. For Helen her father's first affair occurred at the time her mother was pregnant with her. One imagines she would have unconsciously experienced herself as being destructive to her parents' coupling. Was there an unconscious fear that having a child would destroy her and Mitch? Not having sex would have reduced the chances of falling pregnant and having such a 'destructive' child in their own relationship.

I believe that purchasing the family home brought unresolved unconscious anxieties to the fore for both partners. It triggered their different fears of dependency in the face of their parents' relationships. For Mitch, this commitment and the possibility of children touched his fear of being excluded from the marital relationship. For Helen, greater commitment increased the fear of betrayal, as her father had betrayed her mother. Their larger-than-life version of independence and professional status had mitigated feeling small; however, this was no longer offering sufficient protection from these anxieties. When he left his parents' home and became enormously successful, I felt Mitch unconsciously wanted to show his mother that he, not just his father, had a large penis. Was his even bigger than his father's? Did mother notice him now? Young Helen never had a father look at her or acknowledge her loveliness. Father was always saving that for some other woman, not even Mother. In a session about a third of the way through therapy, she said sadly 'My father used to show me off as the "good child" or the "intelligent girl", but he never knew me. He never discussed anything with me.' She had longed for him to know her and her attempts to contact him were never properly reciprocated. Mitch too did not really notice Helen, and when he did it was in a narcissistic way. For example, he worried how she felt about *him* and in sessions he used newspaper headlines to describe her qualities as 'lively', 'intelligent', 'caring'. However, as with Helen's father, these glowing words were always double-edged. They puffed her up momentarily; however, they were also empty, not allowing her to feel that either her father or her husband really knew her at all.

Several months later, their 'niceness' wore off. I noticed that Mitch was subtly cruel when Helen opened up vulnerable parts of herself. He would turn away from her both physically and emotionally. In several sessions I pointed this out and he appeared upset, stating repeatedly 'This is not what I want to be like'. Unconsciously, his actions conveyed to Helen that he could not bear to see the real her. He would not notice her tears nor try to join up with her. Helen became more overtly cruel too; she would repeatedly insist on ending the relationship, frequently reminding Mitch 'I was not attracted to you in the first place', or coldly asking 'Are you sure you're not gay?' There was a brutality to her words. This type of comment caused Mitch to repeat the newspaper headline qualities he so admired in Helen in a rather desperate way. Continuing this cycle, Mitch attempted to butter Helen up by listing her marvellous qualities, which offered Helen a mode of brief self-inflation yet also painfully reminded her again that Mitch did not want to really know her.

As can be seen, both partners had their own manoeuvres for keeping the other at arm's length. Helen revealed 'I never wanted to get married, it's like getting caught.' I imagined her as a wild animal caught in a trap. Another manoeuvre was seen in her relationship with her mother. This overly close pairing came at the expense of her relationship with Mitch. We examined how Mitch remained, in her mind, as a man with the potential to hurt her, like her father had when her mother was pregnant with Helen. By keeping him at arm's length, she was always prepared for a potential departure and frequently pushed him away. This configuration re-enacted Mitch's earlier painful exclusion in an Oedipal triangle as he frequently heard Helen and her mother on the phone, laughing happily together. Once again he was in the position of feeling the small, unspecial boy in the other room, and probably colluded with Helen in creating this dynamic. I wondered about the timing of the referral years after the mother's death. Helen had lost the only close relationship she had been able to trust. Perhaps in the referral there was a desperate hope that they could find a way to trust each other. I wondered about the pregnancy happening at the same time as Helen's mother became seriously ill. Did this confirm some idea of catastrophic inter-course? Once again I was reminded of her mother's pregnancy with Helen and the devastating revelation of her father's first affair. This notion of catastrophic intercourse was reinforced for Helen, as it was during her own gestation as well as in her first pregnancy.

Keeping a no-sex relationship had ensured that they would not be left open to an other who could disappoint them. They found it safer to pair with someone who, unconsciously, would not want sexual intimacy. Clearly it was too dangerous for both of them to have desires, feel lustful or want passionate engagement. For Mitch, he certainly did not want to become like his parents laughing in the other room at the expense of their child. How could such a small boy penetrate Helen when he was never big enough to penetrate his parents' coupling? He paired with a partner who did not want a potent penis inside her, so his penis remained small and inferior. For Mitch, being with Helen recreated the dynamic of a mother who did not look at him lovingly. Neither Helen nor his mother was really attracted to him. Helen and Mitch kept this dynamic in their relationship alive by not desiring each other sexually. Sadly, they both protected their vulnerable selves from being intimately involved with each other so they would not feel so catastrophically let down again.

Progress in the therapy

About five months into the work they were able to take an overseas holiday, without their children. They had sex and they reported enjoying the experience; however, it left them both confused and anxious. Helen worried that being together sexually would take away her right to end the relationship, which she had put on the table at the very beginning of the therapy. To take this away felt terrifying. The partners were finding a new intimacy, which was frightening for both of them. They started to have discussions about their relationship at home instead of avoiding them. They watched TV together when the children went to sleep (this sounds easy; however, for some couples even this is too intimate). Helen still voiced her uncertainty about the relationship, yet they were becoming emotionally closer. They had another overseas holiday, where they held hands and shopped. They described being more playful together. I was struck by their capacity to be more intimate away from home. This highlighted a difficulty integrating their sexual selves into their marriage/home life which they shared with their children. They were also going out for dinners as a couple and hosting dinner parties again. It was an important step in their relationship when these were reinstated. They were both proud of their developments. When Mitch elaborated on these he rubbed his tie from top to bottom in a repetitive manner. This felt to me as if he were pulling his penis, which he was potentially becoming more aware of. In many ways Mitch and Helen were indicating that something more integrated and reliable was building up between them. Their emotional and physical intimacy was developing.

Therapeutic challenges

Approximately ten months into the work, the couple went away for an unscheduled two-week break. Helen returned from this adamant that she no longer wanted the marriage and demanding a separation. She stated 'I feel suffocated by the relationship and a pressure to do something as Mitch does not notice me. I have to escalate the threat so he can take me seriously.' There seemed to be some confusion for her about whom she wanted to leave, as she spoke about leaving therapy too. In her mind all relationships were the same. We explored together how frightening it felt for her when I was not mentally available to her, when she needed me to help them take her emotional experience seriously. This was too frightening to know about and destabilised the very familiar pseudo-independent position that she had held on to for many years. The break had left her feeling vulnerable and alone and she was not going to allow this to be felt again. I felt that her separation from me reminded her of her mother, who had abandoned her through dying five years previously. I was someone she had been trusting, someone whom she allowed herself to open up to. Then during their break, she was in touch with both the distance between us and her need for me and this made her feel vulnerable and small. She was not going to allow herself to feel this way. She enviously attacked her link to me as a benign figure and tried to abort the fragile alliance between the three of us. She stated she was going to stop coming to therapy and insisted she wanted a separation. It all felt hopeless and brutal.

In one session Helen described her attempt to engage Mitch in a discussion about how she was feeling. In essence she was taking a risk and had thought about the sessions where we had explored the way they did not take risks in their relationship. They were out for a drive together and Helen tried to talk to him about her sadness regarding the state of their relationship. Mitch ignored her and pointed out something on the side of the road. She tearfully described that moment and how infuriated and alone she felt. The following weekend they fought. This could have been seen as a sign that something more robust was developing between them. However as the fight escalated, Helen reportedly shouted in fury 'And that's why I am divorcing you'. Mitch did not verbally respond to her. He cleaned the kitchen and appeared to ignore her words. I was reminded of the elephant Mitch described in the first session. Mitch described feeling numb and regretful at what he focused on. He appeared sad describing what they were both losing, 'There are no winners here and we have so much to lose if we're separated'.

Ending the therapy prematurely

Despite Mitch's vocal protests to remain in therapy, I felt Helen sabotaged the therapy for both of them. It felt like an unconscious collusion to stop all intercourse between us. From this time, there were extra holidays with the children that *had* to be taken, and there were many sessions where only one partner was present, and at times both were absent. Neither partner made any real demand for the other to be present nor expressed annoyance or anger when the other was absent. They were giving me the experience of what it was like to be a part of their relationship, where no one shared intimacy and no one expressed any feelings about what was happening. Except for me. I was the holder of many overwhelming feelings they could not know about. They were treating me just like they treated each other. I was not allowed to be of much help or value and I felt I was disposable. At times I felt furious at this treatment. I often wondered whether this was all my fury or was it also theirs, violently projected into me as they could not tolerate it. I felt impotent. They were making me impotent. How could I get them even in the room together so that I could work my counter-transference responses back into the couple work? They were not allowing any intercourse to take place between us, yet I was fed occasional platitudes about how important the therapeutic space was. However with the absences of one or the other, one constantly empty seat reflected the true situation. Helen stated that she would not return to sessions unless we all focused on the separation, especially how and when to tell the children.

During one session Helen was running late. Mitch had started, as he did not know how long she would be. When Helen arrived she was holding an envelope which she rather noisily slapped down on her side table. I assumed the noisy entry was to do with her lateness. She made no reference to the envelope and at the end of the session she handed it to me and left. I had not realised, during the session, that the envelope was for me. I opened it and in it was a furious response to a disagreement regarding the payment of one session they had missed as they were away. She had not raised any of these feelings during the session, yet they were all enclosed in the envelope. I was shocked at her calm manner during the session and her fury that she had left in the envelope. It was so similar to the letter she had written to Mitch. In that moment these parts of her could not be brought together, she could not talk to me about her feelings. The following week we found a way of resolving the financial disagreement; however, more importantly we talked about the feelings located in the envelope and how dangerous they felt, and how for both of them feelings were once again being sealed off from oneself and not communicated to the other.

They persisted with their plan to separate. They were not going to disturb the status quo and they felt immovable. Helen was standing firm as the axe wielder. She was used to being the destructive one. Her mother's pregnancy with her must have ignited her own parents' Oedipal anxieties, as her father concretely sought out someone else to pair with. At some level she must have felt some responsibility for this damage. She wielded the axe in her parents' relationship when she helped her mother 'escape' Father, and here she was repeating this pattern. Marriage was once again equated with feeling 'caught', and for Helen this was akin to annihilation. Perhaps she saw safety in Mitch being potentially gay. He certainly was not a sexually potent man, so something was communicated from their first meeting about the dangers of being physically close. Helen was certainly overtly the one demanding an end to the marriage; however, I had to remember how cruelly Mitch could turn away from Helen and how he also colluded to sabotage the therapy and perhaps his marriage.

In the final two months of working together (well sort of together) separation was firmly on the agenda. This was important work as they both wanted to help their children in the best way to cope with the news of their separation. I respected their capacity to think about their boys' experience at this time. There was one session where the three of us were working on how they would tell their children about the separation. They spoke rather factually without any sense of grief, sadness or emotion, just the how, where and when it would happen. As soon as the session ended I fortunately had supervision in the same clinic where I was working. The minute I saw my supervisor I burst into tears. I cried for all of them, for what I felt they could do if they persevered with sessions, for their children who were soon to hear this news and for what I felt was just a waste. I must say this was not a typical response for me. I would not normally burst into tears during supervision. I was crying the tears and feeling the overwhelming sadness that Mitch and Helen could not. They had unconsciously projected all of these emotions for me to carry. I spoke to my supervisor about all of this and my sense of their wasted relationship. I felt they were becoming more intimate and joined up psychically, and I wanted them to continue to develop – if only they would remain in therapy. My supervisor replied 'Maybe, yet maybe they did all that they could do'.

Despite all of their gains, Mitch and Helen were going to remain a no-sex couple and they had found a solution. Towards the end of therapy they decided to separate yet continue living together 'for the children'. They wanted to have a family meal together every week or even more. This was clearly a nominal separation. The partners were spared the many painful tasks associated with separating. They did not need to mourn the loss of each other, there were no farewells, they were spared the private shame associated with not being a sexual couple and they removed the psychological danger of creating an unsafe coupling. In reality, they legitimised their status of being a no-sex couple who do everything together except have sex. Interestingly this new status enabled them to get closer. They reported having hugs 'as friends'.

Discussion

How do we understand the internal world of Mitch and Helen? Klein's (1946) concept of projective identification described the processes of introjection and projection, which are operative from the beginning of life. Introjection allows the primitive psyche to take in good things, such as food, love and care. It is through repeatedly good experiences that a good internal figure is established. However, if projective processes become extreme, there is a danger that the infant will in phantasy excessively expel its disowned parts into its object, therefore perceiving his mother as holding all the aggression and hatred: the process of projective identification. The child in turn expects retaliation, and this can feel catastrophic as then all is lost.

Bion (1962) extended Klein's concept of projective identification to include his important idea of containment, a primitive form of communication. He proposed that the infant projects into the mother his annihilation anxiety and inchoate primitive elements, that he called beta elements. The mother's role is to unconsciously take in, process and understand the infant's experience and name it. When this happens, the infant can reintroject his projections, modified by understanding, and he also introjects the breast as a container capable of containing and dealing with anxiety. The mother, through her own capacity for thought (her alpha function), has transformed the unbearable beta elements into alpha elements (a higher level of mental functioning). This forms the basis of the infant's own capacity to manage and contain anxiety, as over time the alpha function becomes introjected. Bion also describes the terrifying reversal of this process, which he terms –K, whereby the infant is left to reintroject his own anxieties, unmodified and is left with the terror of the annihilation anxieties. These anxieties are neither understandable nor digestible to the infant, and are perceived as 'nameless dread' (1962).

Both Mitch and Helen lacked containment. Their lack of security and trust in their internal worlds constantly destabilised their couple relationship and led them to project split-off parts of themselves into the other. Further, the unconscious phantasies and conscious experience of their respective parents' relationship were far from benign, revealing unresolved Oedipal issues for both of them. In Mitch's mind, the joining up of his parents represented a most painful and unbearable exclusion. The laughter from the other room was the painful reminder that he was never going to be a special boy for Mother, never to be chosen to pair with her over Father, even momentarily. I believe he saw his parents as a 'combined parental figure'. According to Klein (1928), the combined parent is intrinsic to her conception of the early Oedipus complex, where in phantasy the parents are united in an everlasting sexual embrace. Here the mother contains the father's penis or the whole father, and the father contains the mother's breast or the whole mother. The unconscious phantasy of a combined parental figure is said to be very primitive, highly anxiogenic and terrifying as there is no space for the infant to exist. The combined parental figure evokes the infant's jealousy of and rivalry with the father, who is perceived to be receiving what the child is excluded form. This figure is also imbued with the child's projected rage at this state of affairs. If the child's feelings cannot be contained, then the destructive attacks on the parents feel catastrophic as they lead to his abandonment. This, according to Klein, is a very normal internal phantasy; however, for Mitch it was also his external reality. Therefore, there was no benign parental link for Mitch and there was no possibility of movement into the pairings of their Oedipal triangle. Despite the opposite appearing the case, I feel his parents 'good and loving marriage of sixty years' must have had such a core of fragility that made them cling together in a rather desperate way. Perhaps they shared a fear that if they did not cling together the only other option was to be brutally excluded. For Helen, her parents coming together represented a destructive and unsafe couple who 'smash things up'. Her father's affairs were flaunted and her mother reacted with impotent rage. Both parents were too preoccupied with their own dramas to be containing in any capacity. The four siblings and their fragile mother left home and finally Helen had a figure with whom she could be close to. She became in phantasy and reality her mother's partner. Her parents' relationship had been destructive and Helen was never going to allow herself to be in Mother's position – she would never be vulnerable and needy in relation to a man. She had invested a huge amount of energy preventing her parents from remaining together, and, like Father, Mitch was frequently made to feel an equally dispensable partner.

This couple's early lack of containment in their families of origin, combined with unresolved Oedipal issues, prevented them from developing a sense of their relationship as a third, which Morgan (2005) explains is vital for a creative couple relationship. Without having internalised this third position for their relationship, they had no internal resources to draw upon when breakdown occurred. They reverted to the more familiar position of pseudo-independence they so admired in the other when they met. However, now it put them in touch with the emptiness of isolation. They ensured that their children would never be faced with narcissistically preoccupied parents who excluded them. All neediness, love, dependency and intimacy had been located in their children, who never observed their parents being a loving couple, never choosing each other over them. A major part of the Oedipal triangle was now missing for Mitch and Helen's children. They would not have to negotiate the developmentally important pain of parents who exclude them. Mitch and Helen's no-sex coupling spared the children the pain of acknowledging a parental union that was different from the parent–child relationship. All members of the family slept in separate bedrooms including Mummy and Daddy. I worried for the psychological development of these children and their capacity to form satisfying adult relationships.

Transference issues

The projective processes described by Klein (1946) and Bion (1962) have enormous relevance to what I experienced with Mitch and Helen. At certain times they were able to make use of me and able to make deep contact. I felt they were introjecting the goodness from their sessions with me, as Klein described with the infant taking in goodness from the mother's breast. They were able to know about the awful state of their marriage, to speak honestly and openly about their struggle to be intimate for most of their relationship, how the children for Helen and work for Mitch were used to fill the massive gap in their lonely relationship. They appeared to rely on my presence, my capacity to witness, my empathy, and my way of understanding their relationship. I was offering them their first real contact with anyone able to contain anxieties. However, Mitch and Helen's capacity to use the couple's therapy was severely reduced whenever there was a break or upon returning, whereupon the therapy often felt threatened. Suddenly I heard from Helen (often as the spokesperson for the couple) that 'The sessions took up so much time that they did not have' and how 'It cost them money that was not available' (both of which were not steeped in reality: Helen did not work and they were incredibly wealthy).

Conclusion

Through the phases of the therapy Helen and Mitch were able to develop some aspects of being a more sexual and intimate couple. They were initially unable to have intercourse of any sort unless it related to work or their children. This created an enormously lonely relationship, not offering any sense of containment to either of them. Through the containment that couple therapy offered they were able to know more about their anxieties and fears and how their earlier experiences affected their capacity for intimacy. Their unbearable beta elements were to some degree transformed into more understandable and digestible alpha elements. They were more able to be in touch with the parts of each of them that desired intimacy and were prepared to take risks in the sexual domain. They were somewhat more able to discuss together when these attempts at intimacy were aborted. Sadly for Mitch and Helen their therapeutic gains were rather brutally sabotaged by Helen. Although she was wearing the banner as the one who would destroy the marriage, Mitch was compliant in sabotaging the therapy. I felt some sadness that we could not have had more intercourse in the therapy to help them further, yet I also felt they experienced me as a benign and more or less containing object. At the end of our time together I had been able to process their projections sufficiently that I did not feel so despondent about their departure. I was reminded of the first line of the presenting problem in Mitch and Helen's consultation report which read 'No sex, for which the couple agree Mitch is responsible'. Despite their premature departure from therapy I felt that both Mitch and Helen could each know more about their own sexual and relationship struggles, and I felt they might take further risks with intimacy in the future from a nominally separated state, where they each would feel less 'caught' and therefore safer.

References

Berg, J. (2012). A bad moment with the light: no-sex couples – the role of autistic-contiguous anxieties. *Couple and Family Psychoanalysis, 1*, 33–48. London: Karnac.

Bion, W.R. (1962). *Learning from Experience*. London: Heinemann.

Britton, R. (1989). The missing link: parental sexuality in the Oedipus complex. In J. Steiner (Ed.) *The Oedipus Complex Today: Clinical Implications* (pp. 83–101). London: Karnac.

Glasser, M. (1979). Aggression and sadism in the perversions. In I. Rosen. (Ed.) *Sexual Deviation* (pp. 279–299). London: Oxford University Press.

Grier, F. (2005). No sex couples, catastrophic change, and the primal scene. In F. Grier (Ed.) *Oedipus and the Couple* (pp. 201–219). London: Karnac.

Klein, M. (1928). Early stages of the Oedipal conflict. *International Journal of Psycho-Analysis, 9*, 167–180.

Klein, M. (1946). Notes on some schizoid mechanisms. *International Journal of Psycho-Analysis, 27*, 99–110 [Reprinted in M. Klein, *Envy and Gratitude and Other Works 1946–1963*. London: Hogarth Press, 1980].

Morgan, M. (2005). On being able to be a couple: the importance of a 'creative couple' in psychic life. In F. Grier (Ed.) *Oedipus and the Couple* (pp. 9–30). London: Karnac.

Morgan, M. and Ruszczynski, S. (1998). The creative couple. Unpublished paper presented at Tavistock Marital Studies Institute 50th Anniversary Conference.

Ogden, T. (1989). On the concept of an autistic-contiguous position. *The International Journal of Psycho-Analysis, 70(1)*, 127–140.

Sehgal, A. (2012). Viewing the absence of sex from couple relationships through the 'Core Complex' lens. *Couple and Family Psychoanalysis, 2*, 149–164. London: Karnac.

Winnicott, D.W. (1956). Primary maternal preoccupation. In *Collected Papers: Through Paediatrics to Psychoanalysis* (pp. 145–156). London: Hogarth, 1975.

Chapter 9

Children of Oedipus[1]

Oedipal anxieties in couple and family work

Penny Jools

> Oedipus was the son of Laius, the King of Thebes, and of Jocasta, his queen. To avert the fulfilment of the prophecy that he would murder his father and marry his mother, Oedipus was exposed to die on the mountain and taken in by shepherds. In one version of the myth, he was given to the childless King and Queen of Corinth who raised him as their own. When grown to manhood he unwittingly slew his father, then, having solved the riddle of the sphinx, he was offered the kingdom of Thebes and the hand of Jocasta his mother (although they were both ignorant of the relationship) in marriage. When the truth was revealed Jocasta hanged herself and Oedipus put out his own eyes.
>
> (*Brewer's Dictionary of Phrase and Fable*, 1986)

Introduction

In this version of the Oedipal myth, the focus is on the parents, Laius and Jocasta, who have a murderous need to exclude Oedipus from their relationship. One could say that this was a couple 'who cannot cope with a threesome relationship' (Grier, 2005, p. 1). It is this seminal Oedipal issue of exclusion and inclusion that is the main focus in the clinical cases in this paper. But also of interest is the role of early Oedipal anxieties, relating to a lack of containment in the first year of life, a failure that can compromise normal Oedipal resolution.

These Oedipal anxieties are an aspect of the universal struggle for couples and families to move towards a psychological marriage from previous narcissistic ways of relating (Fisher, 1993). My Australian colleagues and I are interested in the ways in which normal psychological development can be interfered with by developmental anxieties (Berg and Jools, 2004, 2006) that are encountered on the way to mature psychological functioning. We have found a framework of developmental anxieties and their defences useful both in establishing the current psychological functioning of a family or a couple, but also in tracking progress through therapy.

Negotiating these developmental anxieties is a part of a couple or family's normal development, but some families like those discussed in this chapter remain hostage to vulnerabilities that compromise normal psychological growth. In both cases, I am arguing, these vulnerabilities reflect the complex interaction of early and later Oedipal anxieties with external factors, including abuse and transgenerational trauma. In both families, however, one salient manifestation of these anxieties is a sense of exclusion, a feeling also experienced in the transference relationship.

Later and early Oedipal anxieties

In classical theory the Oedipal complex is signalled by the libidinal attachment of the boy to his mother (and daughter to her father), with resolution occurring through the relinquishment of the Oedipal longings by working through fears about castration and loss of love. In dealing with these anxieties, the child must experience and tolerate both inclusion and exclusion from the parental couple. The child's acceptance of their position as a third in the couple relationship is necessary in order for them to find a secure place as a child and to develop a good enough internal parental couple.

Early Oedipal anxieties and their impact on later Oedipal situations are less clearly understood, mainly because they are not mediated by language. Unconscious determinants of these anxieties can be detected in both child and adult analysis (Klein, 1945; Britton, 1989), but also and significantly for this paper in the couple relationship. As a couple psychotherapist, one becomes acutely aware that the couple relationship, and in particular the sexual relationship, is the inheritor of these early conscious and unconscious experiences and phantasies. It is hardly surprising that early internal object relations manifest in the intensely psychosomatic adult sexual relationship since the body is the canvas on which the mother–infant relationship is enacted.

It was Klein who suggested that Oedipal anxieties existed in infants under 2 years of age, thus challenging Freud's assertion that the Oedipus complex extends from three to five years.

She argued that:

> the Oedipus complex starts during the first year of life and in both sexes develops to begin with on similar lines. The relations to the mother's breast is one of the essential factors which determine the whole emotional and sexual development. I therefore take the breast relation as my starting point in the ... beginnings of the Oedipus complex in both sexes.
>
> (Klein, 1945, p. 65)

It was the infant's realisation that the breast is not always available and also the trauma of weaning that causes, in Klein's mind, the turning to the father. It is in this way that the infant's loving and hateful feelings begin to be divided between the parental couple.

Another source of early Oedipal anxieties resides in the infant's experience of and phantasies about parental intercourse, i.e. the primal scene. For Klein (1945) these took the form of a combined parental figure that 'is partly a denial of the parental intercourse, combined the two into one monstrous figure, and also a projection of the child's hostility to that intercourse, making it into a particularly threatening figure' (Segal, 1989, p. 2). These phantasies may involve fear of damage as the infant hears and misinterprets the sounds of parents' intimate moments leading to a phantasy of catastrophic intercourse (Britton, 1989).

Both Klein and Britton saw Oedipal resolution, in its link to the depressive position, as essential in the development of thinking. An acceptance of the parental relationship allows for the linking between external and internal relationships that is essential to psychological functioning, and indeed cognitive development. But Britton also argues that the acceptance of the parental relationship as different, and at times excluding of the child, develops the capacity for an internal triangular space:

> If the link between the parents perceived in love and hate can be tolerated in the child's mind, it provides ... us with a capacity for seeing ourselves in interaction with others and for entertaining another point of view whilst retaining our own, for reflecting on ourselves whilst being ourselves.
>
> (Britton, 1989, p. 87)

Little has been said, however, about the impact on early Oedipal anxieties of the father who is either never present, i.e. a father who impregnates and leaves, or who dies when the child is very young. Both instances can allow a pyrrhic victory: the omnipotent child who becomes the mother's partner, in a situation where his omnipotence remains unchallenged. An absent or dead father is of particular relevance in the history of the two families described in this paper and the consequences of the situation where the child becomes the mother's emotional partner will also be explored.

Early and later Oedipal anxieties in couple psychotherapy

How is this relevant to thinking about couple psychotherapy? Psychoanalytic theory has focused on Oedipus the child who grows up to murder his father and marry his mother. In the original Oedipal myth, however, cited at the beginning of the paper, the focus of interest is Laius and his queen Jocasta in their murderous need to rid themselves of their firstborn son. When we are dealing with a couple relationship that is in difficulty after the birth of a child, we may ask ourselves does the father, like Laius in the original myth, have murderous feelings towards his son? Does the mother have an exclusive relationship with her child thus relegating her husband to emotional exile? These are questions that often arise in couple psychotherapy and alert us to the presence of Oedipal issues in the couple. The perspective of the child, i.e. the early childhood experience of the father and mother, however, is relevant in thinking about early Oedipal difficulties that may result in distorted internal object relations that they bring, as adults, to their couple relationship.

Often, however, the presence of unresolved Oedipal anxiety in couples or families is signalled in a variety of ways that is less obvious than the more overtly murderous feelings of a Laius or Jocasta. One typical sign of these anxieties is a strong feeling of exclusion, with concomitant feelings of envy and jealousy. The second hallmark of Oedipal difficulties is a lack of emotional separation from the family of origin: this can be from poles of idealisation to denigration. Unless the experience in the family of origin, like that of the good enough mother, can be experienced as both good and bad, then the internal objects are projected into the current relationship creating both unrealistic expectations and distorted experiences.

The author suggests that a sense of 'stuckness' and lack of resolution of these Oedipal issues often resides in early Oedipal difficulties. How do these early Oedipal difficulties manifest in couple psychotherapy? While the mother–infant connection is a whole-body experience, the breast has a special significance in its dual role as a source of nourishment to the infant and a source of erotic pleasure to the couple. It thus symbolises the early triangular relationship as anxieties at this level may exist in the rivalry over the breast between the partner and the child. These early Oedipal anxieties are also likely to manifest in the classic hallmarks of paranoid-schizoid functioning. An example of this would be splitting of an extreme form, a very rigid and 'black and white' view of the world. A particularly significant aspect of this is when the father becomes the repository or all the negative or idealised projections that arise from splitting. While this might be an aspect of normal progress through paranoid-schizoid functioning, if the father is absent, then the normal 'working through' is not possible. Further, if the absent father leaves the mother and infant uncontained, at this early stage of development, one might also expect psychosomatic disturbances in one or other of the couple. Also and most importantly if the container is sufficiently damaged, e.g. if the mother is left abandoned by the father without other support or protection, one might anticipate major difficulties in thinking, in linking experience to current reality, This can create a psychological 'blindness' (like Oedipus in his incestuous marriage to his mother) to the psychological reality of the situation, as mentioned earlier, a difficulty in linking internal to external reality. A further aspect of this, clearly outlined in Britton's seminal paper 'The Missing Link' (Britton, 1989) manifests as a major difficulty in seeing the point of view of others in the family, partner or child, an inability to take a 'third' position.

Early Oedipal difficulties were indeed exacerbated in these two cases, by transgenerational dramas of abandonment and loss. In the first case a father impregnated and abandoned the mother of his child, and in the second case a heroic father was murdered while his son was very young. These dramas had not to date been brought into consciousness and worked though. This ongoing trauma, and related early and later Oedipal anxieties, led to the destructive situation that the families presented when I first saw them.

Both families have given me permission to use the material from their sessions for teaching purposes. Identities have been changed and disguised.

Crystal and her family

The family were seen weekly over a two-and-a-half-year period. After a year of family therapy, I continued to see the couple for eighteen months and a colleague saw Crystal on her own for a further twelve months. The couple had been together for fourteen years and married for seven.

Background

The referral started with a telephone call from the mother, who expressed concerns about her 17-year-old daughter, Crystal: 'I'm worried about my daughter Crystal. She has been drinking alcohol at school to deal with stress, although she is happy at school. She attempted to overdose by taking twelve paracetamols. She has also been stabbing and cutting herself.'

Her mother, Maria, said that her behaviour had changed since an incident (that Crystal could not discuss) that had occurred earlier in the year. Since then Crystal, a clever student, had abandoned her studies and was clearly depressed.

Crystal, 17 years old at the time that therapy started, was living with her biological mother, Maria, who was 35 years old and her stepfather, Frank, twenty years older than his wife. Frank was a schoolteacher and Maria worked as a receptionist in a doctor's office. I learned that they had been together as a family since Crystal was 3 years old, but married when she was 10.

Initial interview

The appearance of the family did nothing to dispel the anxieties aroused by the phone call. Crystal was a slightly overweight teenager who appeared at the first appointment dressed like a Goth, with long striped socks, lace-up boots, a short black skirt, a black shirt and dyed black hair worn with no part so that it completely obscured her eyes. Under her hair I could see a heavily made-up face, the eyes circled with black kohl. Her mother Maria was an attractive but obese woman who did not look twenty years younger than her husband. The stepfather, Frank, was a tall good-looking man, neatly dressed in shorts and a shirt.

Frank: *Crystal is quite strong-willed and stubborn. A lot of the conflict is because we try and get her to help at home. We both work full time and we are pretty tired at the end of the day. If we could all chip in then we could spend more time together.*

Therapist: (To Crystal) *So what are you expected to do?*

Crystal: *Feed the cats, tidy the bedroom, pack the dishwasher.*

Therapist: *Do you do it?*

Crystal: (Looking angrily at Maria and Frank) . . . *Mostly.*
             (F. and M. look at each other in a disbelieving way.)

Therapist: (To M.) *Did **you** have a lot to do at home?*

Maria:	Did I ever (she laughs). *I was pregnant with Crystal when I was 17, I was in full rebellion against my mother. I had applied for a scholarship to the Conservatorium.* . . .
Therapist:	*So becoming pregnant stopped you?*
Maria:	*Yes, but I really wanted a child to love and raise. I never resented it. But I had been raising my mother's children since the age of 10. I left school, my mother kicked me out a few days after I brought Crystal home . . . she was born on the day of my final exams. I told the father that I was pregnant but he never wanted any responsibility. I went back to school when Crystal was 3 months old. The father turned up at the school gates and wanted me to marry him. I tried to re-establish a relationship with him but it didn't work. When Crystal was 3 he met someone else – had two children and there was less and less contact.*
Therapist:	*Did you know all this?*
Crystal:	(Nods)

Maria then went on to describe how Frank 'came on the scene' and a photo she has of the three of them – 'it is really beautiful'.

Maria:	*I didn't start with a good life. I wanted Crystal to have a better life. I was a single mother living in Liverpool,* (a working class suburb on the outskirts of Sydney, Australia) *but I was determined to make something of myself. I said to myself 'You can always do better in life'.*
Therapist:	*So I guess you want Crystal to have the things you missed out on?*
Maria:	*That's right. Crystal is very intelligent and artistically brilliant, but she is not focusing on her school work. People love her, but she comes across as sullen and surly. She measures people up, when she decides she trusts you it's OK, but she has a sense of humour.*
Therapist:	(Turning to Crystal) *So I guess you are measuring me up at the moment.*
Crystal.	(Smiles and says nothing)

I turned to Frank and asked him what his thoughts were. He talked about a recent incident where he felt that Crystal had manipulated the situation to get money out of her mother for her birthday and he felt ignored and dismissed. . . .

Frank:	*For me the family unit is one of mutual respect and love. I always thought it was reasonable that Crystal be part of it, an obligation to contribute. For years now Crystal hasn't done that, she doesn't respect the structure. And, God knows, I've asked for a long time: just symbolic contributions, feed the cats and fish, empty the dishwasher, for years she has done virtually nothing. I feel we should not have to ask.*
Therapist:	*So . . . was your family like that?*
Frank:	*Yes, pretty well, I was an only child . . . for medical reasons. My parents had a deep love for one another. When my mother died in 1995 my father was shattered. He died in 2002, we were married in 2001.*
Therapist:	*So he died just after you were married?*

Maria:	Yes, his death had big impact on all of us.
Frank:	I miss him terribly (becomes tearful).
Therapist:	(Turning to Crystal) Do you miss him?
Crystal:	I only met him in 1998.
Maria:	It was only when we were married that we started spending more time with him. You can see what sort of man Frank is through his father. I'm lucky and blessed. I've never had a male figure like him in my life. Frank's parents had a first son that died at birth. Frank was very sick . . . he only just made it.
Frank:	Maria always wanted lots of kids.
Maria:	I was pregnant to Frank. I terminated just after his mother died. It was too early. But we have had no success since. I have polycystic ovarian syndrome. It is hard for me to conceive.

Maria's family

In Maria's family scenario, the age of 17 seems to have a powerful transgenerational meaning. At the time of the referral Crystal was 17 years old and very much at risk. (It is worth noting that the 'incident' that had contributed to her depression and abandoning her studies had, in my mind, the possibility of rape and this hypothesised event had the potential to perpetuate the transgenerational theme of illegitimate births.) Maria had given birth to Crystal illegitimately when she was 17, so Crystal's birth put an end to her dream of a tertiary education. Nancy, Maria's mother, had been abandoned in an orphanage by her mother in wartime Italy where she stayed until she was 17. At that point her mother reclaimed her, and brought her out to Australia to care for the children of her current marriage at which point Nancy promptly became pregnant. Transgenerational themes of abandonment and exclusion are thus powerfully present in Maria's history. Perhaps the most important issue is the absent (or excluded) father. Fathers appear in this story only to impregnate and then abandon their partners. In the case of Crystal's father there is also an incestuous relationship as Crystal's father had an affair with Maria's mother.

Frank's family

Frank described his parents as perfect and loving: yet a first son to the marriage had died after birth and Frank himself was a sickly baby. The idealisation of his family and therefore a denial of its psychological reality persisted through the first year of therapy. I wondered if his denial was a defence against the feeling of exclusion from his parents' grief at the loss of their firstborn.

Transference and counter-transference

Frank's feelings of exclusion were so powerfully expressed in the therapy sessions that I came to see him as voicing something for the whole family, and indeed myself. I approached each session as though I was about to be sacked as a therapist. Even though the family attended regularly it took more than a year of therapy before I felt confident that they would turn up next time. Perhaps this coincided with the time when Frank acknowledged the painful truth of his early experience.

The therapy

In the early sessions, during much of the first year, the feelings of exclusion were expressed by Frank as a litany of complaints about how wounded he was by some (often quite trivial) act of exclusion by his stepdaughter. He would report that she would not inform him of school functions, failed to say goodbye to him when she left the house, etc. (This seemed like normal teenage behaviour.) He was jealous of the closeness between Crystal and her mother.

Crystal often complained about her own feelings of exclusion from the couple: she felt that she got blamed for everything that went wrong yet her mother would often complain about Frank to her. She often felt confused and angry about the way she was treated by Frank and Maria, particularly when Frank complained about her and Maria did not 'stick up' for her for fear of alienating Frank. Maria alternated between a merged relationship with Crystal in which they were very close but excluded Frank and a merged relationship with Frank that excluded Crystal. At other times her own envy and jealousy of her daughter and Crystal's refusal to be a 'parentified child', i.e. become like a mother to her own mother, provoked rage and rejection from Maria.

After eighteen months of therapy, however, Frank revealed that when he was 5 years old his mother had insisted that his father cut off all contact with his extended family because she could not bear any acknowledgment of the death of her first child. She would also never allow him to ride a pushbike because she was afraid he might hurt himself. Frank was angry with me when he acknowledged this as it shattered his previous idealised view of his parents. He struggled over a few months to accept that the emotional reality of his childhood was one of loneliness, overprotection and exclusion. It was this longing to belong that made his feelings about being excluded both so painful and so unrealistic in the family he had formed with Maria and Crystal.

At the end of the first year of therapy, Crystal's fear of exclusion became particularly acute when her mother returned from hospital where she had undergone a stomach stapling operation (resulting in her losing 50 kilos). Maria expected her daughter to 'look after' her (as she had looked after everyone in her family.) Crystal's response to her mother's hospitalisation was a dive into depression, through fear of her mother dying. Her mother failed to understand Crystal's depression and became very angry with her.

Maria: *I just can't go on, I'm fed up, I've had enough!*
Crystal: (Bursts into tears and hides her face in the cushion)
Therapist: *What is going on for you Crystal?*
Crystal: *I just feel like a boarder.* (i.e. I don't feel part of the family)

I asked how long this has been going on. Crystal said that she felt rejected when her mother came out of hospital. I attempted an interpretation about Crystal's fear of losing her mother. Maria continued in an accusing and denigrating way talking about the disgusting condition of Crystal's room. Crystal continued to sob. I suggested it must be hard for Maria to deal with Crystal's apparent lack of care when she had to do so much caring in her family. This was angrily denied by Maria. Frank commented that Crystal's 'neglect' of her mother felt like a 'stab in the back, an act of betrayal'. Maria settled after Frank's comment as this was closer to the mark, closer to the Oedipal nature of Maria's anxieties. Maria's anger may well have been a smokescreen for her fear that in her absence, Frank and Crystal would get together sexually, as indeed her mother had with Crystal's father. It was at this point that Crystal started her own therapy and my focus turned to the couple.

The work with the couple allowed them to consolidate their relationship and at least acknowledge some of the harsher reality of their earlier life, a shared experience of isolation and exclusion. Maria fell pregnant in the second year of therapy with the longed for child of her marriage to Frank, and with the birth of this son, named after Frank's father, the family dynamics were permanently changed. Crystal, helped by her own therapy, completed school and was able to move towards a greater emotional separation from her mother.

Ruth and David

The therapy occurred over an eighteen-month period. I first saw Ruth for six sessions and then the couple weekly. They were in their sixties and had been married for sixteen years.

Background

The way this couple came to see me is unusual. I first saw Ruth who came because she said that she was depressed and that there were issues in her marriage, particularly with her stepchildren. She complained that she felt excluded by her husband from matters that she felt concerned both of them. Over time, the feelings of exclusion focused on the fact that her mother-in-law had excluded her from her will.

In those early sessions Ruth also talked about the death of her father when she was in her early twenties. In one session where she talked, tearily, about her profound sense of loss; she said that she was 'very young' at the time. She has maintained this view, with an increasing understanding in the therapy that 'very young' referred to the strength of her attachment to her father, and also a sense that she was still, at that time, his 'princess'. I only learned recently that she married her first husband shortly after the death of her father. After some months of therapy when her attendance was sporadic and the focus was constantly on the relationship with her husband, I suggested that she come with her husband, David.

He agreed apparently with some enthusiasm, she I felt more reluctantly. I now think this was because she felt that she would be found at fault for the problems in their sixteen-year marriage. As the therapy progressed it became clear that it was the issue of the legacy from David's mother that had contributed to the current state of bitter conflict between the couple. The early months of therapy resembled operating in a war zone as illustrated below. They told me that their previously satisfying sexual relationship had ceased – Ruth was obviously angry and hurt while David was defensive and dismissive. At this point I felt that in the counter-transference I was experiencing their shared despair that anything could change in their marriage; the sense of 'stuckness' was overwhelming.

The following is one in a series of painfully conflicted and 'gridlocked' therapeutic encounters.

David: *But the money came from my mother, it's to go to my children and they're separate.* (To me) *I want to look after Ruth but that thing with my mother and the children and me is very separate, it's an entirely separate issue, it has nothing to do with Ruth.*

Therapist: *But that seems to be the problem, that in fact as Ruth has pointed out, it's not really separate and perhaps that's always been a problem in the marriage that the two of you have not been able to bring those things together to create a marriage where this legacy and your children are part of it.*

Ruth: *That's entirely right, when my daughter had her first child we'd thought about what to call David and we decided to call him papa David, initially we were going to call him papa doc, but we didn't think that was a good idea.*

Ruth: *But I'm just Ruth to his children, I'm just Ruth, I'm just another person, I'm just like one of the friends, I don't have any special kind of meaning in their lives or in their grandchildren's lives. You know when we travel overseas I make a beeline for the baby shops because I love buying the grandchildren things and I always buy for all the grandchildren, I buy equally because I think that's the right thing to do and it's not even the right thing to do it's what I want to do, but it's not like that on David's side of the family.*

David: *No, but my mother and the children and me we're separate, that's a separate thing.*

By this stage I had a headache: the same argument had been going on for weeks.

Therapist: *Look it seems to me that there is a major issue between the two of you. Ruth wants to be part of the family that includes your children and the legacy and you see it as separate. Everything that I've heard from you David to date suggests to me that you're not going to budge – that in your own mind the children and you – in terms of your mother's legacy – are separate and I think that's a major source of hurt for Ruth.*

Ruth: *That's quite right. . . .*

As the therapy progressed Ruth was able to say that she was completely without support for her strong feelings about the legacy; even her brother was not sympathetic. Everyone saw her as greedy and grasping. She was upset about this as she saw herself as a generous woman. She was puzzled herself about why this issue made her so angry and felt ashamed of how it made her look. But once the marital therapy started she came to see that the legacy represented a way in which she was excluded from the marriage. It was not really the money that she was angry about but the fact that in her husband's mind she was not in the least involved in his decision. It was a decision based on his difficulty in detaching from his family of origin. It became clear in the joint sessions that for David the legacy represented a link between himself and his mother. He saw his children as part of this vital link to his family of origin, from which he had not separated.

Ruth's family

Ruth is the younger of two children. Her parents were refugees from war-torn Europe. Her older brother is a successful psychiatrist who has been married several times. Her father died when she was 21 and her mother then took over the business and supported the family. It was her father that Ruth remembered being there after school.

David's family

David is a successful lawyer. His father was murdered during the war protecting his co-workers from the SS. While David is small and dark his father was tall and blonde and has the status of a hero in the family. David sadly commented that the war and his father's heroism were mentioned by his mother every day of his life. David and his mother were alone together for two years hiding in Holland, frightened and without a protector. His mother remarried when he was 3 years old and David did not get on with his stepfather. So David suffered the double trauma of the loss of his father when he was a year old and his mother's remarriage two years later to a man who treated David in a harsh and rigid way.

David's first marriage ended with his first wife's affair. She left him after saying that he was a very inadequate lover – a complete surprise to David and a rejection that has left him deeply wounded. (I have made the point in the therapy that Ruth was able to bring her unhappiness into the marriage rather than just leaving the relationship or looking elsewhere.)

Transference and counter-transference

In the early warring sessions my frequent tension headaches reflected the stuckness of the couple and a projected sense of hopelessness about the situation ever changing. Over time I felt that the couple became quite attached. But there was also a sense of my importance being dismissed. I felt that Ruth was colluding with

David's omnipotence in denying the value of the therapy although I felt I had more of a working alliance with Ruth than I did with her husband. Interestingly, while in some cases this might evoke strong reactions – David could easily have expressed feelings about being left out or excluded – I experienced something different with David. He did not seem to notice this alliance when it happened and I came to think that the lack of jealousy resonated with the Oedipal triumph of his position as his mother's emotional partner. As such he was not threatened by a potential rival. I also noted the couple's difficulty in linking one session to another . . . they seemed never to remember what had happened in the previous week's session.

The therapy

This is an excerpt from a session after six months of therapy, when David is in touch for the first time with his grief about his lost father.

Therapist: *I'm thinking about both of you and this experience that you keep having of something coming between you, sometimes it's called J. (David's ex-wife), sometimes it's the legacy. But it feels like there's this longing to connect but at the same time something comes between you and I'm wondering David when you're really under stress, do you retreat into yourself?*

David: *Yes that's right I've done that all my life.*

Ruth: (Looking very surprised) *Do you think that's really true?*

David: *Yes I think it is true.*

Therapist: *Well I can only imagine the little boy in the room with his mother, his father dead and the sense of terror there all the time and his mother marrying your stepfather. . . . I think emotionally you were on your own for a very long time.*

David: (Looks teary) *It is true.*

Ruth: *Yes I think that is true for David, it was different for me, I always had my family there.*

Therapist: *Yes I think you did and I think in particular your father was there very much to look after you . . . and that is what you want David to do.*

After this session, the sense of the therapy as a battleground changed and the couple seemed more of a couple. This was apparent when they had to face a problem with David's son, an anxious and demanding man who wanted a large sum of money to buy another house and had shouted abuse at David in a public place. David acknowledged his difficulty in saying 'no' to his son, saying that he did not want to be a hard man like his stepfather. He commented that he wanted to be generous like his father who 'could never walk past a beggar in the street without giving him money'. As he said this his eyes filled with tears. 'Yes I'm like my father, my father was like that and that's what I wanted to be like, I wanted to be like my father.' This vignette also reveals David's idealised view of his father, a view not based in experience.

When they came to the next session, David tenderly kissed Ruth on the forehead as they sat down. They told me about how they had discussed together a strategy for dealing with David's son. Ruth had rung her stepson and talked to him and the matter had been resolved. David was very grateful to Ruth for this helpful intervention and it seemed as though his attitude towards her had changed. He said: 'I was very impressed how Ruth handled herself, I thought she handled the whole situation very well and my son apologised for the way he behaved.' They then went on to talk in an easy way about the legacy and how it would be distributed and how it was important to make it clear what his children could expect. There was a moment when David said he needed to talk to a lawyer and Ruth said 'Oh forget it . . .' in a way that excluded her from the consultation, imagining that the lawyer would only think in terms of David's needs. When I pointed this out to her she agreed to go with David to see the lawyer, a decision that resulted in a fair and reasonable discussion about the legacy with them acting as a united and parental couple.

Ruth reflected on the experience and said: 'I realised that if I was to really help the situation then I had to stand up for myself, and that's what I did and I realised that that's what I had to do in general but I have to confess . . . I'm not very comfortable with it.'

I suggested to her that in being a partner she did have to take an equal responsibility for the relationship, but that she had expected David to look after her like her father had. Ruth responded by saying: 'Yes I think that's right, I sort of kinda want him to do it for me but I realised that if I'm really going to be a partner to him then I have to stand up for myself in the partnership.'

Discussion and conclusion

In both families the obvious Oedipal struggle was to deal with a third. In the first family the problem was the integration of a teenage daughter into the family: the presence of a third threatened the safety of the twosome. In the second case the third was represented by a legacy, literally a will from the husband's biological mother, that effectively excluded his current wife and threatened the survival of the marriage. Both families were thus preoccupied with the seminal Oedipal issue of inclusion/exclusion.

In addition both families/couples experienced a failure of maternal containment at the beginning of their lives, exacerbated by major issues of loss and abandonment. This resulted in splitting and projection of a very primitive sort. In the first case, Crystal carried much of the bad feeling in the family, in the second, David's difficulty in letting go of the links to his family of origin caused a split between his wife and his children.

The early loss of the biological father in both cases contributed to a further split. For Maria, her father carried the split-off denigrated aspects of herself (lodged to some degree in Crystal). The phantasised danger in the parental intercourse was exacerbated by the incestuous relationship between Maria's mother and the father of her child and was resuscitated in Maria's anxiety at leaving Crystal at home with her stepfather when she went into hospital. The early loss of David's father, a hero, created him as an idealised figure and denied the psychological and sexual reality of his parents' marriage.

In addition Maria's obesity suggested a major difficulty at the somatic level, an obesity that had caused polycystic ovarian disease and stopped her conceiving. While Frank had his own problems, idealising a family life that had been made isolating and lonely because of his mother's reaction to the loss of her firstborn, he had better self-esteem. Once he had painfully acknowledged the psychological reality of his feeling of exclusion from his parents' relationship and his extended family, he appeared to feel less an intruder in his current family. The conception and birth of his son during the therapy changed the dynamics in the family and as biological father to his son, he no longer felt excluded. The family had some difficulty with symbolic thinking, and in linking one session to the next, but interestingly the therapy perhaps provided enough containment for Maria to conceive a child with Frank.

In the second couple, David's early Oedipal victory was compromised because the child can never be an adequate partner to the mother. As a result, this 'victory' left him with a lifelong sense of inadequacy and responsibility beyond his capacity. David manifested this sense of responsibility by feeling that he had to look after his children to an extraordinary extent. It may also explain why his ex-wife's attack on his sexual inadequacy cut so deep. In his own 'heroic' attempts to be the omnipotent father to his children he was denying his own vulnerability and the priority of the couple in his emotional and financial life. Ruth colluded with this by wanting him to be an indulgent father to her rather than a sexual/financial partner. Couple psychotherapy helped David to acknowledge the grief of the lost father and therefore his own vulnerability, previously located in his children. Ruth, less damaged, was able to relinquish her longing to have a partner who was an indulgent father and struggle to become a real partner in the marriage. She also helped David to see his own need for a real partner.

The work of therapy was in containment, not just in maintaining boundaries and the frame, but in giving each of them the experience of a third mind that could take in their anxieties and think about them. The therapist also challenged each of the relationship dyads by her presence as a third person in the consulting room. The couples thus had a different experience of inclusion and exclusion as I listened to each of them while holding the couple and the family in mind. In the first family, both Frank and Maria were denied this experience in their families of origin – Maria's mother because of her abandonment and neglect, Frank's mother because she lost her mind to grief over her dead son. In the second family, David's mother also failed to provide maternal containment, since grief-stricken and terrified, she recruited her baby son as a partner.

> A failure to internalize a recognizable oedipal triangle ... results in a failure to integrate observation and experience ... I suggest that it is a consequence of a prior failure of maternal containment.
>
> (Britton, 1989, p. 92)

In each of these couples/families, the more obvious Oedipal issue of a feeling of exclusion was exacerbated by earlier Oedipal difficulties. My work was to provide the 'maternal containment' that each parent had missed in their families of origin. In the first family, my containing mind facilitated the separation of the merged dyads, Frank/Maria, Maria/Crystal, sufficient for them to form a more real and realistic family, even one that could include a child. In the second family, the work of therapy allowed David an opportunity to separate from the traumatic attachment to his family of origin and experience the value of a real partnership with his wife Ruth. David's wife Ruth in turn relinquished an idealised view of her father and accepted with difficulty the reality of a partner with whom she had to make her needs known.

The importance of an exploration of early Oedipal difficulties is vital in understanding the complexity of more overtly Oedipal issues, like exclusion, particularly when the couple or family seems stuck in a destructive way. An exploration of these earlier Oedipal issues, particularly the absence/loss of a father (and therefore the lack of an internal parental couple), the anxieties and defences against this loss, was an essential part of both these therapies and led to better psychological functioning in both cases.

Note

1 This article was first published in slightly different form in *Couple and Family Psychoanalysis*, Vol. 2 No. 2 in 2012, pp.198–214. It is republished here by kind permission of the editor Molly Ludlam and the publisher, Karnac.

References

Berg, J. and Jools, P. (2004). Holding on and letting go: developmental anxieties in couples after the birth of a child. *International Journal of Applied Analytic Studies*, *1(3)*, 224–233.

Berg, J. and Jools, P. (2006). Holding on and letting go: from family to couple therapy. In J.S. Scharff and D.E. Scharff (2007). *New Paradigms for Treating Relationships*. Lanham, MD: Jason Aronson.

Britton, R. (1989). The missing link: parental sexuality in the Oedipus complex. In J. Steiner (Ed.) *The Oedipus Complex Today: Clinical Implications*. London: Karnac Books.

Fisher, J.V. (1993). The impenetrable other: ambivalence and the Oedipal conflict in work with couples. In S. Ruszczynski (Ed.) *Psychotherapy with Couples*. London: Karnac Books.

Grier, F. (2005). *Oedipus and the Couple*. London: Tavistock Publications.

Klein, M. (1945). The Oedipus complex in the light of early anxieties [Reprinted in Klein, M. *Love, Guilt and Reparation*. London: The Hogarth Press, 1967].

Segal, H. (1989). Introduction. In J. Steiner (Ed.) *The Oedipus Complex Today: Clinical Implications*. London: Karnac Books.

Attachment Theory and affective learning groups: applications of our model

Introduction to Part III

Penny Jools

Any book that presents a model of working with couples and families is incomplete without some discussion of Attachment Theory. In Chapter 10 Noela Byrne looks at couple psychotherapy through the lens of Attachment Theory. Her case study demonstrates the value and shortcomings of an attachment perspective in understanding the complex dynamics of the couple she worked with.

The final chapter in this section incorporates the hypothetical work of an affective learning group in reacting to and reflecting on a conference that incorporates many of the ideas in the book. As an organisation we have used Affective Learning Groups in our workshops and conferences that extend over more than one day. We are committed to the value of these group experiences in deepening the understanding of projective processes in the group as they experience the impact of the emotional and intellectual challenges of the conference.

Finally, the conclusion presents the unfinished issues that remain in the minds of the editor, issues that need further thought and exploration in the context of the contribution that this volume makes to the international discourse on couple and family psychoanalysis.

Chapter 10

Couple psychotherapy through the lens of Attachment Theory[1]

Noela Byrne

What is attachment?

John Bowlby has become known as the architect of Attachment Theory. His interest in attachment was sparked by his studies of delinquent and institutionalised children and the effect on them of maternal deprivation. He noted that: 'the propensity to make strong emotional bonds to particular individuals [is] a basic component of human nature' (Bowlby, 1988, p. 3) and he described attachment as a 'lasting psychological connectedness between human beings' (Bowlby, 1969, p. 194). Bowlby's assertion seems to fit with Object Relations Theory introduced by Fairbairn (1952) who, in a radical departure from Freudian Instinct Theory, hypothesised that the infant is relationship-seeking from birth, and that early experiences in childhood are not only formative for the development of psychic structure but also underpin personality formation and behaviour later in life. These ideas have been discussed in detail in Chapter 1 in this volume.

Bowlby argued that security and attachment are prime motivators in humans and he saw secure attachment as an important precursor to stable adult relationships. Bowlby's ideas were subsequently vindicated by substantial empirical data showing that unsatisfactory attachment patterns can lead to interpersonal maladjustment and destructive behaviour in oneself which can be replicated in family relationships in the next generation (Cowan and Cowan, 2001).

Attachment Theory, however, does not place emphasis on the unconscious or unconscious phantasy as does Object Relations Theory. This is an important distinction as object relations theorists believe that change results from a modification of the internal objects that can only be accessed through psychic phantasy via transference and counter-transference. In addition, Bowlby's Attachment Theory does not take into account constitutional differences in infants and the way these might influence the experience of the relationship with the primary caregiver. In addition, it does not readily suggest therapeutic interventions and how internal change might be achieved. Nevertheless, Attachment Theory is helpful because it provides an empirical way of describing the styles of relating that individuals and couples employ.

Ainsworth and empirically-derived attachment styles in children

Mary Ainsworth was influenced by Bowlby's reformulation of Attachment Theory to the extent that in 1963 she embarked on an observational project, the thoroughness of which no researcher has since equalled: the now famous *Strange Situation Test* (SST). This now familiar scenario involves a mother and her infant exposed to the presence of a stranger while the mother leaves the room and returns (in various combinations). Ainsworth concluded that the key to the reaction of the infant was the sense the infant makes of the mother's sudden departure based on the infant's existing anxieties. This therefore raised the question, 'How does the infant respond when the security with the attachment figure is perceived as threatened?'

As an end result of these studies, Ainsworth described children as being secure, avoidant or ambivalent in their attachment style (Ainsworth *et al.*, 1978). Later research carried out by her students identified a 'disorganised' category of attachment style (Main and Hesse, 1990). What do these categories mean in terms of the infant's behaviour?

Secure attachment

Securely attached children seem to trust that the missing parent will return. When frightened, they seek comfort from their caregivers and are confident that their parent will provide reassurance.

Ambivalent attachment

Children who have an ambivalent attachment status tend to be suspicious of strangers, display considerable distress when separated from a parent or caregiver but do not seem reassured or comforted by their return. They may passively reject their parent or caregiver and refuse comfort from them. In addition, they may be openly aggressive. As these children develop they may remain clingy and over-dependent.

Avoidant attachment

Children with an avoidant attachment style appear to avoid parents and caregivers especially after a period of absence. They do not seek out comfort or contact and often show no preference between a parent and a complete stranger.

Disorganised attachment

Children with a disorganised-insecure attachment style manifest a mixture of responses to caregivers, including avoidance or resistance. These children are described as appearing to be either confused or apprehensive in the presence of the caregiver.

This classification system for describing children's observed behaviour moved Attachment Theory out of the domain of psychoanalysis and led to further research into child development. Ainsworth's work also opened the way for more consideration of internal representations of mother and infant and how these might interact. It is now widely accepted that the parent's capacity to provide a secure base from which the growing child can explore and develop will influence the child's confidence in the availability of the caregiver.

Later research explored the categories described by Ainsworth as it might be applied to adult attachment, as follows.

Empirically-derived attachment styles in adults

These empirically-based categories were based on Ainsworth's Adult Attachment Interview (AAI) methodology that used the verbatim text of interviews where a subject had been asked to give adjectives to describe their experiences of their primary caregivers.

As distinct from Ainsworth's childhood attachment categories which are primarily a description of patterns of behaviour, and reflect the asymmetrical nature of parent–child relationships, her adult attachment descriptions appear to take into account the reciprocal nature of attachment of the adult relationship (Ainsworth, 1982; Hesse, 1999).

Secure attachment

Securely attached adults experience their intimate relationships as mutually warm and responsive, and have positive views of themselves and their partners. They feel comfortable with both intimacy and independence and are able to balance these in their relationships.

Anxious-preoccupied attachment

These adults focus on seeking approval, intimacy and responsiveness from their partners. This focus on intimacy can lead to them being seen as 'clingy'. They tend to have less positive views about themselves and doubt their worth as a partner. They are also inclined to see others as unreliable or untrustworthy. In addition, high levels of emotional expressiveness, worry and impulsiveness are observed in their relationships.

Dismissive-avoidant attachment

Adults with this category of attachment often appear to be overly independent and appear to desire independence seemingly as an attempt to avoid attachment altogether. They perceive themselves as self-sufficient and invulnerable to feelings associated with being closely attached to others. Thus, they frequently deny the need for close relationships, and may even view close relationships as relatively unimportant.

Fearful-avoidant attachment

These adults are ambivalent about relationships. They wish to have emotionally close relationships but feel uncomfortable when emotional closeness occurs. This is linked to their negative views about themselves and their partners. They often mistrust the intentions of their partners and anticipate rejection. At the same time they can feel unworthy of responsiveness from their partners (Bartholomew and Horowitz, 1991)

Wanda and Heath

With this theoretical background in mind, let us meet the couple whose interactions in their relationship we will be thinking about in attachment terms. First, what do we know about their history?

Wanda is the younger of two children. Her older sister suffered from a childhood illness, which meant that Wanda's mother was preoccupied with her and overly protective of her. This was not the case with Wanda who was encouraged to be independent. Wanda was closer to her father, but at times he was unpredictable and would lash out at Wanda in a rage. He died when Wanda was 12 years old and it was not until many years later that she realised how attached she had been to him and how much she missed him when he died.

Heath was an only child, whose father was absent for the first five years of his life, fighting in the Second World War. Throughout his childhood, his mother would regularly erupt in a rage, criticising him and threatening to abandon him. Similarly when his father returned, he was frequently violent towards Heath and his mother. On some occasions after a fight between his parents, Heath's father would either retreat to the pub or would escape with Heath to the movie theatre.

The couple was referred by Wanda's individual psychotherapist who had seen her for sometime because of bouts of depression and several suicide attempts. The couple had been married for twenty years, but had not had a sexual relationship for the past seven years. Heath had a drinking problem and would spend many hours at the pub with his friends. Wanda complained about his absences but when he returned she would attack him for his drinking. Consequently, they were unable to achieve any real closeness.

How then can we think about these two troubled individuals in their struggle to relate to each other?

Assessment session with Wanda and Heath: identifying the characteristics of adult attachment style

Wanda and Heath were full of complaints about each other.

Heath: *Wanda is always angry with me. And if she's not angry, she's depressed and spends the weekend in bed.*

Wanda: *Whenever I get angry you pathologise me. You make me feel as if I am mad. You become so defensive that I feel I can't say anything. Everything has to be done your way.*

Heath: *I don't know what you mean by that. We don't do anything together at the weekend because you are in bed. When you get depressed I am terrified you will try to kill yourself again. I just feel overwhelmed with anxiety.*

Wanda: *How do you think I feel when you disappear to the pub? You leave me to do most of the housework and that's not fair when I work full time and you don't. You spend all the money I earn at the pub or on your movie collection. It's not fair!*

Heath: *I do a lot for you. I drive you to work every day and I am looking for part-time work. You don't appreciate what I do for you!*

So far in discussing the history of attachment and its relationship to work with couples, we have focused on the individual. This vignette with Wanda and Heath clearly illustrates the *interactive* nature of attachment styles.

In this segment of session material, Wanda's dismissive style is demonstrated in her compulsive self-reliance (belief that she was the sole provider for the couple) and withdrawal from Heath. In addition it reveals a more 'thick-skinned' narcissistic style as described by Rosenfeld (1988). Wanda uses projective identification to place the unwanted parts of herself, the need to be cared for, in Heath. She then denigrates and devalues this part of herself that she has located in him.

For Heath, the material suggests something about his preoccupied/fearful attachment style. He does not contest her emotional withdrawal but retreats (into alcohol and DVDs as self-soothing behaviours). Thoughts of his own unworthiness lead him to fear closeness because he expects rejection. Thus, Heath appears to display a more 'thin-skinned' narcissistic style (Rosenfeld, 1988) in which his dependency needs leave him feeling vulnerable, because he fears rejection. He attempts to avoid these feelings by either angrily complaining to Wanda about her unavailability or alternatively by withdrawing to protect himself.

Together they demonstrate functioning typical of narcissistic coupling, which highlights the projection ('projective gridlock' (Morgan, 1995)) of unwanted dependency needs and insecurity into each other. Clinicians have noted how confusing it can be when they are confronted with the interchangeability in these patterns of relating in a couple and observe that this can render the relationship unstable (Bateman, 1996; Fisher, 1995).

Attachment and couples: an interpersonal perspective

The Tavistock Marital Studies Institute (TMSI) later known as Tavistock Relationships has developed a methodology to begin to explore the nature of couples' attachment. This research focuses on the bi-directional system whereby each partner depends on or is depended on by the other partner. This is referred to as 'complex attachment' because it involves two sets of mental representations of childhood attachment that are influential in the couple relationship.

The following putative categories of couple attachment have been suggested (Fisher and Crandell, 2001).

Secure attachment

The individual who is securely attached will enjoy the freedom to move between the dependent and depended-on positions in an intimate relationship. In securely attached couples there is a capacity to perceive the other as a separate feeling person and each is free to express the need for comfort and contact, as well as being open to receive that contact.

Insecure couple attachment

In contrast to secure attachment, insecurity in couple attachment manifests in a marked lack of flexibility, and mutuality with each of the partners stuck in one position, with little movement between them. There is also little recognition of the other's experience. More specific insecure dyad descriptions have been proposed as follows.

Dismissing/dismissing couple attachment

In this instance there is a pseudo-independence based on a denial of dependence. Any expression of neediness is perceived as threatening. Both partners collude to deny their dependency needs, and they may function well until there is a crisis brought about by such occurrences as the birth of a child, illness or unemployment.

Preoccupied/preoccupied couple attachment

With such a dyad individuals may have been involved in a role reversal with their caregiver or have been given inconsistent care.

In the couple relationship there is a deep-seated sense of deprivation. Each will demand emotional contact but is often angry because it will always be experienced as inadequate or unsatisfying. With these couples there is a high level of disagreement. Each partner competes for the dependent position while simultaneously resisting it.

Dismissing/preoccupied couple attachment

This attachment dyad configuration is a common pattern in couples presenting for help. There is a highly conflictual pattern with the preoccupied partner expressing most of the discontent and the dismissing partner asserting that the only problem in the relationship is the other's discontent. The preoccupied partner feels chronically deprived while the dismissing partner expresses disdain towards the other's expression of dependency needs.

Secure/insecure couple attachment

It is possible that through pairing with a secure partner, the insecure partner is able to engage in a more flexible, balanced way. However, the balance might go in the opposite direction and the secure partner could become less flexible.

Wanda and Heath are a couple who display features of a *dismissive/preoccupied* or *fearful* couple attachment. In such coupling there is self-reliance in the dismissive partner because intimacy is not valued and in response, the 'fearful' partner retreats because of fears of unworthiness and expectation of inevitable rejection.

A vignette from the work with Heath and Wanda demonstrates this. Heath and Wanda began arguing about how much housework each does. As this progressed, Heath became more and more enraged. Nevertheless, there was a repetitive feel about it, as though they had embarked on a well-worn path.

Heath stood up and said: 'I'm not going to stay and listen to this. I'm going!'

He stormed out. The following week, Heath reported that Wanda had taken an overdose that night.
The therapist said, 'Is this what happens when Wanda isn't heard?'
Heath turned on the therapist in a rage, saying 'I'm not taking the blame for her overdose!'

It seems that at the point when Heath stormed out, Wanda was put in touch with her vulnerability and her need of Heath. This she found both shameful and intolerable.

When she took the overdose, she was not only attempting to omnipotently control these feelings, but also, through projective identification, was forcing Heath to feel something that she could not feel: her vulnerability. Thus, he was overwhelmed by his need of her and his terror of losing her.

Here we see how the problematic pairings are perpetuated via a projective gridlock (Morgan, 1995) and how each contributes to the insecurity of the other.

Marrying attachment and objects relations theory

As distinct from childhood attachment which is primarily a description of patterns of behaviour, adult attachment appears to be based on a mental representation of childhood attachment that is re-enacted in subsequent relationships. This is similar to the Object Relations concept in that an internal representation becomes the means of seeing oneself and others and therefore can be predictive of certain behaviours in adult relationships.

Like many marriages, the relationship between Attachment Theory and object relations theory is not necessarily an easy one. Historically, psycho-analysts were unwilling to embrace Bowlby's approach that focused more on observation of behaviour rather than on internal processes of representation. This is a valid distinction because often in our clinical experience we meet a parent or parents who are loving and caring parents, but their secure attachment to the infant was compromised by external events such as illness, either in the infant or in the caregiver. Despite loving behaviour on the part of parents, the child has internalised a negative representation of the relationship. In addition, distortions may arise from the child's internal state (fantasies, or cognitions), leading to an inaccurate internal representation of the parental figure. However, there is general agreement between attachment and object relations theorists about what is necessary for the infant's optimal development: the development of good internal object relationships.

There is also broad agreement about the important role of the therapist in providing the patient with a secure base from which to explore and rework internal or representational models of self, others and relationships.

In Chapter 2 a hierarchy of developmental anxieties was described. Here we might consider some specific points where links can be made between this aspect of Object Relations, or Psychoanalytic Theory, and Attachment Theory.

1   In a state dominated by autistic-contiguous anxieties, primitive anxieties such as dissolving and spilling out could be thought of as underlying disorganised attachment.
2   Paranoid-schizoid defences against anxiety such as splitting and projective identification are perhaps more characteristic of insecure attachment styles.

Contempt and/or denial of vulnerability and idealisation of stoic self-sufficiency could be seen as the child's attempt to incorporate (that is, introject) the experience of a mother who is so preoccupied with her own distress that she cannot accurately mirror the child's experience.

These defences of contempt and denial of dependency and idealisation may be used as a defence against depressive anxieties in couples and are characteristic of a dismissive attachment style. This leaves the couple in a regressed state where they are functioning in a continual state of war.

Thus, with the couple we have discussed, Wanda shows contempt for Heath's need of her and Heath denies any awareness of the anger his withdrawal to the pub elicits in Wanda. He is thus repeating the pattern of his father's avoidance of coping with his mother's needs.

3   As discussed in Chapter 1, Fairbairn (1952) describes the splitting that occurs when the infant experiences frustrating and unsatisfying interactions with the mother or caregiver. These exciting and rejecting objects are split off and repressed. This splitting is sometimes seen in the couples who present for therapy, with one carrying one aspect, and the other the opposite. This is the case with Wanda and Heath. Wanda has internalised a rejecting object and demonstrates a dismissive attachment style. Heath has internalised an object exciting of anxiety which leaves him with a fearful or preoccupied attachment style.

4   In contrast to the Paranoid-Schizoid Position, the depressive position shares characteristics with attachment security, where the mother is able to respond appropriately to assist the child in processing his experience. In this mode of functioning (which entails the resolution of Oedipal anxieties), the other is perceived as a separate thinking and feeling person. This recognition of the other's reflective capacity and an ability to coherently describe the actions of oneself or one's caregiver in mental state terms is crucial to a secure attachment.

Attachment and Oedipal anxieties

Oedipal anxieties, which are discussed in Chapter 9, have particular relevance for work with a couple, and address a dimension of the internal world of the couple that attachment theories do not address. As outlined in that chapter, the child in the couple relationship needs to be able to tolerate the exclusion that the couple's intimate and sexual relationship demands. If the child is able to tolerate this, then as an adult he is able to move from a two-person pre-Oedipal constellation to a three-person Oedipal constellation. In Britton's terms (1989, p. 87) he is 'able to be both an observer and a participant' in the couple relationship. The importance of this in the capacity to form a couple relationship of one's own cannot be overestimated. These ideas about Oedipal resolution introduce the importance of the father and the couple itself into the complex world of attachment. The focus is no longer exclusively on the mother–child relationship. The relevance of this resolution to the capacity to be a couple is of contemporary interest (Britton, 1998; Clulow, 2001). In attachment terms resolving Oedipal issues is the pathway to secure couple attachment, the ultimate marker of working through developmental anxieties.

Sexuality and attachment

Many of the couples that are seen for couple psychotherapy present with sexual difficulties. Often this means that the couple no longer have a sexual relationship with each other. This is puzzling because many of these couples seem genuinely attached and want to stay together. In the case of Wanda and Heath, there had been no sexual relationship for many years and each blamed the other for its absence. In working with them, it soon became apparent that there was a collusive element operating, in that each projected their abandoning, rejecting internal object into the other, thereby repeating their childhood experience.

Psychoanalytic ideas about sexuality focus more on the internal representation of the relationship rather than the external expression of sexual behaviour, in particular the capacity to integrate love and hate. Kernberg (1995) notes that securely attached individuals are able to merge with the other in a sexual union without a fear of annihilation of self. With secure couples there is an integration of ambivalent feeling and confidence that the level of aggression (which can add to the pleasurable experience of sex) can be managed, that it is contained by love. In couples where each is insecurely attached, intimacy or autonomy might be compromised as each struggles to find a secure base.

In addition, in an earlier chapter of this volume, the importance is highlighted of early experiences of touch and sensory experience in establishing the context for satisfactory sexual relationships. We do not know what the early experiences of Wanda and Heath were. However, it is likely that Wanda was not held or touched enough by her parents. For Heath, particularly in his first five years when his mother was a single parent, he may have experienced her as inconsistent, being alternatively smothering and rejecting.

The following is a vignette from a session late in the work with Wanda and Heath.

In the course of entertaining friends, Heath had drunk too much. In the morning, he was angry with himself. For the first time the couple are displaying an ability to view the relationship as an entity in itself, that is, as a third.

Heath: *I just have to cut down on my drinking, for my health, for my weight . . .*
Wanda: *For our relationship.*

(Heath ignored the comment.)

Therapist: *Did you hear what Wanda said? She wants to know that she is an important reason for you to cut down your drinking.*
Heath: *Yes, of course that is an important reason.*
Wanda: *I told him the other night that I love him and I want to be with him, that he is a great companion and my best friend.*
Therapist: *And what about you, Heath, can you tell Wanda what she means to you?*
Heath: *Yes, I sometimes say it, especially in bed, I say I love you.*

The work with Wanda and Heath gradually brought them to a place where their need to dominate and exclude their feelings of need were replaced by compassion for this aspect of themselves. Wanda moved to a more secure attachment style, while Heath did not move as far as Wanda but he did move to a more preoccupied attachment style.

Implications for treatment

What can be understood from the observation of this couple, Wanda and Heath, and the progress their relationship made in therapy?

The work with this couple demonstrates the usefulness of Attachment Theory in understanding some of the destructive patterns the couple had developed over the twenty years of their relationship These patterns, reflecting a shared sense of insecurity, functioned to destroy intimacy and prevent their growth both as individuals and as a couple.

In terms of the application of Attachment Theory for treatment, one of the central implications is that a secure base/container provided by a consistent, reliable and non-judgemental therapist can also serve as a potential new template for an internal working model or an internalised couple. Initially, both Wanda and Heath were so ambivalent about couple therapy that they cancelled several early appointments. Later, as they became more firmly engaged, the therapist's even-handed and non-judgemental attitude to both of them enabled them to begin to perceive themselves and each other in a more positive light.

Conclusions

A couple psychotherapist may find it useful to consider the attachment styles of each member of the couple and how these may be influencing the couple's functioning. Potentially, each partner can serve as a secure base for the other, so that through therapy, as the relationship becomes more stable and more of a priority for each of them, a secure base can be established. Ultimately each partner is provided with a greater security than each is able to establish on their own.

The work with Wanda and Heath saw a shift in the attachment styles of each of them. Heath's addiction to alcohol remained a problem for the couple. In spite of their efforts to nurture their relationship as a 'third' from which they could both derive security and comfort, Heath's drinking remained as a malignant 'third' in the relationship. He had been referred for individual therapy but continued to struggle with his addiction, which could be seen as a destructive way of dealing with his own significant dependency needs.

Note

1 The case material used in this chapter was also used in a chapter published earlier in M. Ludlam and V. Nyberg (Eds.) *Couple Attachments: Theoretical and Clinical Studies*, London: Karnac in 2007, and is reprinted with kind permission of the editors and Karnac books.

An earlier version of this chapter was written in collaboration with Dr Timothy Keogh and presented as part of the CCAFPAA lecture series.

References

Ainsworth, M.D., Blehar, M.C., Waters, E. and Wall., S. (1978). *Patterns of Attachment: A Psychological Study of a Strange Situation*. Hillsdale, NJ: Erlbaum.

Ainsworth, M.D. (1982). Attachment: Retrospect and prospect. In C.M. Parkes and J. Stevenson-Hinde (Eds.) *The Place of Attachment in Human Behaviour*. New York: Basic Books.

Bartholomew, K. and Horowitz, L. (1991). Attachment styles among young adults: A test of a four category model, *Journal of Personality and Social Psychology, 61,* 226–244.

Bateman, A. (1996). The concept of enactment and 'thick skinned' and 'thin skinned' narcissism. Paper presented at the European Conference of English-speaking Psychoanalysts. London.

Bowlby, J. (1969). *Attachment and Loss,* (Vol. 1). New York: Basic Books.

Bowlby, J. (1988). *A Secure Base.* New York: Basic Books.

Britton, R. (1989). The missing link: parental sexuality in the Oedipus complex. In J. Steiner (Ed.) *The Oedipus Complex Today.* London: Karnac.

Britton, R. (1998). *Belief and Imagination: Explorations in Psychoanalysis.* London: Routledge.

Clulow, C. (2001). Attachment theory and the therapeutic frame. In C. Clulow (Ed.) *Adult Attachment and Couple Psychotherapy.* New York: Brunner-Routledge.

Cowan, P. and Cowan, C. (2001). A couple perspective on the transmission of attachment patterns. In C. Clulow (Ed.) *Adult Attachment and Couple Psychotherapy.* New York: Brunner-Routledge.

Fairbairn, R. (1952). *Psychoanalytic Studies of the Personality.* London: Hogarth.

Fisher, J. (1995). Identity and intimacy in the couple: three kinds of identification. In S. Ruszczynski and J. Fisher (Eds.) *Intrusiveness and Intimacy in the Couple.* London: Karnac.

Fisher, J. and Crandell, L. (2001). Patterns of relating in the couple. In C. Clulow (Ed.) *Adult Attachment and Couple Psychotherapy.* New York: Brunner-Routledge.

Hesse, E. (1999). The adult attachment interview: historical and current perspectives. In J. Cassidy and P. Shaver (Eds.) *Handbook of Attachment.* New York: The Guildford Press.

Kernberg, O. (1995). *Love Relations.* New Haven, CT: Yale University Press.

Main, M. and Hesse, E. (1990). Parents' unresolved traumatic experiences are related to infant disorganised attachment status: Is frightened and/or frightening parental behaviour the linking mechanism? In M.T. Greenberg, D. Cicchetti and E.M. Cummings (Eds.) *Attachment in the Preschool Years* (pp. 161–182). Chicago: University of Chicago Press.

Morgan, M. (1995). The projective gridlock: A form of projective identification in couple relationships. In S. Ruszczynski and J. Fisher (Eds.) *Intrusiveness and Intimacy in the Couple.* London: Karnac.

Rosenfeld, H. (1988). Contribution to the psychopathology of psychotic states: The importance of projective identification in the ego structure and object relations of psychotic patients. In E. Spillius (Ed.) *Melanie Klein Today.* London: Routledge [First published in 1971].

Chapter 11

Learning from experience

The use of affective learning groups

Laurie Lovell-Simons and Penny Jools

We begin our chapter with a hypothetical scenario: We are in the final meeting of an affective learning group held during a psychotherapy conference titled 'Loss and Trauma within the Family'.[1] One of the participants, 'Bruce', has not arrived; nor has he let anyone know he will be absent. His absence could be ignored, reacted to without reflection, or could be used in the service of learning about group process, as illustrated in this chapter. Given the topic of the conference, the significance of his absence (a not infrequent occurrence in small group work) will not be lost on anyone with a background in psychoanalytically-based psychotherapy.

So how then can we make use of Bruce's absence? We suggest that it has a conscious and unconscious impact on everyone in the group, including the group leaders. This impact can be understood as an extension of the idea of the use of the self in psychoanalytically-based therapy. Just as the therapist is able to use the complex transferences and counter-transferences in each individual and the couple to better understand the couple or family dynamics, the '*family within*', these same processes can be understood and examined in the group.

So this chapter is about what happens to a hypothetical affective learning group in the context of a conference on Loss and Trauma within the Family. Our major focus is on how the individuals, and the group as a whole, express aspects of the clinical and theoretical material presented during the conference through projective processes: transference, counter-transference, splitting and projective identification. The capacity of the leaders to hold and contain anxieties about being in a group of comparative strangers, and exposed to confronting and distressing clinical material is also examined. Bion's (1961) ideas on work group and basic assumption mentalities can be illustrated in some of the small group interactions.

Finally, a group has its own life and will be seen to evolve through different phases of development. These phases have characteristic anxieties, defences, ways of thinking, and themes – latent and overt. This idea of developmental change is, of course, one of the major theoretical themes of working with couples and families explored in this book.

Small groups in clinical practice

Small groups have long been used for reflection in clinical practice and training (Gosling *et al.*, 1967). While these groups have often been conducted in an idiosyncratic manner, dependent on the leader's personal style, some group models have been developed. These models have their own traditions and organisations dedicated to using and promoting them: examples are Balint Groups (Balint, 1957) and Affective Learning Groups (Scharff and Scharff, 2000). The Scharffs make the case for the value of 'affective learning groups' in their training of couple and family psychotherapists, based in part on Bion's thinking about groups; we use a similar model in this chapter.

Bion's contribution to affective learning groups

Bion pioneered many developments in his work with groups, and analysed their functioning in terms of 'work group mentality' and 'basic assumption mentality' (Bion, 1961).

Briefly, 'work group mentality' describes a group that 'tries to look at itself and the group process scientifically, to observe itself, and to contain and speak about feelings rather than discharge them' (Symington and Symington, 1996, p. 126).

Bion noted that when primitive feelings, and their accompanying defences, are aroused in the group, work group functioning was compromised by what he came to call 'basic assumption mentality'. This expresses itself in three mutually exclusive patterns or cultures: dependency on a leader, fight against or flight from some perceived threat to the group, and pairing between two group members, where the rest of the group become onlookers. A group may switch between these cultures many times within the one group meeting, or remain stuck in one for a long time.

The use of affective learning groups in our organisation

Our organisation, CCAFPAA (Couple Child and Family Psychotherapy Association of Australasia) first began using affective learning groups in 2006. Dr Stan Tsigounis, an American group analyst, who was our invited guest speaker and group facilitator at a conference we called 'Family As Group', deepened our understanding of the role that affective learning groups could play for psychoanalytic psychotherapists working with couples and families. He also emphasised the value of someone holding a thinking space for the group leaders, parallel to the leaders holding the participants in the groups.

CCAFPAA now incorporates affective learning groups into conferences or workshops that run over at least two days. Our experience suggests that when the groups are well led and the whole experience is contained, they can greatly enhance the participants' learning process at both intellectual and emotional levels. It is this deep appreciation of their value, in particular for the felt experience of projective processes in the group, that has led to the writing of this chapter.

What is an affective learning group?

Affective learning groups are premised on the following:

- That all learning involves the integration of cognitive and affective aspects of experience.
- That all learning takes place in an affective matrix: we are incapable of feeling nothing about the material we are learning and of feeling nothing about ourselves while we are learning.
- That unconscious processes are activated in everyone in a small group and the emergence and understanding of these processes can be engaged to deepen learning.

What happens in an affective learning group?

Participants are invited to explore their reactions, thoughts, feelings and fantasies to the conference material.

There are designated leaders who understand group processes as well as having a good grasp of the theoretical material that is the subject of the conference or training. The leaders' task is to promote a space for reflection, thought and integration of the conference themes. They help contain anxieties that might interfere with this process, providing emotional 'safety' by establishing and maintaining an appropriate small group frame. While not a therapy group, participants may reveal personal information, which should be treated respectfully.

Our hypothetical two-day conference: 'Loss and Trauma within the Family'

The content of the three conference presentations have been summarised. Our focus is on the descriptions of some key moments of the subsequent, ninety-minute meetings of one of the affective learning groups. We have chosen interactions that we hope will illustrate how the affective learning group can channel and deepen the understanding and integration of the theoretical and clinical material, but also have a life of its own.

Lecture 1: Case Study: 'Annabelle and Barry'
Laurie Lovell-Simons

Background

LL-S was the couple's third therapist in two years. The first therapist they 'sacked' as they did not feel he understood them. The second therapist had stopped seeing them prior to the birth of her own baby and going on extended leave.

Barry and Annabelle, both in their early sixties, have been married for thirty years, and live with their single 29-year-old daughter, Margaret.

Barry has a sister two years younger. He suffered from severe asthma and was obese as a child. He felt he was the 'black sheep' in the family. In late adolescence, Barry was driving his father's car home from university one evening when he accidentally killed a cyclist who swerved in front of him without warning. Barry's family blamed him for the cyclist's death, even though it was not his fault. After the accident, which seemed to unleash an internalised sense of 'not being good enough', he never fulfilled his previously promising potential. His working life has been characterised by disorganisation and procrastination that have escalated as he has moved towards retirement.

Annabelle is also the elder of two, with a brother three years younger. Her family were 'strugglers'; her brother was encouraged academically, she was not. When she misbehaved as a young child, she recalls her mother threatening to send her to an orphanage. Later as a teenager, when her parents discovered she had been to a church dance with a boy without their permission, her father shaved off all her hair. After this event both her parents became more punitive and controlling of Annabelle and she left home as soon as she could leave school. She has never developed a career, though in recent years has developed some creative pursuits which have brought in minimal income.

Relationship history

Annabelle and Barry's relationship began as a highly sexualised whirlwind romance that led to marriage within months of their meeting. Their daughter, Margaret, was conceived soon after their marriage, and her arrival had a catastrophic impact on their relationship. Annabelle developed serious postnatal depression and is still on medication three decades later. At the height of her depression, Barry suggested they could adopt out their daughter. Annabelle has never forgiven Barry for this.

Barry's disorganisation intensified after Margaret's birth and he was physically violent towards Annabelle on several occasions. He sought help, and has not been physically violent since. However, their relationship has continued to be conflictual and unsatisfying. Mutual affection is limited, their sexual relationship sporadic and almost always sought by Annabelle and reluctantly engaged in by Barry. She blames Barry for the state of their relationship, and feels desperately unloved and unnoticed. Barry feels put upon by Annabelle, constantly anxious about his capacity to earn as a consultant, and worried about their financial future as he nears retirement.

Annabelle initiated the referral for couple psychotherapy. The therapist sensed that for Annabelle coming to therapy was a make or break endeavour for the relationship. She doubted Barry would ever leave.

During sessions Annabelle often interrupts Barry. The therapist frequently felt like she had two needy babies in the room; Annabelle desperate for her attention, Barry secretly longing for it but unable to directly let her know.

Summary of a session after five months
of weekly psychotherapy

The couple had missed the previous session. Annabelle looked haggard and some-what dishevelled, Barry was tense. Annabelle insisted that Barry start, but without much apparent interest in what he said. Barry talked about the up and down nature of the relationship, Annabelle's depression and how he feels responsible. He described a conflict from the weekend. A green waste collection was due in a few days and Barry had agreed to prune a large shrub for the collection. He gave up on the job before it was finished, stating it was far too hot to work outside. Annabelle was upset, they had a fight and she became depressed and withdrew.

The therapist commented on Barry's feeling of responsibility and wondered whether he had felt this way with his mother, whom he had previously described as demanding and needy. Barry had not thought of his mother this way before, but it brought to mind how often he had been left at home from the age of 3, with his 1-year-old sister, while his mother taught next door at the school, where his father was the principal. On one of these occasions, he had smeared faeces all over the hall wall. In the discussion that followed Barry began to be able to acknowledge that he did feel abandoned by his parents, and this might have had something to do with why he smeared faeces.

While Barry talked, Annabelle sat on the edge of her seat, eager to speak. Much to Barry's and the therapist's astonishment, she revealed that she too had an experience of smearing faeces. In her case she manipulated her brother, the family's 'golden boy', into smearing his excrement on the wall so he would get into trouble. She also talked about the discomfort of her childhood eczema and how she had comforted herself for years with a dummy. Her teeth decayed at a very young age, involving considerable expense and inconvenience for her parents, who frequently reminded her of this. She expressed distress at her mother's failure to intervene when her father cut off her hair, at how her mother had joined in with her father over this. She wondered if her mother had been too afraid of her father to speak up.

In a poignant moment, Annabelle exclaimed 'My brother got the hugs, I got none'. The room was raw with the feelings of the three of us. After the therapist gathered herself, she was able to share some thoughts with them. She commented that over the months she had noticed how her attempts to reach out to Annabelle had often been responded to with a scratchy rejection, and she had felt discouraged. She had noticed how Barry had also often tried, but never could get things right. She had felt for Barry, but was reluctant to comment on his struggle as she felt Annabelle was hypersensitive to any attention she gave Barry, and might feel that Barry was the brother who got the hugs.

The therapist suggested that when Annabelle was a baby, hugs may have been painful when her skin was so raw with eczema, and that her emotional skin continued to feel raw and easily damaged, making it hard for her to feel 'touched' by Barry, but also by the therapist.

She spoke to their shared feelings of emotional abandonment as young children, and the hurt and angry feelings that resulted, expressed by smearing faeces. She could see how these dynamics of abandonment were alive in their relationship, but expressed in different ways: Barry withdraws and/or gets angry while Annabelle gets depressed.

After the therapist had spoken, Annabelle revisited the incident with the green waste, and said that she was coming into the garage to tell Barry that it was too hot to keep working. However, before she could say anything he had exploded at her, and she had felt traumatised. This experience reminded her of her father cutting her hair, and the threat of being sent to the orphanage.

At the end of the session they expressed a greater appreciation for how each had suffered as children, and empathy for how they felt abandoned by each other as adults. They expressed gratitude for the work we had done, and we all three shared some hope that something loving and useful could develop.

Our hypothetical affective learning group

The requirement for attendance is that participants are in clinical practice and have committed to attending the full conference, including all the affective learning groups. They have been asked ahead of time to check they have no boundary issues in the group to which they have been assigned and have been sent reading material about affective learning groups. Normally in a conference of this sort a plenary session for all the affective learning groups would be held at the end of the conference. Since the focus is on the trajectory of only one group, this potential final meeting has not been discussed.

We have created a brief thumbnail 'impression' of our hypothetical leaders and participants as follows:

Bronwyn – a senior couple and family therapist, and **Steven**, a newly trained couple therapist, have not worked together before as *co-leaders*.

April – experienced couple and family psychotherapist in her fifties, eager to fit in and looks up to Bronwyn.

Bruce – recently graduated clinical psychologist, in his mid-thirties, intellectual, keen to impress, highly defended against his own vulnerability. He does not attend the third group.

Chloe – in training as couple and family psychotherapist, is in her mid-thirties. She asks searching questions and is able to think about the theory. Her female partner is also at the conference, in another group.

Denise – counsellor for an NGO, in her late sixties, speaks from her experience as a mother and wants to see the good in everyone.

Edward – minister of religion, and counsellor for a church organisation, in his mid-sixties.

Fiona – a psychologist working for a government child and family mental health clinic, in her late twenties. She seems overwhelmed by the conference and feels her previous training has ill prepared her.

Gary – psychiatrist, working in hospital-based unit for adolescents, in his early forties. He wants to extend his thinking beyond the medical model. His family moved to Australia from China when he was toddler.

Heather – experienced individual psychotherapist in her late forties. She is now beginning to work with couples and families, and is finding it difficult to make this change.

Summary of the first affective learning group

The group leaders, Bronwyn and Steven, are waiting in the room when the participants arrive. Bruce and Edward sit either side of Steven, Heather and April either side of Bronwyn.

After brief introductions, Bronwyn explains their task and confirms the contract they have with each other about the conduct of the group. She reminds them they may experience uncomfortable and unexpected feelings during the group and after.

Bronwyn invites comment on their experience of the clinical material.

April: (After a long silence) *I was struck by the fact that Annabelle and Barry have been together all these years, and both had this early experience of smearing faeces, yet have never talked about it before.*

There is more silence and Edward, Bruce and Steven all look uncomfortable.

Bronwyn: *Perhaps we all feel a bit shocked. It seems like some very shitty feelings have been brought into the group right from the beginning.*

There are further long pauses and eye contact is minimal, as if something shameful is unfolding.

Steven: *It seems hard to talk about this, perhaps it feels exposing . . . and we have only been together for ten minutes, we hardly know each other.*
Bruce: *Well we are sure not having fun like Annabelle and Barry did when they first met!!*

Gary rolls his eyes, Denise tries to muffle a giggle, Edward swallows with embarrassment.

Heather: *Yeah, I found it shocking what they did with their faeces . . . but I just felt really angry with the parents of both of them.*
Denise: *I felt sorry for the kids, they were so neglected.*

Bruce: *Yeah, but I also thought it was a bit funny* (chuckling awkwardly) – *I mean 3-year-olds play with their poo, don't they?* (Looking around for an ally)

Fiona joins Bruce in the chuckling and reminisces about her nephew's play with his dirty nappy. Everyone else squirms silently, at the same time watching a little excitedly to see where this conversation might lead.

Bronwyn: *Perhaps we feel embarrassed talking about faeces, so we have to make a bit of a joke about it. . . . It is easier to do that than think about what it might communicate about what was going on for Annabelle and Barry as children and their families.*

Further silence. Bronwyn wonders if she sounds critical of Bruce.

April: *I was thinking about how that the therapy had been going for five months, and they married after only knowing each other for a few months and . . .*
Edward: (Interrupting) *. . . they got pregnant soon after they were married, so that was too soon for them too. They did not really know each other.*
Gary: *They married when everything was still all exciting. No wonder she got so depressed when Margaret was born.*
Heather: (Cutting off Gary) *Why would that mean you get depressed? Lots of women get pregnant just after they get married . . . and are happy about it. I was!*

Edward and Bruce both wonder if Annabelle was pregnant before they got married and that maybe Barry didn't want to have a baby.

Denise: *Well even if that was the case I just felt so angry with Barry because he suggested they adopt out their baby.*
Chloe: *Having babies seems to signal all sorts of difficulties for this couple. The smearing happened when Barry's sister was born.*
Fiona: *And Annabelle and Barry were dropped when their second therapist was having a baby. That must have been painful.*
Edward: (Emphatically) *But it was **their** decision to stop seeing their first therapist.*

Edward's comment cuts the linking the group had just begun to make.

Bronwyn: *Annabelle and Barry seemed to have trouble creating space to bring their baby, a third person, into their relationship . . .*
Bruce: (Sounding frustrated) *How this is helping me understand how to work with couples. Seems we are all just sounding off without any purpose!*

Bronwyn is feeling pulled in different directions, and anxious about where the group is going. She feels irritated with Bruce, and disconnected from her co-leader Steven, who briefly looks out the window.

Denise: *I just keep thinking about that poor little boy left in the house on his own when he is only 3 years old.*

Bronwyn wonders if this is also Bruce. She says nothing.

Edward: *And the father cutting Annabelle's hair in the garage; that felt so brutal. But she did go behind her father's back.*
Steven: (Attempting to connect with Bruce) *I am thinking about what Bruce said, how will talking about individual histories and their early trauma help us work with couples? . . . So what do we think about how they are functioning as a couple now?*

Bronwyn wishes Steven had not commented at this point and given the group some space.
The group continues to jump around with seemingly unconnected comments.
In the final moments . . .

Chloe: *Remember the green waste. . . is that like the shit that got smeared, something that could not be dealt with in the relationship . . . a different kind of waste between them . . . they could not get it together even though they both wanted to . . . for Barry it was too hot, and Annabelle wanted the task done no matter what.*
Gary: *She had no empathy for Barry and how hot it was. She just blamed him.*
Heather: *And then they have this horrible fight . . .*
Gary: *And then she gets depressed . . .*

A long silence follows.

Steven: *I wonder if something like that is happening in the group. It feels too hot to deal with some of these difficult feelings. . . . Perhaps we all get a bit depressed.*

The group are silent, and some are checking their watches as it is nearly time to finish.

Bronwyn: *After hearing how abandoned they felt as children and how they are unable to function as a couple, it is hard for us to contain all our feelings in the group.*

Commentary

Like the couple when they first met, the group begins in an excited manner. Bion's basic assumption of pairing could be considered to be at play when Bruce and Fiona engage in an animated coupling about toddlers and poo, leaving the rest of the group as onlookers, and the group task unattended.

We could also consider this moment as enactment in the group of the unresolved shitty feelings the couple unconsciously brought into their relationship and how the group feels about having to do the work.

The group avoided engaging with what it would have been like to be Annabelle and Barry as little children whose only way to communicate some awful feelings was through smearing faeces. It was easier for the group to feel angry with the parents rather than deal with feelings of vulnerability, abandonment and depression.

In response to the trauma of being exposed to this material, the group responded with thinking that was disorganised and disconnected, reminiscent of Barry's losing his capacity to use his mind well after he accidently killed a cyclist all those years ago.

The leaders struggle to function as a couple, mirroring in some ways the dysfunctional couple in the case. They are each feeling a need to be heard by the group, to each feel 'hugged'. Both leaders jump in quickly after each other's comments, leaving the group no space to digest what each has just been said. Perhaps the group is mirroring the difficult early years that Annabelle and Barry experienced in their marriage, after the birth of their daughter, and the therapist's experience of the couple interrupting each other in the sessions.

The participants organised their seating around the leader of the same gender. This could suggest they were hoping that they could depend on the nominated group leaders to lead them away from their anxieties of 'not knowing' how to do the work of understanding the clinical material, and of 'not knowing' each other in the group. Bruce's questioning whether the group experience will help them learn anything could be seen as expressing something on behalf of the whole group: will our parental couple be of any use to us? Has he an underlying wish to fight the leaders and take over leading?

Lecture 2: The Couple and Family in Mind

JENNY BERG

Dr Berg discussed the internalisation in the mind of relationships formed in infancy between the infant and his mother/object. She introduced key contributions to this theory of Object Relations made by Fairbairn (1952) and Klein (1946). Fairbairn described the infant as 'object seeking' and suggested that early processes of internalisation of relationships help to create the blueprint for future 'object' relationships. This suggests that the way people relate to others in their adult lives is shaped by family experiences during infancy, particularly the relationship with the mother. Both these theorists described the infant's need, when faced with a mother who was not always available, to split the mother (object) into good (satisfying) and bad (frustrating), and to repress the bad experience into unconsciousness. In addition, Fairbairn thought the unsatisfying object was further divided into an exciting (of anxiety) or a rejecting part, and that the infant's relationships with these various split-off aspects then formed different parts of a dynamic, though unconscious, mind or self.

She also discussed Bion's (1962) idea of container/contained: the capacity of the mother to transform infantile distress (beta elements) through her capacity for 'reverie' into something more manageable (alpha elements), so that experience can be thought about and learned from. Dr Berg also noted the importance of Winnicott's (1960) idea of the holding environment for both the parents and the child. The mother needs to feel supported and held by her husband, and the couple held by their own 'internal parental couples' in order to hold the child.

Summary of the second affective learning group

The leaders start the group on time, even though Bruce has not arrived. Bronwyn invites the group to comment on the theory just presented and how it could be used in understanding and working with Annabelle and Barry.

Fiona:	*Shouldn't we wait until Bruce gets here?*
Gary:	*I am keen to get going. Being at the conference instead of being with my family is a big sacrifice. My son has not long come home from his last bout in hospital.*

No one responds to Gary's personal disclosure.

Heather:	*I agree. It is not fair if we miss out.*
Denise:	*I'm with Fiona, I want to wait for Bruce.*
Edward:	*(Stiffly) I agree with Gary. Bruce knows we are meant to start on time.*

There is rising tension in the group. Steven looks unsure and says nothing. He turns to Bronwyn in the hope she will take the lead. Bronwyn appreciates that although Steven knows the importance of keeping the frame of the group he has not been faced with this before. She remains silent.

April:	*Well I am going to start. I found the lecture really helpful; I think I understood the case material much better after the lecture.*
Fiona:	*I was struggling with all the theory . . . I am new to these ideas. I tuned out a bit.*
Heather:	*I was struggling to grasp it too, it was quite complicated. I am finding it difficult to think about the histories and dynamics of two people rather than just one. I feel pulled one way and then another and wanting to take sides.*

Denise looks unhappy and uncomfortable. She is upset with the leaders for not waiting for Bruce.

Bronwyn is struggling to feel that they are good enough to help the group (siblings), and feels flat. She wonders if the participants' anxiety and sense of inadequacy are being projected into Steven and her as leaders.

At this point Bruce arrives, carrying a coffee. He doesn't seem to register that he is late, and offers no apology. Denise smiles at him, as if apologising on behalf of the group for not waiting for him.

Bronwyn: (Looking in Bruce's direction) *We are talking about struggling with all the material . . . and how to relate it to Annabelle and Barry's difficulties . . . maybe we are feeling a bit overwhelmed by so much new information, perhaps like when we meet a couple in our consulting rooms for the first time?*

There is some discussion about beginnings, as infants, as couples, and as couples beginning therapy. It is recalled that Annabelle and Barry missed the previous therapy session but it was not referred to in the session.

Chloe: *I think I understood a bit more about object relations, I had always imagined something like a photo inside the mind, but it is the relationship that the child takes in.*

Heather: *So I guess both Annabelle and Barry had pretty awful internal relationships with their mothers . . . what was it that Jenny said, something about bad internal objects . . .*

Gary: *Yes, I guess with Annabelle and Barry, in the beginning it was exciting and then later the relationship became rejecting . . . of each other, like their parents really rejected them . . . Annabelle was punished and Barry was blamed. . . .*

Steven: *Why do you think that Barry was unable to support her, even suggesting that the baby be adopted?*

Gary: *Maybe he was frightened that the baby would take his wife away from him. . . . I know how that feels . . .* (anxiously)

The group looks at Gary sympathetically.

April: *And he was frightened of the responsibility, for the baby, and for Annabelle. He probably has no idea how to nurture her because he was left to nurture himself.*

Chloe: *Barry lost out to his baby sister . . . and Annabelle lost out to her brother.*

April: *Annabelle was so sensitive and, to be fair to Barry, he had to get it exactly right for her.*

Denise:	*My son had eczema . . . it was really hard to soothe his itchy skin. I felt a failure as a mother, really powerless. I found myself wondering, Gary, about your little boy in hospital. . . .*
Gary:	*Yeah, I didn't want to distract from the case . . . he was born very premature . . . but he is going OK.*

The group again look sympathetically at Gary and he thanks them for their concern. . . .

Edward:	*And what about her bad teeth, I found myself really wondering about that.*
Bronwyn:	*What were you wondering?*
Edward:	*Well, why were her teeth so bad? I thought that she had been given too much sweet stuff. That it was the parents' fault.*
Denise:	*I wondered if her dummy had been covered in honey. It was comforting, but it was rotting her teeth. Poor little girl, given the wrong stuff, and then blamed for her bad teeth, it is awful.*

For the first time the group is in a state of quiet reverie, able to bear with Annabelle's pain and vulnerability.

Bronwyn:	*They are not able to offer themselves as emotional containers for all her bad feelings, her pain and discomfort, her aloneness. The only comfort that her parents could offer her was something that is bad for her.*
Chloe:	*I found the stuff about splitting really interesting. . . . I see a lot of families where there is a good child and a bad one. And often that repeats something in the couple's background, one or other of them was the 'bad' child in their own family.*

There is a flurry of anecdotes about the fighting couples they see in their own consulting rooms, and how very often there are histories of neglect in both families of origin. The group returns to Annabelle and Barry.

Bronwyn:	*We have been talking about Annabelle and Barry. In terms of the lecture, neither of them felt 'good' about themselves, they were not 'contained' in their families, but they dealt with it in different ways.*
Gary:	*Yes, Barry withdraws but can get enraged. Didn't he attack Annabelle early in their marriage?*
Edward:	*But to his credit, he stopped after some counselling . . .*
Chloe:	*And Annabelle is angry, but then gets depressed.*
Heather:	*(Hesitantly, and looking towards Bruce) I was wondering about Bruce coming in late, and you were firm about us starting on time. I have just started to work with couples, and I am never quite sure*

what to do . . . when one person comes first and the other is late,
what should you do? Or if one person does not turn up at all . . .

Various opinions are expressed. No one asks Bruce why he was late, nor does he offer
any explanation. He sits rather nonchalantly, as if oblivious. Bronwyn feels concerned
that despite his presentation, Bruce is very fragile. She feels torn. If she comments
will he feel blamed like Barry, or if she says nothing will he feel abandoned.

The group returns to discussing blame and how it can be difficult for the couple
to function as a couple, without blaming one child over the other, or blaming each
other as parents.

Bruce: *Almost all the couples we see blame each other for everything that*
            has gone wrong. So what's new about this approach?

There is awkward silence. Bronwyn and Steven both feel criticised and inadequate.

Steven: *Well what do you think is different about this approach?*
April: *Well wasn't Jenny trying to show that blaming is a stage that couples*
            go through? Until they can think about their own part in what has
            gone wrong.
Heather: *But how does that bring about change?*
Bruce: *It doesn't seem to me that much changes at all in the couple.*
Bronwyn: *Just as we can feel stuck as therapists, perhaps we are feeling a bit*
            stuck with much to still process in our group. This is a painful moment
            for us to have to finish and wait for tomorrow's final small group.

Denise tries to continue the conversation, but Steven stands to signal the group is
finished.

Commentary

The group begins with emerging tensions about whether or not the group should
start before Bruce arrives. At this point the group is in danger of splitting and is
under the sway of the fight/flight basic assumption mentality. The leaders are
anxious about holding the group and containing the emerging differences.

Throughout the group Bruce seems to be neither in nor out of it, and could be
seen as expressing the group's ambivalence, in particular about working on understanding the difficult theory on object relations and its relationship to the case, as
well as the feelings evoked.

The group begins to integrate some of the theoretical themes around splitting
and unite as a group when the group experiences and demonstrates concern for
Gary and his premature son. This could be understood as an unconscious expression of the empathy that was missing in Barry and Annabelle's parents, and
subsequently in the couple's own relationship.

The sense of helplessness of Annabelle and Barry as infants, and as a couple, is projected into the leaders who sometimes struggle to offer something to the group. No one asks about Bruce's absence at the beginning, even though it is noted. Nor is his late arrival commented on. Is there a fear of making him the 'bad' one in the group, as are the leaders who did not wait for Bruce, while the rest of the group are the 'good' ones?

The group is feeling stuck in the middle of the work, like our couples do. There is a struggle to end on time, and the anxieties in the group feel uncontained at times.

Lecture 3: The developmental framework

NOELA BYRNE

Ms Byrne traced the normal emotional development of the infant and his developing capacity to deal with the anxieties inherent in life. A couple's relationship can be seen to mirror the infant's psychological development. This hierarchy of developmental anxieties can also reflect the changes over time as a couple or family benefit from therapy, and are able to move on emotionally from stuck and destructive patterns of behaviour.

The earliest level of relating, which we call the Autistic-Contiguous Position, refers to the way in which an infant exists in a sensory world where the sensations of the skin, touch in particular, are pre-eminent. A failure of care at this level can manifest somatically.

In the couple, this primitive level of relating can lead to narcissistic fusion, a clinging together in denial of their difference, an 'adhesive identification' (Meltzer, 1975). Early difficulties at the somatic level can also lead to sexual difficulties in the couple, since touch and skin contact form such an important part of the adult sexual relationship.

The next level of development in the infant has been called the Paranoid-Schizoid Position (Klein, 1946) and describes a way of relating characterised by splitting and projection. These processes are familiar to us in our work with couples, who, when they can no longer find anything lovable about each other, blame each other for problems they have encountered and are in constant conflict.

A later stage of development, which everyone goes through, and is never fully resolved, is often precipitated by the birth of a child. There are painful feelings of exclusion, rivalry and jealousy provoked by this intrusion of a third into the couple relationship. These anxieties about exclusion, rivalry and jealousy, known collectively as Oedipal anxieties, herald the beginning of the depressive position.

The hallmarks of the depressive position are the capacity to see the other's point of view while being able to maintain your own, to feel remorse for hurt you have caused others and to learn from experience. This mature way of relating may be disrupted, however, by traumatic events or something experienced as traumatic. The hope is that depressive level functioning becomes a 'default' position that individuals and couples can return to.

Summary of the third affective learning group

Bruce does not appear, and has not let anyone know he will be absent. His chair is left empty. Apart from a brief acknowledgement that he is not present, nothing further is said.

Bronwyn: *This is our third and final small group. We have heard some new theory and how it relates to the clinical material we heard yesterday.*

Chloe: *I started to understand a bit more about the autistic-contiguous phase, it is such a clunky term, but both Annabelle and Barry had awful problems with their skin and their bodies . . .*

Gary: *Yes, I found that interesting as a doctor. . . . I have seen lots of eczema and asthma, like Annabelle and Barry had. I am starting to think more about its meaning, not just seeing it as a medical condition . . .*

Ten minutes later.

Heather: (Who had been quiet to this point) *I was so tired last night and it was an effort to come today. I am feeling a bit overwhelmed with all the new stuff . . . opened up, and raw.*

Edward: *I think we are all a bit exhausted. Maybe that is why Bruce has not turned up . . . has anyone heard from him?* (No one had) *Maybe he feels a bit tired and overwhelmed too?*

Gary: *I saw him after today's lecture. He looked sad.*

Everyone looks uncomfortable. Steven speaks to the group's exhaustion and Bruce's absence, to these physical responses in the face of raw feelings evoked by the lectures, as well as tensions within the group. The group avoids taking this up.

Gary and Chloe make further complimentary references to Noela's lecture. Bronwyn and Steven feel brushed aside and left to watch.

April: *I think you are right Chloe. You have really understood the lecture well.* (Everyone looks at Chloe and she shines with pleasure.) *I really liked Noela's lecture too. I think I am beginning to understand how couples have their own development. I remember when I was first married and I felt really annoyed when my husband wanted to spend time with his mates. I took that as a rejection of me, rather than he needed to have friends in his life as well as me.*

Edward: *I remember what that was like . . . now that I am in semi-retirement my wife gets fed up that I am home so much.*

The group laughs at Edward's and April's disclosures, then gets on with discussing the lecture in an excited and busy manner. A couple of times Bronwyn invites the group to link their comments to the theory, but she is squeezed out and feels redundant. She also wonders what has happened to Bruce.

Bronwyn: *If we think about the developmental model, how do you think the couple changed during the therapy?*

Heather: *They are still like needy children, not grown up at all, I keep thinking about Annabelle's rotten teeth because of the honey on the dummy . . .*

Bronwyn: *But if we go back to the theoretical model.*

Heather laughs.

Bronwyn: *Ok, I give up . . . but I am not going to withdraw like Barry or leave the room, like Annabelle threatens to leave the relationship. . . . Maybe we are struggling to find space for each other . . .*

Some in the group smile . . . they seem to relax.

Gary: *I would like to understand more about those paranoid-schizoid processes . . .*

Theoretical ideas are tossed around. There is an absence of affect in the group.

Chloe: *Isn't that mainly about splitting . . .*

Bronwyn: (Aware she invited the group to think about theory a few minutes ago) *It is easier for **all** of us to withdraw into theory rather than relate it to feelings, Annabelle's and Barry's, or our feelings in the group.*

Denise: (Connects with what Bronwyn had just said) *Why would Barry want to give up his daughter for adoption, maybe I am a bit naïve, but I find that really shocking?*

Heather: *It is awful! I find it hard to work with a couple where I don't like one of them . . . and I could not warm to Barry.*

Others concur. Edward says he felt kindly towards Barry, and what follows is a discussion about how differently they feel about the various couples they see.

Bronwyn: *Just as happened with Annabelle and Barry, we too are affected by our own histories, our own families and our own internal families as well as our personal likes and dislikes.*

The group continues to discuss themes around transference and counter-transference and what aspects of themselves they might bring to their clinical work.

Heather: *I am so used to working with individuals, it is hard to think about working with a couple, keeping in mind that you have to hold two points of view all the time . . . to know what feelings belong where.*

Gary: *It is hard, especially when I meet a couple or a family for the first time.*

Bronwyn: *It is the same with this group, we only met yesterday and it takes time to sort out what we might be projecting into each other, what any one member of the group might be carrying and expressing for any of us.*

Gary: *I wonder if Laurie felt really shocked at the idea of the baby being adopted out. Would Barry have picked up on that?*

Bronwyn is wondering if this reference to someone being sent away is a reference to Bruce, who is absent. She waits to see if someone else mentions this . . .

Steven: *What difference do you think Laurie's processing of her own feelings made to the therapy?*

April: *Well, it is like what was talked about yesterday, the idea of containment. Laurie did what neither Annabelle's nor Barry's mothers could do . . . She thought about what was going on in the couple, but also her own feelings. She didn't just react when she felt irritated, she wondered what this meant about what was happening in the therapy.*

Chloe: (With exasperation) *I sometimes think that none of the couples I see have had much of an experience of real containment in their own families!*

Denise: *I can't stop wondering why Bruce wasn't here for this last group.*

Everyone looks startled by the 'return' of Bruce to the group. Bronwyn and Steven wait to see how everyone will respond.

The mood of the group drops; the earlier excitement and sense of mastery of the lecture material diminishes. Heather, Chloe and Fiona express disappointment, hurt and resentment about Bruce's absence; Denise and Edward wonder what this has to do with understanding the lecture material. April says nothing . . .

Bronwyn: *Until now it has been easier to feel excited about the theoretical material we are trying to understand than to get in touch with other less comfortable feelings to do with Bruce's absence. Someone mentioned Barry wanting to send his daughter off for adoption. Have we somehow sent Bruce off there too?*

Denise: *Even though Bruce said a lot in our first group, he was quiet in the afternoon and looked really tired. I'm a bit worried about him.*

Fiona: *But why didn't he let us know he wasn't coming or what the matter was?*

Edward: *I think it is rude to not turn up.*

Chloe: *Perhaps he just did not feel safe enough . . . after all we hardly know each other and we didn't always agree with what he said yesterday. I remember when he said smearing was funny, well I didn't like him saying that . . . and I think others in the group felt the same.* (Some of the others nodded.) *He must have noticed that . . .*

Gary: *I should have reached out to him when I saw him just after the last lecture.*

Chloe: *I think I will email him tomorrow and see how he is.*

Chloe and Gary are both briefly looked to for some direction and leadership about Bruce's absence. After a while the group moves towards a state of reverie and reflection and the leaders begin to feel more enlivened and involved.

Steven: *We have had varied responses to Bruce's absence. Even though Bruce never said so, maybe he was deeply affected by the confronting and difficult material of the lectures. Maybe the way he expressed it was by being confrontational, and expressing different views to everyone else . . . and leaving.*

There is acknowledgement from Gary and Chloe. Denise looks a little baffled.

Bronwyn: *Steven is pointing out that Bruce actually left, but in a way we were also left, as a group. Perhaps you were hoping Steven and I had reached out to Bruce, as leaders?*

Denise and April agree. Gary and Chloe feel badly about doing nothing themselves.

Bronwyn: *Perhaps we experienced Bruce's absence as a break, a trauma even, to our sense of being a group. We largely avoided talking about his absence earlier. We cut ourselves off from what happened, and from what Bruce might be experiencing. We were in denial of the loss. In a similar way, when Barry could not deal with the difficult feelings that his daughter's birth provoked in him, his solution was to suggest sending her away, to abandon her . . .*

After some further discussion . . .

Steven: *Maybe this is also about us leaving each other? This is our last small group and we are soon to finish.*

Denise: *Oh is this our last group?* (Looks surprised) *It seems to have gone so quickly!*

What followed was an outpouring of feelings and associations to the lectures and the group. There was a little alarm and sadness, but also some relief that the group was soon to finish. There was recognition that they were not able to say goodbye to Bruce or share with him their experience of his absence and what they had learned from it. There was recognition of ambivalence towards each other and the group. Loss, abandonment and trauma in the clinical material and the group were more directly spoken about in ways that suggested the participants were listening and reflecting, rather than reacting.

Commentary

Some of the earlier themes of the first two groups are repeated: splitting, particularly around feelings about Bruce's absence, and the discussions about disliking Barry. There are still several occasions where the group protects itself from feelings of abandonment and vulnerability by retreating into excited discussions about theory. This repetition and reworking of themes from a slightly different perspective from one group to the next parallels our reworking with couples and families over time.

The leaders' linking of the group's exhaustion and Bruce's absence, a comment made to address the somatic response to anxiety and the flight/fight state of mind, is ignored in favour of the excitement of Chloe's mastery of the theory. At this moment the group briefly looked to Chloe to lead (basic assumption dependency), which left Bronwyn and Steven feeling redundant.

The group spoke to the difficulty in digesting so much new material in the group, mirroring the experience of couple therapists with a new referral.

The leaders have become more of a couple, and are therefore better able to contain the group and each other although they too are subject to the same unconscious processes. Some processes of splitting and projection, transference and counter-transference present in the clinical material have been initially enacted in the group and later understood better at an emotional level.

When the impact of Bruce's non-attendance is properly thought about, the group becomes more alive, as do the group leaders. They are then able to help the group to acknowledge and reflect on the meaning of Bruce's absence as a metaphor for the ending of the group itself, and to mourn.

Summary and conclusions

This is a brief account of how an affective learning group might function in an attempt to grapple with clinical and theoretical material in a two-day conference. Mirroring the processes that happen with the couples and families we meet in the consulting room, concepts such as transference and counter-transference, splitting and projective identification are enacted in the group. Being (mostly) well contained by the leaders allowed the participants to understand these processes at the level of felt experience.

We have noted some occasions where the group was under the sway of basic assumption mentalities; where the group's anxieties and defences against that anxiety interfered with the task of learning (work group mentality). In the hope of finding an easier solution to the difficult feelings in the group, dyads are briefly formed leaving the leaders to feel left out and redundant (pairing). At times the group tries to get the leaders to do the work of making sense of the material presented to them, and working out what to do with Bruce's lateness and absence (dependency). There is a flight from reflecting on the painful feelings and their meaning in the clinical material and the leaders' authority and their usefulness is questioned (fight/flight).

The group also demonstrated its own development over time; the excitement and anxiety of first coming together, and the frustrations of beginning to make sense of the middle phase. In the end phase, the absence of a group member brings the group sharply in touch with denial of loss, which mirrored the splitting, denial and projective defences present in both the case material and the theory. Towards the end of the last group, the leaders are able to process the split-off aspects of this absence, enabling the group to experience something akin to the depressive position, when it mourns its own ending.

Note

1 The lectures by Dr Jenny Berg and Ms Noela Byrne referred to in this chapter are summarised versions of Chapters 1 and 2 in this volume.

References

Balint, M. (1957). *The Doctor, His Patient and the Illness*. New York: International Universities Press.

Bion, W.R. (1961). *Experiences in Groups and Other Papers*. London: Tavistock Publications.

Bion, W.R. (1962). *Learning from Experience*. London: Heinemann.

Fairbairn, W.R.D. (1952). *Psychological Studies of the Personality*. London: Routledge & Kegan Paul.

Gosling, R., Miller, D.H., Woodhouse, D. and Turquet, P.M. (1967). *The Use of Small Groups in Training*. London: Karnac.

Klein, M. (1946). Notes on some schizoid mechanisms. *International Journal of Psycho-Analysis*, *27*, 99–110 [Reprinted in M. Klein, *Envy and Gratitude and Other Works 1946–1963*. London: Hogarth Press, 1980].

Meltzer, D. (1975). Adhesive identification. *Contemporary Psychoanalysis*, *11*, 289–310.

Scharff, J.S. and Scharff, D.E. (2000). *Tuning the Therapeutic Instrument*. London: Jason Aronson.

Symington, J. and Symington, N. (1996). *The Clinical Thinking of Wilfred Bion*. London and New York: Routledge.

Winnicott, D. (1960). The theory of the parent–infant relationship. *International Journal of Psycho-Analysis*, *41*, 585–595.

Concluding thoughts

Penny Jools

The purpose of this book is to provide a developmental model of couple and family psychotherapy, which is intended as a helpful framework for thinking about the largely unconscious dilemmas of the people we meet in our consulting room, *their family within*. Like any model of development it leaves us with some questions. An underlying aim of this book is to contribute to further discussion and sharing of ideas about some of the issues that the book raises. Just as with psychoanalysis and psychotherapy of individuals, the body of theoretical knowledge and good practice in couple and family psychotherapy evolves: theory too has a developmental trajectory.

Strengths and weakness of a developmental theoretical model

The idea of a developmental model for psychological growth is not original; from Freud to Klein there has been a linking of the internal world of the adult to the child's normal development. For Freud, part of his theory suggested that the child's relationship with the world was shaped through erotogenic phases – oral, anal, phallic and genital modalities. Klein contributed a focus on infant development – and a move from paranoid-schizoid functioning to the depressive position. The movement, according to Klein, was from ways of relating characterised by splitting and projection, to ones where the child was able to see the parent(s) as whole people, both good and bad; experiencing guilt for real or phantasied attacks on the (m)other; growing into a capacity for concern and the ability to make reparation.

The model the authors have developed includes the contribution of very early experience, at the level of the skin and touch, to difficulties in the couple relationship, (Ogden, 1989) as described in several of the preceding chapters. We consider it important to extend the Kleinian idea of development to include this sensory experience. The main reason for this is because of the power of projective identification in the communication between the couple and the family and the therapist. We also suggest that when these early sensory experiences are compromised it affects the couple's capacity to connect in an intimate sexual relationship, thus compromising the relationship's containing function, as demonstrated in Chapters 2 and 6 in particular.

The authors have all been trained to work with children, and have experienced an infant observation. Our training has brought us into a direct encounter with the internal world of the child. We have learned about the powerful impact such encounters have on the psyche of the therapist, and consider they are an essential grounding in working with the intensity which is the natural expression of couples in therapy. The 'use of the self' is an important conduit to understanding the complex inner worlds of the couples and families we see. Working with, and through, the counter-transference is the primary tool of a therapist working with a psychodynamic developmental model of the couple. Experiences with the real infant or child are helpful, indeed in our view essential, to working in couple and family psychotherapy, since often the couple in the consulting room is in the grip of regressed ways of interacting that are capable of both disturbing the therapist and disrupting the therapeutic frame if not understood.

Many of the cases in the book demonstrate the use of the therapist's mind in processing feelings that are expressed unconsciously, through projective processes. One of our aims in writing the book from this theoretical perspective was to give a therapist, whether at the beginning of their career or well established in it, a model to hold on to when it is difficult to think. The model has the potential to provide a map for the difficult emotional terrain of a couple's internal world, but can also provide a way of thinking about changes in the couple or family's internal world in therapy.

One issue that this focus on early somatic experience raises is the possibility of greater communication between couple psychotherapists working from an object relations model and those trained in a Jungian theoretical perspective. The Jungian idea of 'psychoid substance', which refers to psychosomatic communication seems to have much in common with the role of autistic-contiguous anxieties in our developmental model. This area of very early experience and its effect on the couple's relationship seems ripe for some exchange between these two perspectives.

While Klein's ideas are familiar to therapists working with a psychodynamic model, Fairbairn's (1952) potential contribution is less well known, but is of special value to the couple psychotherapist. We agree with the Scharffs (2005) in championing the importance of Fairbairn in understanding the interactive and feedback aspects of mother–child interactions and its application to couple and family psychotherapy. Fairbairn's approach challenged the model of development based on instincts, arguing that the child is born 'object seeking'. His endopsychic model described the real interaction between the mother and child, which in turn created an internalised representation of relationship that then impacted on the sense of self. Development was thus not internally generated but progressed through a constant interplay between the child and the environment, in the first instance the mother.[1]

The notion of a feedback loop helps us, for instance, to understand the impact on the child of the overanxious mother, who intrudes her presence into the child's world in a manner that excites longing for soothing contact but does not satisfy. This sort of mother can seem like a good mother, and indeed she is, but her anxiety, a legacy of her own early experience, can disrupt the child's emotional growth. We often witness in our consulting rooms an equivalent pattern operating between couples who act out these internalised exciting/rejecting interactions, one partner demanding of more attention, while the other experiences the atmosphere as claustrophobic and retreats from the threat of intrusion.

Problems with a developmental theoretical model

The problem with a developmental model, however, is that it carries an expectation of improvement, and a tendency to see progress in black and white terms. Readers will have noticed that not all cases described in the book have a happy ending. In reality most people and couples move in and out of what might be called 'mature' ways of relating. The progress of couples and families is never linear; it is common for families and couples to regress under the strain of traumatic external events, death, divorce, dislocation. The case studies in our book have been chosen primarily to illustrate our model, and the ways we work with a couple or family, including the problems we encounter. Generally the cases that are able to use the therapy to move on are less likely to be recorded. These cases could be regarded as our 'successes'.

But also the cases we present in this book are those that have engendered a lot of thinking precisely because they have been so challenging. We have learnt most from couples and families that challenged us. These are also the cases that have been brought to supervision and therefore represent the additional thinking of a group of colleagues.

Indeed, the fact that not all interventions are successes may provide some relief for therapists, by tempering our ideals with the challenges of reality. But it is also perhaps evidence of the inevitable tendency of therapists to consider our work within a black and white paranoid-schizoid paradigm, which leads us to judge the complexity of couple psychotherapy work in terms of success or failure.

Clinical challenges to containment in couple and family psychotherapy

In Chapter 2 we present some ideas for how we might treat couples and families at various stages of psychic development: these ideas are developed in Chapters 4 and 5. This area of clinical practice merits greater sharing and discussion among our local and international colleagues.

Somatic presentations

Somatic disturbance is more likely to be treated medically than from a psychological perspective: this was particularly so for the generation of the parents we see in therapy. If we consider that somatic complaints may be a physical enactment of Bion's (1962) 'beta' elements, the medicalisation of these symptoms when the couples were children may have reduced their possibility of containment at a psychological level. This in turn may increase the likelihood that as adults the damage is repressed into the unconscious or projected through projective identification into the couple's children.

When we meet a couple or family for the first time, we often feel that this therapeutic encounter is their first experience of containment: this then becomes the primary task of therapy whatever the family or couple's level of insight and integration.

We are not denying the important therapeutic work of holding and reflection of feelings, but as we emphasise in Chapter 5 the containing function of the therapy is to hold and bring into consciousness the 'beta' elements of the couple's shared histories. These elements can often be communicated unconsciously.

Paranoid-schizoid process: splitting and intergenerational trauma

Many couples and families come to psychotherapy with intergenerational trauma and secrets that have never been properly metabolised. In Chapter 5, the writer describes the impact on a father and son of the grandfather's suicide. The boy who was referred for treatment was carrying the father's unresolved grief and shame that had never been talked about. The boy's depression was in projective identification with the father's: it was concern for the son that brought the family and the father in particular into treatment.

This case demonstrates the importance of a family history that includes the emotional impact of trauma from previous generations. This is another aspect of paranoid-schizoid processes in the couple or family, where intergenerational trauma is 'split off' from consciousness, but unconsciously enacted in the current generation. Research on children of the Holocaust, the 'Stolen Generations' in Aboriginal Australia, as well as the more recent treatment of refugee families in detention, are constant reminders of the impact of the trauma experienced by one generation on their children. This leads to another important aspect of the intergenerational experience of the couple, establishing an understanding of the *internal parental couple*. We are not just interested in the history of each of the grandparents of the couple, but rather how the couple came to understand and internalise their parents' relationship. We often find that some of the splitting in the current generation can resonate with a split and unhappy internalised parental couple.

The malign influence of narcissistic ways of relating is one of the issues highlighted by the difficult cases described in the book. These cases frequently bring couples into difficulties, both with each other and with the therapist, as the book amply illustrates.

Narcissism in couple and family relationships

Couples caught up in narcissistic ways of relating continue to be a source of challenge and are puzzling for us as clinicians. We have hypothesised in our developmental model that narcissistic relating inhabits a 'borderline' area between autistic-contiguous and paranoid-schizoid ways of relating, but how to help narcissistically engaged couples remains a clinical challenge. When these couples seek help, they are often locked into a merged relationship that allows them little freedom or growth as a couple, clinging to an idealised idea of what the relationship 'should be'. As they emerge from this state in therapy, towards greater acknowledgment of each other as individuals within the relationship, paranoid-schizoid functioning can ensue, with splitting and projection, as is illustrated by the interactions of Wendy and Hilton in Chapter 2. It is easy for the therapist to be caught in the splits that inevitably occur for couples in this state. This may be a crucial dilemma when one or both of the couple are unwilling to relinquish the previous merged state, but wish to go back to it, preserved, perhaps a bit like Miss Havisham's cobwebbed wedding dress. This longing is echoed in Wendy's plaintive cry: 'where has all the good gone?'

This is a precarious crisis for the therapy, where the possibility of real change is present, but is undermined by the often sadomasochistic dance of the couple, a crisis in which therapy can be broken off or the therapist spat out.

Symington (1993) has described narcissistic ways of relating as an attack on the 'lifegiver'. He sees it as an existential choice. While Symington's new theory of narcissism is controversial, his idea of the attack on the 'lifegiver' seems to resonate with Fairbairn's notion of the 'internal saboteur', a force that attacks the possibility of change for the better. As therapists we have all been struck by what seems like sheer bloody-mindedness in some narcissistic partners in maintaining an 'anti-relating' stance (Colman, 2005). The degree to which they have 'turned away' from the other in the relationship can seem to express an element of choice. This may also represent an envious spoiling attack.

But the real point is how to help these couples to construct a more robust and realistic relationship? We believe that the ways in which these narcissistic ways of relating develop and how to treat them merits more thought and sharing of ideas. Our developmental model suggests that in these cases their earliest relationship with their mother or caring person was disturbed, leading to an inability to separate from and an inability to connect with the maternal figure. Therapeutic work, in our view, needs to be slow and patient, focusing on holding both partners until some evidence of introjection of the therapist as a 'good enough' person is evident. There will be much resistance, however, as for many of these couples the 'internal saboteur' is firmly established.

Popular culture is no ally in challenging narcissism, in its universal idealisation of the couple relationship. We are part of that culture in our desire to see our couples and families get better. The resistance of narcissistically engaged couples can challenge the therapist's sense of competence and compassion but also challenges our own therapeutic narcissism.

Part of the cultural idealising of the couple includes the idealising of the arrival of the baby. While for some couples this is indeed a happy experience, for many couples the birth of a child can resonate in a painful way with their own early experience. For many of the couples we see, difficulties seem to have arisen with the birth of one or other of their children. This is often a painful issue for a couple to acknowledge and can resonate with unresolved Oedipal difficulties. In some cases this leads to a projection of the difficulties onto the child.

Oedipal issues: the child is the problem

Several of the cases presented in the book start with the child as the 'problem'. In the cases described, a change of focus to the couple's difficulties freed the child from carrying the parents' projections and they were able to get on with the normal developmental tasks of childhood. This outcome should not be lightly brushed aside. While parents may find it difficult to let go of their narcissistic defences, many come to see a therapist out of genuine concern about their child. Some of them are able to see how the child is carrying projections that come from their own difficulties more readily than they can own what they are projecting into their partner. If the parents turn their attention away from the 'problems' in their child, which they may both be blaming each other for, and focus on their own difficulties, the child has an experience of parents who are working together to try to help each other and the child.

We are presenting a challenge here to ways of working therapeutically with children and families where the child receives therapy and the parents are met within an 'educational' framework. Much as we support child psychotherapy, work with the couple, in our view, needs to focus on taking back as far as possible the projections the child is carrying on behalf of the parents. We would argue that this can only be done if the parents are themselves treated psychotherapeutically.

Reverie in psychotherapy with couples and families

A friend asked what role reverie plays in work with couples. It seemed like a legitimate question. Reverie is, according to Bion, how the beta elements expressed by the child are transformed by the alpha function of the mother.

Silence is a rare occurrence in a couple or family psychotherapy session. The lived experience of psychotherapy with couples can often find the therapist struggling to interrupt the torrent of accusations and counteraccusations.

Group supervision may play an important role in the reverie process. A family's story listened to in a group supervision, often over a period of years, can be an essential part of understanding the couple or family dynamics. Sometimes it is the group reverie which does greatest justice to and offers the most insight into the complex transferences and counter-transferences of the couple and family.

The sexual relationship: a theoretical and clinical issue

At the beginning of this chapter the impact of early somatic difficulties on the couple's sexual relationship was raised.

A number of couple psychotherapists have commented on the absence of focus on a couple's sexual relationship in couple psychotherapy (Kahr, 2009), and indeed the prevalence of 'no-sex' couples in their consulting rooms (Grier, 2005). Several of the chapters in the book highlight how difficult it can be for couples to maintain a satisfying sexual relationship. In Chapter 2, the authors argue for the role of very early anxieties at the level of the skin as a factor in these sexual difficulties. We believe there is a need for the couple psychotherapy community to think more about sexual difficulties in the couple. David Scharff is an advocate of sensate focused therapy as an adjunct to couple psychotherapy (Scharff, 1998). Given the authors' hypothesis that some of a couple's sexual difficulties may reside in very early experience at the level of skin and touch, one might anticipate that a sensate approach could be helpful, at least at the level of gathering more information about the nature of the difficulties. Some might argue that there is a caveat here for couples who have experienced sexual abuse; however, each case is individual, and these couples need help too. In any case, as we have said in a number of places, the couple needs to be 'held' by the therapy for long enough to establish a more secure internal object relationship before they are able to constructively and more openly discuss their sexual difficulties.

Is there a 'cure' in psychoanalytically-based psychotherapy with families and couples?

There has always been a tension in the literature on outcomes in psychoanalysis and psychoanalytic psychotherapy about whether they provide a 'cure'.

> ...much will be gained if we succeed in transforming your hysterical misery into common unhappiness. With a mental life that has been restored to health, you will be better armed against that unhappiness.
>
> (Freud and Breuer, 1895)

This quote from Freud is usually cited without the second sentence. It is this second sentence, however, that resonates with the experience of all therapists working from a psychoanalytic perspective. Freud is not suggesting that the best outcome is 'common unhappiness', but rather that a healthy personality has the resources to deal with the vicissitudes of ordinary existence.

In couple psychotherapy, similarly, the hope for change lies in creating a better relationship between the couple in the consulting room, one that can deal with the challenges of life. Sometimes a good outcome in couple psychotherapy is for the couple to separate; sometimes it is for the couple to consolidate their commitment to each other through marriage. Some of the more useful work we can do is with separating families around the psychological care of the children. Whether the couple stay together or separate, we would hope that we have created a space to think about their relationship, thus internalising the space that has been created in the consulting room.

On a positive note, there is increasing evidence of the usefulness of psychotherapy with couples. David Hewison reports that recent research in the UK suggests that psychoanalytically-based couple and family psychotherapy 'is amongst the best couple therapies that have been delivered in ordinary settings with ordinary couples, and we make an argument that it's as good as that done in the highly controlled experimental settings of Randomized Controlled Trials' (Hewison, 2017).

The developmental model we have proposed and described in the case studies in this volume recognises the inevitable regressions of the couple through the layers of internalised experience that reflect the experience of being fully human and connected. Thus, to be 'married', to make a real commitment to the other, is in direct opposition to narcissistic ways of relating that reflect some of the current values of our society. The subtitle of Fisher's seminal book, published nearly twenty years ago, was 'emerging from narcissism towards marriage' (Fisher, 1999). A developmental model can recognise the need for tolerance, containment and flexibility in the shared work of therapist and family in the movement towards maturity. Our hope is that this model can form part of an international dialogue about the theory and practice of psychotherapy with couples and families and include the possibility of research. Research needs clinically informed questions if it is to usefully serve its community.

On a final note, this book has been written by a group of people who have worked together for more than twenty years. They have shared ideas, frustrations and supervision groups. They also share a passion for the work they do with couples. Why is it so interesting? Perhaps as we are present with a couple in our consulting rooms, we are filled with all the Oedipal longings and emotional intensity we experienced as a child witnessing our own parents. The Oedipal drama is still within us as part of our own internal parent; as Britton puts it: 'the idea of a couple coming together to produce a child is central in our psychic life, whether we aspire to it, object to it, realise we are produced by it, deny it, relish it, or hate it' (Britton, 1995).

In psychotherapy with couples and families we offer our own minds to our couples and families and in the process there is, often enough, a shared experience of giving birth to a third, a more creative relationship. Maturity is the achievement of the capacity to think, to play and to work, but most crucially to relate deeply and intimately.

Note

1 This is not to deny the role of phantasy in shaping the infant's response to the world. But as Piaget pointed out nearly 100 years ago with his observations of object constancy, the phantasies of the child are in part informed by cognitive development.

References

Bion, W.R. (1962). The psychoanalytical study of thinking. *International Journal of Psycho-Analysis*, *43*, 306–310.

Britton, R. (1995). Foreword. In S. Ruszczynski and J. Fisher (Eds.) *Intrusiveness and Intimacy in the Couple* (Introduction, p. xi). London: Karnac.

Colman, W. (2005). The intolerable other. *Psychoanalytic Perspectives on Couple Work*. Society of Couple Psychoanalytic Psychotherapists, Issue 1, London.

Fairbairn, W.R.D. (1952). *Psychological Studies of the Personality*. London: Routledge & Kegan Paul.

Fisher, J. (1999). *The Uninvited Guest: Emerging from Narcissism towards Marriage*. London: Karnac.

Freud, S. and Breuer, J. (1895). *Studies on Hysteria*, translated and edited by James and Alix Strachey. In A. Richards (Ed.) *The Pelican Freud Library, Vol. 3, Studies on Hysteria*, 1974. London: Penguin.

Grier, F. (2005). No sex couples, catastrophic change, and the primal scene. In F. Grier (Ed.) *Oedipus and the Couple* (pp. 201–219). London: Karnac.

Hewison, D. (2017). Tavistock Alumni News, 2 of 3, 19 January 2017.

Kahr, B. (2009). Psychoanalysis and sexpertise. In C. Clulow (Ed.) *Sex, Attachment and Couple Psychotherapy*. London: Karnac.

Ogden, T. (1989). *The Primitive Edge of Experience*. New York: Aronson.

Scharff, D.E. (1998). *The Sexual Relationship: An Object Relations View of Sex and the Family*. London: Jason Aronson, p. 221.

Scharff, J.S. and Scharff, D.E. (2005). *The Legacy of Fairbairn and Sutherland*. London and New York: Routledge.

Symington, N. (1993). *Narcissism: A New Theory*. London. Karnac Books.

Glossary
Meaning of terms and application to couple and family work

Penny Jools

The glossary is intended to help readers to understand the terms discussed in this book. It is also intended as way of cross-referencing from one chapter to another when the meaning of a term needs to be recalled.

Affective learning groups (Lovell-Simons and Jools, Chapter 11)

Affective learning groups are small groups that are an integral part of the structure of a workshop or conference. Their aim is to enrich the learning experience of individuals attending by facilitating an understanding and integration of the conference/workshop material on an affective as well as cognitive level. The affective learning group is not a therapy group.

The assumption underlying these groups is that theoretical and clinical material evoke feelings that both impact on and enhance the learning process. It is also the case that unconscious processes evoked by the material will be enacted in the group setting, and this can also be utilised as part of the learning experience. Further, that it is an essential part of working with couples and families to be able to be in touch with and work with feelings evoked by material brought to the sessions.

Attachment (Byrne, Chapter 10)

Bowlby described attachment as a 'lasting psychological connectedness between human beings' (Bowlby, 1969, p. 194). In many ways Attachment Theory has dominated the thinking about mother–child relationships for forty to fifty years. It has been developed empirically by the work of Mary Ainsworth *et al.* (1978) and the Strange Situation Test.

Relevance to work with couples and families:

Tavistock Relationships has developed an empirical way of exploring adult couple attachment. They suggested a number of couple pairings based on insecure attachments in each of the individuals. The patterns have predictive value in terms of the nature of the relationships they can describe, including those most likely to be problematic. These include:

(1) Dismissing/Dismissing: a pseudo-independence based on a denial of dependency needs;

(2) Preoccupied/Preoccupied: these couples carry a perpetual feeling of deprivation, a high level of disagreement where each partner competes for the dependency position while also resisting it;

(3) Dismissing/Preoccupied: this is a common pattern in couples who present with difficulties. It is a highly conflictual pattern with the preoccupied partner expressing much discontent and the dismissing partner believing the only problem in the relationship is the other's discontent; and

(4) Secure/Insecure: if one partner is securely attached, the other is able to engage in a more flexible, balanced way. It can go in the other direction however.

Bodymind (Meyerowitz-Katz, Chapter 7)

This is a clinically useful Jungian concept that represents the idea that somatic process and experiences, and mental experiences, are a single entity (Grotstein, 1997; Clark, 2008). It is related to *psychoid* and *psychoid substance* (Clark, 1996, 2006, 2008, 2010; Meyerowitz-Katz, 2016).

Claustro-agoraphobic anxieties (Berg, Chapter 6; Abrahams, Chapter 8)

These are anxieties that stem from the most primitive phase of development, the autistic-contiguous phase, and often result from early trauma to or dysfunction of the mother–infant bond. As a result patients are extremely insecure and unable to find a safe distance for relating to their objects. Closeness is associated with feeling engulfed, losing one's sense of self, being entrapped or taken over (claustrophobic); distance is equally terrifying and the emptiness of this is felt as a threat of psychic disintegration (agoraphobia). There is both an intense longing for and yet a profound fear of attachment (Glasser, 1979).

Combined parental figure (Abrahams, Chapter 8; Jools, Chapter 9)

The combined parental figure is a phantasy in the infant's mind that the parents, or rather their sexual organs, are locked together in permanent intercourse. It is the earliest and most primitive phantasy of the Oedipal situation. 'These united parents are extremely cruel and much dreaded assailants' (Klein, 1929, p. 213). The infant's fury and rage towards this figure imbues it with violence so there is mutually assured destruction in the intercourse and the terror of what this means for the child, who sadistically triumphs only to be completely bereft and abandoned. The violence and sadism connected with this phantasy was seen by Klein as derived from envy of the parental intercourse, and exclusion from it.

So on the one hand this figure represents the chaos of an explosive and destructive coupling. It also represents very early feelings related to the child's sense of exclusion, and is a precursor to Oedipal anxieties.

Relevance to work with couples and families:

While bearing in mind that the sense of exclusion is a normal and necessary part of the path to emotional growth, some couples and families carry an internal sense of the combined parental figure, i.e. real intercourse, whether with each other or the therapist, as being destructive and annihilating. This has profound implications for the couple's relationship, and the transference relationship with the therapist.

Complex (Meyerowitz-Katz, Chapter 7)

Complexes can be thought of as autonomous part-selves with their own energy and consciousness. They are internal structures 'focal or nodal points of psychic life' (Jung, 1921, para. 925) which are imbued with powerful affect whose source is hidden from consciousness and by which individuals can be gripped; as Jung writes: 'complexes can *have us*' (Jung, 1960/1969, para. 200, italics original); i.e. complexes can powerfully drive our emotions, thoughts and actions. They are related to *intra- and interlocking traumatic scenes* (Pickering, 2006, 2008).

Conjoint personality: unconscious complementariness (Byrne and Kourt, Chapter 3)

If the ego boundaries between individuals in a couple are sufficiently blurred, a joint personality can be created from lost, split-off or repressed aspects of the self located in the other. They are then re-experienced by introjective identification, as creating a sense of belonging, of being re-united with these unconscious split-off parts of the self, in the other. This sense of belonging can be understood only if we allow that at a deeper level the partner is seen as part of oneself. The partner is then treated according to how this aspect of themselves was treated in childhood, either spoilt and cherished or denigrated and persecuted (Dicks, 1967).

Container/contained (from a Jungian perspective) (Meyerowitz-Katz, Chapter 7)

Jung's (1954/1991) notion of marriage as a problematic bilateral unconscious psychological container. This is an image of an undeveloped, pre-symbolic couple state of mind. It is imbued with each partner's nuanced developmental achievements and lacks, intergenerationally transmitted 'unconscious motivations' and expectations deriving from their experiences within their families of origin, and particularly in relation to how they experienced their parents. Each partner unconsciously seeks containment in, and therefore healing by, the other, expecting the other to function as a parent in order to repair early environmental failure. This is a shared predicament as each seeks something from the other that relies on a developmental achievement that neither has negotiated successfully.

Containment

The idea of containment comes from Bion's (1962) model of container/contained and Klein's (1946) concept of projective identification. It describes the capacity of the mother to contain the infant's projected experiences and needs. Bion proposed that the infant projects into the mother his inchoate primitive anxieties that he called beta elements. The mother's role is to unconsciously take in, process and understand the infant's experience and name it. When this happens, the infant can reintroject his projected fears, modified by understanding, and at the same time he also introjects an experience of breast/mother as a container capable of dealing with anxiety. The mother, through her own capacity for thought (her alpha function), has transformed the unbearable beta elements into alpha elements (a higher level of mental functioning). This forms the basis of the infant's own capacity to manage and contain anxiety. According to Bion (1962), it is the mother's reverie that allows for the metabolising of the infant's split-off feelings and the returning of them to the infant in a way that can be taken in. Thus the infant learns from experience.

Relevance to work with couples and families:

Often couples and families who come for therapy are experiencing containment for the first time, as the consulting room provides a space where strong feelings can be expressed and unconscious anxieties brought to the surface. Transference feelings can be strong and complex. The therapist needs to maintain a sense of themselves as a good object to be able to help the couple or family to internalise the experience as a good internal container.

Counter-transference

The concept of counter-transference has a long history. It refers to subjective feelings that the therapist has in relation to what the patient brings with them into the therapy room, especially at an unconscious level. Originally, counter-transference was seen as a failing on the part of the therapist. Later the value of understanding and processing these projected feelings and the mechanism of projective identification was acknowledged in both individual and couple and family psychotherapy.

Relevance to work with couples and families:

In couple and family psychotherapy various members of the family may be carrying split-off parts of the complex projective and introjective identification processes. A depressed child, for example, may be carrying the parents' denied grief about an earlier abortion. The therapist can also experience these unconscious anxieties in the couple or family. Understanding the counter-transference sometimes needs the assistance of supervision, individual or group. As Jill Scharff stated (1994) 'Transference enables us to detect the problem. Countertransference is the medium for its resolution'.

Creative couple or a couple state of mind; see also Internal parental couple (Abrahams, Chapter 8)

This is a level of psychic development, where different thoughts and feelings are allowed and are able to come together in one's mind, and where it is possible for something to develop out of them. These psychic developments (such as Britton's concept of the third position) form a vital part of the individual's psychic structure, which sustains them in a couple relationship. Morgan (2005) referred to the crystallisation of these psychic developments as the internalisation of a 'creative couple' (Morgan and Ruszczynski, 1998).

During infancy, the baby is in a close relationship with its mother. Later in life, this becomes an urge to link up with another in an intimate adult relationship. During childhood, the child develops an awareness of the parents as a creative couple operating in a relationship that excludes him. The internalisation of this positive parental intercourse requires a mourning of the loss of the one-on-one parent–child coupling, and leads to the resolution of Oedipal issues. This is the third position referred to by Britton (1989) where the child has the experience of being both included and excluded. In mature relationships, if the individuals concerned have developed this 'couple state of mind' (Morgan, 2005) they are able to nurture their relationship as a third entity and use it as a psychological container in times of stress.

Depressive position (see Developmental positions)

Developmental positions (Berg and Byrne, Chapter 2):

Autistic-Contiguous Position/anxieties (Berg and Byrne, Chapter 2)

This refers to an early stage of psychic development prior to Klein's Paranoid-Schizoid stage. It is described as 'a sensory-dominated mode in which the most inchoate sense of self is built upon the rhythm of sensation' (Ogden, 1989, p. 31). It builds on the work of Bick (1968) and Tustin (1986) in which they argue that the skin functions to contain and provide a distinction between inner and outer experience. A failure at this stage of development results in disintegrative anxieties, feelings of leaking, dissolving, disappearing or falling into shapeless boundless space' (Ogden, 1989, p. 68).

Relevance to work with couples and families:

A lack of containment very early in life (a depressed mother who struggles to handle her baby in a responsive way, an infant raised in an orphanage) can lead to an adult who may have difficulties in relationships that involve touch and skin contact, as in the sexual relationship. Without this capacity of being held, the psychic danger is of annihilation either through merger or abandonment.

Paranoid-Schizoid Position (Berg and Byrne, Chapter 2)

This stage is characterised by the splitting of the object (and the self) into good and bad. The same mother who both satisfies and frustrates is split into a good or bad mother, the two are not integrated. The world of the infant thus exists in parts, or part object terms. This can also lead to persecutory anxiety as the infant fears a retaliatory attack from the projected bad mother that has later been reintrojected and internalised.

Relevance to work with couples and families:

Many couples and families who present for therapy are in the grip of paranoid-schizoid anxieties. They are functioning with much projection and projective identification. Couples are often blaming of each other without a capacity to see the other's point of view. Children in the family may be split into the 'good' compliant child and the 'bad' acting out child. This split may reflect intergenerational losses that have been denied. Each child carries part of the family. Work with the couple or family hopefully leads to a more integrated view of themselves and the family, where good and bad can be acknowledged and there is more space for thought and growth. This leads to the . . .

Depressive position (Berg and Byrne, Chapter 2)

The infant gradually comes to see the mother as a whole person, and is able to experience ambivalence, to appreciate that satisfaction and frustration both emanate from the mother. The infant also feels concern for the survival of the mother from their prior persecutory hostile attacks and attempts at reparation are made. The working through of the depressive position is always a work in progress.

Relevance to work with couples and families:

We can see evidence of depressive position functioning in couples and families when there is less repetitive conflict and a developing understanding and acceptance of the partner and his or her differences. There may also be more evidence of curiosity about the partner's feelings and thoughts. An improved sexual relationship may reflect this greater intimacy and trust. There may also be evidence of the internalisation of the containment that therapy offers.

Oedipal position (Jools, Chapter 9)

In classical theory the Oedipal complex is signalled by the libidinal attachment of the boy to his mother (and girl to her father), with resolution occurring through the relinquishment of the Oedipal longings by working through fears about castration and loss of love. In dealing with these anxieties, the child must experience and tolerate both inclusion and exclusion from the parental couple. The child's acceptance of their position as a third in the couple relationship is necessary in order for them to find a secure place as a child and to develop a good enough internal parental couple.

Relevance to work with couples and families:

Early disruption of Oedipal issues, such as the loss of a parent, the birth of a sibling, can build on later Oedipal situations, with a particular focus on exclusion, and sometimes a sense of catastrophic intercourse. See **Combined parental figure** in Glossary (Britton, 1989). Later Oedipal issues can be brought to light in couple and family psychotherapy when a child has become the 'partner' of one parent or there are major intergenerational relationship issues where the husband or wife is excluded or feels excluded from the family of origin. Although these feelings of jealousy and envy are difficult to deal with, they signal the possibility of the depressive position in the acceptance of the other as different and separate.

Embodied (Meyerowitz-Katz, Chapter 7)

'Embodied' is a Jungian term that refers to a process within the psychotherapeutic relationship in which a part of the patient's inner world is experienced in the analyst's body. '"Embodied" is intended to suggest a physical, actual, material, sensual expression in the analyst of something in the patient's inner world, a drawing together and solidification of this, an incarnation by the analyst of a part of the patient's psyche' (Samuels, 1985, p. 52). It means that 'in analysis, the analyst's body is not entirely his own and what it says to him is not a message for him alone' (Samuels, 1985, p. 60). Embodied counter-transference is a 'highly informative analytic lens' into the 'difficult zones' associated with 'oversensitive and defensive narcissistic and destructive borderline conditions, and to chronically and acutely regressed states' (Clark, 2010, p. 88). Embodiment implies 'a becoming, with its consequent involvements, and also a suggestion of the medium for counter-transference communications from the patient; this, it will turn out, is the analyst's body' (Samuels, 1985, p. 53). See **Psychoid** and **Psychoid substance**.

Endopsychic structure (Berg, Chapter 1)

This is Fairbairn's term to describe the structure of the ego or structure of the internal world as it is split into various object relations. Fairbairn's ego was split between conscious and unconscious aspects. These are: (1) the 'ideal object relationship', between the central ego (or self) and the 'ideal' object, a relationship associated with the affect of **satisfaction.** The use of 'ideal' is confusing, and this is better thought of as a 'good enough' object relationship, borrowing the term from Winnicott (1953). This object relationship is located in the conscious realm of the mind. (2) There are two other main types of object relationships, both of which are unsatisfying: the **exciting and the frustrating object relationship** (Scharff, 1994) or **libidinal and anti-libidinal** object relationships (Fairbairn, 1952). They are associated with painful emotions, and are therefore repressed into unconsciousness by their accompanying ego aspects.

Relevance to work with couples and families:

Fairbairn's ideas seem to be particularly useful in understanding certain couple dynamics, where the basis for the coupling is where one partner seems to be 'exciting' and the other 'rejecting and frustrating'. Work in therapy aims to provide a shared understanding of the cause of these positions relating to shared unsatisfactory early object relationships, which have produced different defences. The focus in therapy can be on helping the couple to understand their shared deficit in a compassionate way.

False self couple (Byrne and Kourt, Chapter 3)

When the mother is unable to contain and respond appropriately to the communications of the infant, but responds with her own gesture, the infant may experience this as a compulsion to fit in or comply with the mother. This can result in a compliant 'false self' as described by Winnicott (1960).

Relevance to work with couples and families

The term 'false self couple' describes a couple relationship where the partners share a history of lack of parental containment. In this couple dynamic, there will be a tyrannical self and a compliant other, and the tyrannical partner pressures the compliant one to fit in. However, the roles can reverse, the compliant partner waiting for their chance to become the tyrant. In describing this phenomenon, Fisher (1993) states that 'this is the two sides of the interactional experience that leads to the false self organisation'. He adds that here 'there is little possibility of any creative understanding of difference'.

Holding (Berg and Jools, Chapter 4)

Winnicott (1973) argued that the infant's internal world was moulded in part by the environment in which it existed. There needed to be enough holding in the environment for the baby to develop. Winnicott distinguished between the 'environment mother', the mother who keeps the child safe, warm, clothed and fed, and an 'object mother'. A 'good enough' environment mother will allow the 'object mother' to exist; this is the mother who is the object of love, hate and other emotions. There is a distinction here between Bion's idea of containment which refers to the mother's function in terms of unconscious internal processes and Winnicott's idea of holding which refers to the external environment the mother (and father) provide for the infant.

Relevance to work with couples and families:

Scharff and Scharff (2005) have developed these ideas in their work with couples and families and distinguish between *contextual* and *focused* holding. Contextual holding refers to the frame of therapy and conscious feelings about the therapy experience. In this sense it is like Winnicott's idea of holding. Focused holding is more about the unconscious aspect of the relationship between the therapist and the couple or family. Both aspects are important in work with couples and families.

Interlocking traumatic scene (Byrne and Kourt, Chapter 3)

This is an 'interpenetration of two memory systems' (Pickering, 2006, p. 257). 'Couples superimpose their respective scripts to create an entangled drama, which hijacks the relationship' (Pickering, 2008, p. 11), in which each partner 'conscripts' the other to replay these stories. The person finds themselves gripped by the traumatic memory system which is experienced as a here and now reality, and not a memory, so that opportunities to 'improvise' are foreclosed (Pickering, 2008, pp. 135–136).

Internal parental couple (Byrne and Kourt, Chapter 3)

Relevance to work with couples and families:

This is a different concept from the 'combined parental figure' (see Glossary), referred to by Klein (1929). It is an idea that represents the concept of a couple in the mind of the individual, a cooperative functional and sexual parental couple, or 'mature internal parental couple or combined object' (Fisher, 1995, p. 79). This internal parental couple is derived from a person's own good enough experiences of their own parents in their family of origin. If internalised adequately, which is to a large extent a function of the parental relationship the infant is exposed to, the link between the parents provides stability and generativity. This idea is linked to Oedipal resolution, where the link between the parents is recognised and the child is able to let go of exclusive rights to one parent, i.e. suffer loss, and progress to depressive position functioning.

If this object relationship has not been able to be reliably secured the patient has problems being part of a couple, and also can tend to attack the psychoanalytic couple. Early Oedipal issues are one likely cause of a difficulty introjecting a stable internal parental couple and therefore also a capacity to parent adequately.

It is also a source of containment for difficulties the couple may experience in creating their own coupledom and family. It is linked to the idea of the 'creative couple' (see Glossary).

Intralocking traumatic scene (Meyerowitz-Katz, Chapter 7)

A term used by Pickering (2006, 2008): 'Traumatic memory systems tend to be organised in the form of a particular scene' (Pickering, 2006, p. 256). Intralocking traumatic scenes trap the individual in a sealed and impenetrable intrapsychic system which they are unwittingly driven to replay repetitively and which forecloses on capacities to think, and learn from experience or tolerate uncertainties. They represent unconscious scripts which individuals bring to their couple relationships.

Introjective identification (Byrne and Kourt, Chapter 3)

> In introjective identification, infants take in that modification of earlier feelings that the mother has provided ... If the mothers are not able to contain their infants' worries, the babies then receive a view of themselves that confirms their poor sense of themselves as unmanageable. When the mothers are good enough, the infants take in the mothers' good containing function and then become able to manage themselves and their feelings now and in the future in a progressively more competent and reliable way.
>
> (Scharff and Scharff, 2005, p. 38)

Relevance to work with couples and families:

This can happen when the couple or family is able to introject the therapist as a positive figure and one from whom they can learn. This comes up sometimes in couple or family therapy when one member of the family will repeat what the therapist has said or suggested in a helpful way.

Narcissistic (object) relating (Berg, Chapter 1; Berg and Byrne, Chapter 2; Byrne and Kourt, Chapter 3)

There are a number of different theories of narcissism, notably in Australia; Symington (1993) defined narcissism as the **rejection** of the lifegiver, composed of the healthy part of the self and aspects of the mother (or most significant other).

Relevance to work with couples and families:

James Fisher (1999) defines narcissistic object relating as:

> a relationship where there is an intolerance of the reality of the independent existence of the other. Narcissism in this sense is in fact a longing for another who is perfectly attuned and responsive and thus not a genuine other at all.

He adds, 'It is not the state of identification or oneness that is problematic, but the rigidity that cannot allow for the reality of difference' (Fisher, 1999, pp. 1–2). In our work with couples and families we have come to see narcissistic ways of relating as occupying a 'borderline' state between autistic-contiguous and paranoid-schizoid functioning.

Object relations (Berg, Chapter 1)

Object Relations Theory is a theory of the human personality developed from study of the therapist–patient relationship as it reflects the mother–infant dyad. The theory holds that the infant is driven to relate and that the infant's experiences in relationship with the mother is the primary determinant of personality formation and that the infant's need for attachment to the mother is the motivating factor in the development of the infantile self (Scharff and Scharff, 2005, p. 3).

Relevance to couple and family work:

An internal object is an internal manifestation of a relationship. It is important to remember that these internal relationships are encoded by the emotions that accompany the quality of what the experience has felt like to the infant/child. They are very affecting. While this internal object (relationship) carries some semblance to the real life relationship with the external figure (mother, father, sister, brother), one of the fundamental tenets of object relations theory is that the *internal objects* have been modified, distorted by unconscious phantasy. In therapy, the patient (the couple or family) is able through the transference and counter-transference experience in the consulting room to bring the phantasy aspects of these internal objects into consciousness and thus modify and ameliorate the intensity of his internal world.

Oedipal position (See Developmental positions)

Paranoid-Schizoid Position (see Developmental positions)

Participation mystique (Meyerowitz-Katz, Chapter 7)

A term that Jung derived from Lévy-Bruhl. Although dependent on unconscious projective and introjective processes, and having characteristics which resonate with the Kleinian concept of projective identification, participation mystique carries with it an added flavour of two people being swept up as participants in the same shared experience which consequently blurs the boundaries between them (Winborn, 2014).

Phantasy

There is a long and complex history to the idea of phantasy. Klein argued that it was the psychic manifestation of instinct (paying homage to Freud). Segal (1964) suggested that phantasy played an important role in the development of the infant, as it was constantly in interplay with external reality. Phantasies can distort the infant's experience and it is the work of therapy to try to bring phantasy and experience more in line through the medium of transference. Some aspects of phantasy can be thought of as relating to the highly sensory nature of experience, particularly early pre-verbal experience, but also highly emotionally charged experience.

Relevance to work with couples and families: (see also **Shared unconscious phantasy**)

While individuals in a family and the couple may have phantasies about their own early lives, and therefore what they project onto their partners, it is in the transference with the therapist that these will be enacted.

Pre-symbolic (Meyerowitz-Katz, Chapter 7)

This concept rests on the premise that the capacity to symbolise, i.e. to understand that one thing can represent another, for example, that a word can represent a feeling or an idea and that there is a quality of 'as if', is a developmental achievement. They are expressions of primitive undigested infantile experience and part of psychotic experience. Pre-symbolic states and communications are part of the Paranoid-Schizoid Position where experience is concrete. Pre-symbolic experience can be transformed through processes of mourning in the depressive position and through the transcendent function into symbolic experience.

Projective identification (Haralambous and Jools, Chapter 5)

The term comes from Klein (1946) and refers to part or all of the self being projected into the other and then identified with. Klein felt it happened with infants from the beginning of life. If projective processes become extreme, there is a danger that the infant will in phantasy excessively expel its disowned parts into its object, therefore perceiving its mother as holding all the aggression and hatred: the process of projective identification.

The term has come to have a variety of meanings. Bion suggested one of these was that projective identification was a normal part of communication and development. It can lead to a loss of the sense of self.

Relevance to work with couples and families:

This concept is crucial to thinking about the internal processes of couples and families in therapy. Most couples and families who seek treatment have split off and projected parts of themselves into a family member who is pathologised or projected outside into a persecutory world. The therapist will be involved in this process through both negative and hopefully ultimately positive transferences. Projective identification is the keystone to understanding the difficulties couples experience but also an essential part of the therapeutic process as the therapist in counter-transference enters the projective world of the family or couple. Progress in therapy depends in large part on the therapist's capacity to contain and understand the split-off parts of the couple or family's inner world.

Psychoid (Meyerowitz-Katz, Chapter 7)

A term used by Jung which refers to an unconscious mindbody process and, importantly, out of which psyche emerges (Addison, 2009). It contains both regressed *as well as* unrealised, and therefore unborn, mindbody potential. Clark (1996, 2008, 2010). There is resonance with Grotstein's concept of a 'bodymind'. Psychoid experience is fundamental to all psychic experience – its structures and energies – and may therefore be considered its source (Clark 1996, 2006, 2008, 2010).

Psychoid substance (Meyerowitz-Katz, Chapter 7)

A term used by Clark (1996, 2006, 2010) to denote an energy that brings together psyche and soma, both internally and interpersonally. Clark defines psychoid substance as a 'consubstantiating psychoid energy which is experienced psychoidly (psychosomatically) inside us and between us' (Clark, 1996, p. 354). He is referring to experiences that are signalled and communicated via projective identification intrapsychically as well as through somatic sensations – via somatic infection through the autonomic nervous system. In other words they are communicated unconsciously in an embodied form in order to 'painfully unite us in something we unconsciously make together, arising out of an as yet un-met need to share in something undeveloped and unco-ordinated' (ibid., p. 354); and they are communicated in this way, because psychoid potential has not become integrated into symbolic communication; there is no 'as-if'.

Shared unconscious phantasy (Byrne and Kourt, Chapter 3)

This term refers to a shared defence, used by both partners to ward off a common fear which will be based on a shared phantasy. For example, the couple may have a shared unconscious collusion to maintain their initial illusory expectations of each other, rather than deal with disappointment and potential conflict. It is as though conflict must be avoided at all costs, for fear of disastrous consequences.

Transcendent function (Meyerowitz-Katz, Chapter 7)

Identified by Jung, this refers to an ordinary psychological process which has to do with bringing opposites together. The opposites can be conscious and unconscious experience that exist in compensatory relationship to each other. It is how 'one part of the mind can find out what another part is experiencing' (Knox, 2005, p. 626). It is a process that compares and integrates internal objects and the self, a new event and past experience, explicit and implicit knowledge, cognition and emotion, left and right brain, orbito-frontal cortex and sub-cortical networks (ibid.). It is a mediating function and is comparable with Bion's concept of 'linking' or alpha function, and in couple work, with Morgan's (2005) concept of 'mating'. Because it results in two opposite points of view becoming united, the transcendent function offers a route to symbolising; the opposites are transcended, and a new, third position is achieved – an analytic third, a symbol. Modelling the mechanism of the transcendent function is a useful clinical tool.

Transference

In the context of therapy, refers to all that is projected into/onto and experienced in relation to the therapist and the treatment setting through the unconscious phantasies in the experience of the patient–therapist relationship.

Relevance to work with couples and families:

Transference in couple or family work is complex and can be negative and positive. Together with counter-transference it is one of the major ways in which the shared anxieties and defences in the family or couple can be understood. A split transference between one partner and the other can signal Oedipal issues that need to be addressed.

Triangular space or the third position

The concept of triangular space comes from Britton (1989), who, along with his analytic colleagues, reinstated Oedipal anxieties as seminal in understanding the intrapsychic world. He also argues that a resolution of Oedipal anxieties (which is never complete) is crucial in the transition to depressive position functioning. The idea of triangular space refers specifically to the capacity of the couple to have another perspective, to see the other's point of view. It can also apply to the space created in the consulting room, where there is a space to reflect and understand.

Relevance to work with couples and families:

Britton has highlighted the importance of the relationship of the individual to their *internal couple*, the internal object relationship to the parents as a couple.

'The capacity to envisage a benign parental relationship influences the development of a space outside the self capable of being observed and thought about, which provides the basis for a belief in a secure and stable world' (Britton, 1989, p. 87).

References

Addison, A. (2009). Jung, vitalism and 'the psychoid': An historical reconstruction. *The Journal of Analytical Psychology, 54(1)*, 123–142.

Ainsworth, M.D., Blehar, M.C., Waters, E. and Wall, S. (1978). *Patterns of Attachment: A Psychological Study of a Strange Situation.* Hillsdale, NJ: Erlbaum.

Bick, E. (1968). The experience of the skin in early object relations. *International Journal of Psycho-Analysis, 49*, 484–486.

Bion, W. (1962). *Learning from Experience.* London: Heinemann.

Bowlby, J. (1969). *Attachment and Loss*, (Vol. 1). New York: Basic Books.

Britton, R. (1989). The missing link: parental sexuality in the Oedipus complex. In J. Steiner (Ed.) *The Oedipal Complex Today: Clinical Implications.* London: Karnac.

Clark, G. (1996). The animating body: psychoid substance as a mutual experience of psychosomatic disorder. *The Journal of Analytical Psychology, 41*, 353–368.

Clark, G. (2006). A Spinozan lens onto the confusions of borderline relations. *The Journal of Analytical Psychology, 51*, 67–68.

Clark, G. (2008) The active use of the analyst's bodymind as it is informed by psychic disturbances. In *The Uses of Subjective Experience.* Proceedings of the Conference *The Uses of Subjective Experience: A Weekend of Conversations between ANZSJA Analysts and Academics who Work with Jung's Ideas*, 20–21 October, Melbourne, Australia.

Clark, G. (2010). The embodied countertransference and recycling the mad matter of symbolic equivalence. In G. Heuer (Ed.) *Sacral Revolutions: Reflecting on the Work of Andrew Samuels – Cutting Edges in Psychoanalysis.* London: Routledge, Taylor & Francis Group.

Dicks, H.V. (1967). *Marital Tensions: Clinical Studies towards a Psychological Theory of Interaction.* London: Routledge & Kegan Paul.

Fairbairn, W.R.D. (1952). *Psychological Studies of the Personality.* London: Routledge & Kegan Paul.

Fisher, J. (1993). The impenetrable other: Ambivalence and the Oedipal conflict in work with couples. In S. Ruszczynski (Ed.) *Psychotherapy with Couples.* London: Karnac.

Fisher, J. (1995). Identity and intimacy in the couple: Three kinds of identification. In S. Ruszczynski and J. Fisher (Eds.) *Intrusiveness and Intimacy in the Couple.* London: Karnac.

Fisher, J.V. (1999). *The Uninvited Guest: Emerging from Narcissism towards Marriage.* Karnac: London.

Glasser, M. (1979). Aggression and sadism in the perversions. In I. Rosen (Ed.) *Sexual Deviation.* London: Oxford University Press.

Grotstein, J.S. (1997). 'Mens sana in corpore sano': The mind and body as an 'odd couple' and as an oddly coupled unity. *Psychoanalytic Inquiry, 17(2)*, 204–222.

Jung, C.G. (1960/1969). The Transcendent Function. *The Collected Works, Vol. 8 The Structure and Dynamics of the Psyche.* Second Edition. Bollingen Foundation, New York. Princeton: Princeton University Press.

Klein, M. (1929). Infantile anxiety: Situations reflected in a work of art and in the creative impulse. In *Love, Guilt and Reparation and Other Works 1921–1945 (The Writings of Melanie Klein, Volume 1).* London: Hogarth Press, 1957.

Klein, M. (1946). Notes on some schizoid mechanisms. *International Journal of Psycho-Analysis, 27*, 99–110 [Reprinted in M. Klein, *Envy and Gratitude and Other Works 1946–1963.* London: Hogarth Press, 1980].

Knox, J. (2005). Sex, shame and the transcendent function: The function of fantasy in self-development. *The Journal of Analytical Psychology, 50*, 617–639.

Meyerowitz-Katz, J. (2016). Navigating ambivalent states of bodymind: Working with intergenerationally transmitted Holocaust trauma in couple therapy. *Couple and Family Psychoanalysis, 6(1)*, 25–43.

Morgan, M. (2005). On being able to be a couple: The importance of a 'creative couple' in psychic life. In F. Grier (Ed.) *Oedipus and the Couple*. London: Karnac.

Morgan, M. and Ruszczynski, S. (1998). The creative couple. Unpublished paper presented at Tavistock Marital Studies Institute 50th Anniversary Conference.

Ogden, T. (1989). *The Primitive Edge of Experience*. Northvale, NJ: Jason Aronson.

Pickering, J. (2006). Who's afraid of the Wolfe couple: The interlocking traumatic scene. *Journal of Analytical Psychology, 51*, 251–270.

Pickering, J. (2008). *Being in Love: Therapeutic Pathways through Psychological Obstacles to Love*. London: Routledge, Taylor & Francis Group.

Samuels, A. (1985). Countertransference, the 'Mundus Imaginalis' and a research project. *Journal of Analytical Psychology, 30*, 47–71.

Scharff, J.S. (1994). *Projective and Introjective Identification and the Use of the Therapist's Self*. Northvale, NJ: Jason Aronson.

Scharff, J.S. and Scharff, D.E. (2005). *The Primer of Object Relations*. Second Edition. New York: Jason Aronson.

Segal, H. (1957). Notes on symbol formation. *International Journal of Psycho-Analysis, 38*, 39–405.

Symington, N. (1993). *Narcissism: A New Theory*. London: Karnac.

Tustin, F. (1986). *Autistic Barriers in Neurotic Patients*. London: Karnac.

Winborn, M. (Ed.) (2014). *Shared Realities. Participation Mystique and Beyond*. Skiatook, OK: Fisher King Press.

Winnicott, D.W. (1953). Transitional objects and transitional phenomena. *International Journal of Psycho-Analysis, 34*, 89–97.

Winnicott, D.W. (1960). Ego distortion in terms of true and false self. In *The Maturational Process and the Facilitating Environment* (pp. 140–152). London: Hogarth Press (1965).

Winnicott, D.W. (1973). *The Child, the Family, and the Outside World*. London: Penguin.

Index

Page numbers referring to pages containing tables are given in **bold**; those referring to pages containing figures are given in *italic*.

For Product Safety Concerns and Information please contact our EU
representative GPSR@taylorandfrancis.com
Taylor & Francis Verlag GmbH, Kaufingerstraße 24, 80331 München, Germany

9 781138 079892